Apocalyptic Ruin and Everyday Wonder in Don DeLillo's America

Apocalyptic Ruin and Everyday Wonder in Don DeLillo's America

Michael Naas

BLOOMSBURY ACADEMIC
NEW YORK • LONDON • OXFORD • NEW DELHI • SYDNEY

BLOOMSBURY ACADEMIC
Bloomsbury Publishing Inc
1385 Broadway, New York, NY 10018, USA
50 Bedford Square, London, WC1B 3DP, UK
29 Earlsfort Terrace, Dublin 2, Ireland

BLOOMSBURY, BLOOMSBURY ACADEMIC and the Diana logo are trademarks of Bloomsbury Publishing Plc

First published in the United States of America 2022

Copyright © Michael Naas, 2022

For legal purposes the Acknowledgments on pp. 242–243 constitute an extension of this copyright page.

Cover design: Eleanor Rose
Cover image: Manhattanhenge, May 2011 © Eileen O'Donnell / Getty Images

All rights reserved. No part of this publication may be reproduced or transmitted in any form or by any means, electronic or mechanical, including photocopying, recording, or any information storage or retrieval system, without prior permission in writing from the publishers.

Bloomsbury Publishing Inc does not have any control over, or responsibility for, any third-party websites referred to or in this book. All internet addresses given in this book were correct at the time of going to press. The author and publisher regret any inconvenience caused if addresses have changed or sites have ceased to exist, but can accept no responsibility for any such changes.

Library of Congress Cataloging-in-Publication Data
Names: Naas, Michael, author.
Title: Apocalyptic ruin and everyday wonder in Don DeLillo's America / Michael Naas.
Description: New York : Bloomsbury Academic, 2022. | Includes bibliographical references. |
Summary: "An innovative look at the relevance of DeLillo's work to contemporary literature and thought through the lens of "last things," like death, mourning, and the decline of the American empire"– Provided by publisher.
Identifiers: LCCN 2022006035 (print) | LCCN 2022006036 (ebook) |
ISBN 9781501390692 (hardback) | ISBN 9781501390685 (paperback) |
ISBN 9781501390708 (epub) | ISBN 9781501390715 (pdf) | ISBN 9781501390722
Subjects: LCSH: DeLillo, Don–Criticism and interpretation. | DeLillo, Don–Themes, motives. | American fiction–20th century–History and criticism. | American fiction–21st century–History and criticism. | Apocalypse in literature. | United States–In literature.
Classification: LCC PS3554.E4425 Z7569 2022 (print) | LCC PS3554.E4425 (ebook) | DDC 813/.54–dc23/eng/20220422
LC record available at https://lccn.loc.gov/2022006035
LC ebook record available at https://lccn.loc.gov/2022006036

ISBN:	HB:	978-1-5013-9069-2
	PB:	978-1-5013-9068-5
	ePDF:	978-1-5013-9071-5
	eBook:	978-1-5013-9070-8

Typeset by Integra Software Services Pvt. Ltd.

To find out more about our authors and books visit www.bloomsbury.com and sign up for our newsletters.

In Memory of

*Nancy (Ropiak) Naas
(1936–2021)*

&

*Stanley R. Ropiak
(1939–2021)*

Contents

Abbreviations of Works by Don DeLillo		ix
Preface: Last Things		xi
1	Countermovements	1
	America	1
	New York, New York	1
	"USA! USA! USA!"	4
	The West, the Desert, and, Inevitably, California	9
	Automobiles	14
	Airplanes	17
	Beyond America	21
2	Countercurrents	27
	Sports, Games, Sports Gaming	27
	Academia	35
	Philosophy	41
	Technologies of Life and Death	47
3	Counterproductions	57
	Empire, Capital, the Corporation	57
	Money	66
	Advertising	69
	Consumerism and Waste	77
4	Counterhistories	85
	American History 2.0	85
	Terrorism	87
	9/11, The Twin Towers	96
	Creation and Ruin	101
	War and Peace	104

5	Countermeasures	113
	Self and Others	113
	The Individual and the Crowd	119
	Prophylactics and Purifications	125
	The Shit, the Shower, the Shave, and the Haircut	133
6	Counterforces	145
	Life and Death	145
	Mourning	151
	The Afterlife	154
	The Apocalypse	159
	The Omega Point, the Death Drive	160
7	Counterworlds	169
	Space	169
	Time	172
	Space-Time	177
	Religion	179
	Miracles	190
	The Everyday	197
	Earth, Moon, Sun	205
	Radiance	212
Conclusion: Silent Mode (The Future of Contraband)		219
Acknowledgments		242

Abbreviations of Works by Don DeLillo

Novels

A	*Americana*. Boston: Houghton Mifflin, 1971. Rev. Ed. New York: Penguin, 1989.
AZ	*Amazons: An Intimate Memoir by the First Woman Ever to Play in the National Hockey League*. Written under the pseudonym Cleo Birdwell. New York: Holt, Rinehart and Winston, 1980.
BA	*The Body Artist*. New York: Scribner, 2001.
C	*Cosmopolis*. New York: Scribner, 2003.
EZ	*End Zone*. Boston: Houghton Mifflin, 1972. Paper: New York: Penguin, 1986.
FM	*Falling Man*. New York: Scribner, 2007.
GJ	*Great Jones Street*. Boston: Houghton Mifflin, 1973. Paper: New York: Vintage, 1989.
L	*Libra*. New York: Viking, 1988.
M	*Mao II*. New York: Viking, 1991.
N	*The Names*. New York: Knopf, 1982.
P	*Players*. New York: Knopf, 1977.
PO	*Point Omega*. New York: Scribner, 2010.
RD	*Running Dog*. New York: Knopf, 1978.
RS	*Ratner's Star*. New York: Knopf, 1976.
S	*The Silence*. New York: Scribner, 2020.
U	*Underworld*. New York: Scribner, 1997.
WN	*White Noise*. New York: Viking, 1985.
ZK	*Zero K*. New York: Scribner, 2016.

Short Stories

AE	*The Angel Esmeralda: Nine Stories*. New York: Scribner, 2011.
"AE"	The Angel Esmeralda
"BM"	Baader Meinhof
"C"	Creation
"HM"	Human Moments in World War III
"HS"	Hammer and Sickle
"IA"	The Ivory Acrobat
"MD"	Midnight in Dostoevsky
"R"	The Runner
"S"	The Starveling

Plays

EM	*The Engineer of Moonlight*. *Cornell Review* 5 (Winter 1979): 21–47.
LL	*Love-Lies-Bleeding*. New York: Scribner, 2006.
DR	*The Day Room*. New York: Knopf, 1987. Rpt. Viking/Penguin, 1989.
V	*Valparaiso*. New York: Scribner, 1999.

Essays

"PH"	"The Power of History"
"RF"	"In the Ruins of the Future." First published in *Harper's Magazine* (December 2001) and then republished in *The Guardian* on December 22, 2001.

Preface
Last Things

Everybody wants to own the end of the world.

ZK 3

They were drenching me in last things. I thought about these two words. This is eschatology, isn't it?

ZK 144

This is a book about what theologians call "last things" in the work of Don DeLillo—things like death, mourning, and inconsolable loss, the last judgment and heaven and hell, the decline and fall of the American empire, just to get us warmed up, but then the apocalypse or the end of the world more generally. It is about a great American writer's vision of the decline not just of a single nation but of an entire world, one that is today threatened on so many fronts by violence and ruin, death and destruction, by human catastrophes and environmental disasters of all kinds, a world that seems to be edging ever closer, as if under the influence of some inexorable death drive, toward that omega point where all things come to end. Last things, then, because—no one can deny it—nothing lasts, and the works of Don DeLillo have been there to remind us of this simple and yet profound fact for more than half a century.

And yet—because you just know there had to be an *and yet*—this work is also about all the things that double or shadow those last things in the very same works of DeLillo, things like the wonder of language or the radiance of everyday events, a sunset between buildings in Manhattan, for example, or a young girl's face on a billboard in the Bronx, or a baseball game under the lights in the Polo Grounds. The argument here is thus not that in the works of DeLillo wonder has been forever replaced by apocalyptic ruin or that the once-great American empire—or the once great planet earth—is today in the midst of a decline or degeneration that it could and should have avoided. The news is both better and worse than that. The point is that in DeLillo's works last things will have been there from the beginning, last things as the hither side of first things, ruin and apocalypse going hand-in-hand with everyday miracles and wonder. Life will have thus been from the beginning haunted by death, creation always shadowed by destruction, the beginning of the American empire accompanied from the start by its end. This is a book, then, that looks at the way in which Don DeLillo has, from the beginning of his career up to the present, and perhaps like no other American author, created meaning by contrasting, juxtaposing, or, as I shall call it here, *contrabanding* first and last things, conflicting values or opposing forces such as life and death, creation and destruction, consumption and waste, everyday wonder and apocalyptic ruin, the origins of language and end of the world.

In one novel after another, from *Americana* (1971) and *End Zone* (1972) through *Zero K* (2016) and *The Silence* (2020), Don DeLillo will have contrabanded last things with first not simply at the level of the themes that run through his fictions—though that is the most visible aspect of the phenomenon—but also at the level of the different narrative lines that run through them, even at the level of individual sentences or words, where differing or contrasting meanings are set against one another in an absolutely unique and uniquely powerful way. For DeLillo teaches us that it is almost never by looking at something directly, head on, that we learn anything about it, but rather through juxtaposition, detour, and contrast. It is the sidelong glance as opposed to the stare that teaches us most about other people, the unexpected glimpse of ourselves in a mirror as opposed to concentrated introspection that tells us best who we are, a surprising or jolting reframing of themes as opposed to a straightforward or direct treatment of them that helps us learn best about our world. These are the techniques that have allowed DeLillo to teach us so much about the trajectory of the American empire and the world more generally, though also, and perhaps especially, the techniques that make the reading of his work so pleasurable and so powerful. This is a book, then, about how Don DeLillo, who has been prescient about so much in contemporary American life, has tried to make sense of what has been happening in America and in the world more generally by reframing and reinterpreting through his fictions such things as war, terrorism, the events of 9/11, and, as we shall see, because they are related, the deep meaning of facial hair, such things as science, religion, technology, and role of condoms in contemporary life, things like capitalism, consumerism, and the radiant beauty of an eclipse, or the American automobile, air travel, and the place of New York City in the American imaginary, or life, death, the apocalypse, the afterlife, and the promise of cryogenics.

While this book is meant to stand alone and to be read on its own, it can also be read as the sequel—the double—of *Don DeLillo, American Original: Drugs, Weapons, Erotica, and Other Literary Contraband* (Bloomsbury, 2020). It was in that book that I first argued that the unique power and insight, as well as the unparalleled humor, of DeLillo's work comes from its unexpected, inventive, and always pleasurable juxtaposition of different narratives and media, its incorporation in counterpoint of various kinds of narrative doubling and reproductive technologies, everything from radio, photography,

TV, and film to the internet. The word under which all these diverse but related phenomena were gathered was, there too, *contraband*, at once a narrative technique, a way to describe the incorporation and juxtaposition of various narratives lines or "bands," and a way of rethinking the doubleness or duplicity of literature itself, that is, literature itself *as* contraband. Whereas that earlier work thus concentrated on DeLillo's notion of contraband as a narrative technique and on the way that technique inflects the *form* of DeLillo's writing, this work focuses essentially on the *content*, if I may be allowed such an opposition, that is, on all those last things that have been central to DeLillo's work for over five decades now. Like that earlier work, this one too tries to develop a single line of argumentation about DeLillo's uniquely contrapuntal or contraband writing through a series of very short sections that can be read more or less independently of one another, while waiting at the gate for your plane to board, or at the hairdresser's waiting for your time in the chair, or, why not, in the bathroom before a shower or a shave. With an abundance of quotes from DeLillo's works and brief manageable sections on close to forty different topics, I hope that this book will be of interest not just to philosophers or literary critics but also, and perhaps above all, to the avid DeLillo reader who already knows why they enjoy the work of DeLillo but who might like to think a bit further about how novels on such seemingly diverse themes as college football, 9–11, academia, the Kennedy Assassination, climate change, the sudden appearance of an unknown person in a house by the sea, and a breakdown in the electrical grid, fit together into a larger whole.

This book is thus also intended to be as much a celebration of DeLillo's work as a scholarly analysis of it, a taking stock of an incomparably original and inventive corpus in American literature, one that still has much to teach us about who we are and where we are going. It is meant to be read as a serious scholarly book, with a single thesis regarding the way in which DeLillo develops his narratives and narrative themes through contrast or juxtaposition, in a word, through the contrabanding of opposite or contrary values and forces. But, once again, what I have attempted here is a different kind of literary criticism, one whose primary concern is to underscore DeLillo's writing itself rather than commentaries on it. I thus forgo references to the enormous secondary literature on DeLillo, much of it excellent and insightful on many of the themes treated here, for the simple reason that incorporating such works would have turned the focus away from DeLillo's own unique writing and shifted attention away from the unique way opposites or contraries are developed and deployed in them.

Opposites or contraries, then, because Don DeLillo has been since his first novel *Americana* in 1971 up to his most recent, *The Silence* in 2020, the ultimate contrarian in American literature (though he would no doubt dispute that characterization). At the level of narrative, syntax, semantics, even tone, DeLillo's texts *work* through counterpoint or opposition, through the juxtaposition of contraries, and that is the source of both their pleasure and their power, their insight and their humor. But it should be noted that the *explicit theme* of opposites—indeed even the combining or contrabanding of them—has itself been central to DeLillo's work from the very beginning, even if, as always, this deep and heady theme often taken up in philosophy and religion classes is always treated with both the reverence or seriousness it deserves and a certain degree of distance and skepticism, even cynicism, and, once again, humor.

Perhaps the fullest or at least most explicit exploration of this juxtaposing or combining in counterpoint, this contrabanding of opposites, is to be found in one of DeLillo's most important but least read works, *Ratner's Star*. The title itself, *Ratner's Star*, already begins this work of contrasting opposites by bringing together low and high, that which lives below ground and that which shines above, the "rat" inside *Star* with the "star" inside *Ratner's*, the two words combined into a single work of "art." The entire novel is then itself a reflection of this juxtaposition or contrabanding of conflicting or opposing values. It begins, for example, above ground, inside an enormous cycloid, the "most gorgeous curve in nature," "a figure of magical properties" (*RS* 78), built somewhere out in the desert. But as the narrative progresses things go further and further underground, thirteen levels down, in fact, "into the darkness of the inverted cycloid" (*RS* 283), where there is "no day or night" (*RS* 286), the cycloid above ground being mirrored, we come to understand, by a subterranean cycloid of the same size below. It is thus the "same shape upside down" (*RS* 282), and the central mission of those working inside this enormous double cycloid research facility is to interpret a mysterious coded message supposedly sent by extraterrestrials on or near Ratner's Star. We are then treated to various juxtaposed narratives within the novel, some traveling up, some down, some following the search for meaning in the stars and some an archaeological dig into man's distant past. Eventually, all these narrative bands running parallel to one another intersect as scientists discover that the signals thought to be coming from outer space were actually produced by an ancient human civilization here on earth capable of "beaming radio signals into space" (*RS* 403), so that what seemed to be furthest away ended up coming from what was closest to home. That which was long ago thrown out into space had thus ended up, like a boomerang, returning to its origin, a "curious juxtaposition of the primitive and the extraterrestrial" (*RS* 104–5). The distant past thus turns out to be just as advanced as the present, with a long period of devolution and decline followed by a long period of evolution and development, a sort of V-shape model of history, if you want to sketch it out—another sort of cycloid or boomerang—that puts the two extremes, past and present, into proximity. Once again, what is farthest away teaches us about what is nearest, the lowest always right next to the highest, the rat with the star, the aboriginal with the extraterrestrial: it is no coincidence that "religion and art probably began in caves" (*RS* 386). Because opposites co-exist—as band and contraband.

Always a bit tongue-in-cheek, though never simply just tongue-in-cheek, this contrabanding of opposites, that is, this "solidarity," "interlocking," or "reconciliation" of opposites (*RS* 35, 438, 313), can be seen to permeate every aspect of *Ratner's Star*, right down to the way one reads items on a Chinese menu: "Sweet and sour pork. Diametrically opposed entities partaking of each other's flesh…. The reconciliation of opposites" (*RS* 313). With chapter titles like "Substratum," "Dichotomy," "Opposites," and "Pairs," the relationship between band and contraband becomes both the form and the subject of the novel. Hence the venerable Shazar Lazarus Ratner, a Jewish scientist from Brooklyn, will speak of science and mysticism as producing states of mind that pass "beyond the opposites of the world" (*RS* 226). It sounds like a drug-induced one-liner, but Ratner has a whole theory or theology to back it up:

> The universe, what is it?… It began with a point. The point expanded so that darkness took up the left, light the right. This was the beginning of distinctions. But before expansion, there was contraction. There had to be room for the universe to fit. So the *en-sof* contracted. This made room. The creator, also known as G-dash-d, then made the point of pure energy that became the universe. In science this is what they call the big bang.
>
> (*RS* 217)

If all of DeLillo's narratives work with opposites or oppositions (light/dark, above/below, sweet/sour), *Ratner's Star* speaks explicitly—and at length—about these opposites and of the reconciliation of them or the coincidences between them. It is Ratner himself, together with Endor, the mentor of Billy Twillig, the fourteen-year-old math prodigy at the center of the novel, who has the lion's share of these remarks. The theory seems to be that things begin as one, without opposition, in childhood or at the beginning of the universe, since, as Ratner says, "the only nonmystical state where the opposites are joined is infancy" (*RS* 222). But then sometime after infancy opposition enters the world. As another character argues early on:

In a very short time everything falls apart. The solidarity of opposites is completely shattered. Before you've learned to put two words together, you are mired in an existence full of essential dichotomies.

(*RS* 35)

The idea of religion, then, or of various mystical states, is to reconcile or reunite these opposites as best one can, to juxtapose them—just as the novelist will—in order to show that "all things are present in all other things. Each in its opposite" (*RS* 219). Oppositions or dichotomies will thus scan *Ratner's Star* from beginning to end and front to back. Here's a little conversation between Ratner himself and Billy Twillig, whose name also seems to contain opposites (like "twig" and "twinkle"). Ratner gets the ball rolling:

> "Our beginning and end are made in the stars. Light, dark. High, low. Big, little. Go ahead, take it from there."
> "East, west."
> "Up," Ratner said.
> "Down."
> "In."
> "Out."
> "Give me a few, to test my fading powers."
> "Love."
> "Hate," Ratner said.
> "Innocence."
> "Kilt."
> "Very good," Billy said after a thoughtful pause.

(*RS* 224)

We see how serious the discourse is until all of a sudden, since the serious and the playful is another of those oppositions, it is not (though the covering over of a perfectly good word like "guilt" with an off-kilter "k" is never a wholly innocent gesture in a work by the author of *Zero K*). This play of opposites seems to bring together origin and end, childhood and advanced technology, religion and science, mysticism and pharmaceuticals: "True or false. Yes or no. Zero or one.... Computers are like children. Yes-no, yes-no, yes-no.... A little bit of yin in yang. A microdot of yang in yin. This machine is a science in itself. Bi-Levelism, I call it" (*RS* 65).

Ratner's Star can be read as a primer on opposition or contraband, a novel that takes contraband as its central theme. But it can also be read as a primer or preparation for all of DeLillo's other works, a series of hints or clues about the kinds of things we should be on the lookout for elsewhere. Here's a brief example from *The Names*, where we see again how DeLillo's exploration of a serious topic can veer off into a humorous and, in this case, nonsequitous contraband, demonstrating in the process just how DeLillo's mind or writing works:

> "How does his mind work?"
> "On-off, zero-one."
> "Binary. How do minds in general work? Anyone's. Christ, we're out of beer. Are there stores open seven days a week after death?"
>
> (*N* 97)

Binaries or opposites are thus everywhere in DeLillo, beginning with statements about how they interact. For example, in *Underworld*: "It's not enough to have your enemy. You have to understand how the two of you bring each other to deep completion" (*U* 51). It's a general statement that is then reflected in the details of the novel, which are also the details of everyday life. It informs, for example, the batter-pitcher duel or duo at the center of the famous baseball game in the Polo Grounds in 1951, as well as the debate between two of the physicists responsible for the technology that would lead to the nuclear test blast that takes place in Kazakhstan on the same day as that game: "Thomson and Branca, Bobby and Ralph, the binary hero-goat inseparable to the end," though it "could just as easily be Oppenheimer and Teller" (*U* 466), not to mention, since DeLillo mentions them more or less in the same breath, the double-stemmed mushroom itself, the one that grows beneath the earth in dark, dank places and the one that, thanks to those once feuding physicists, towers above the earth, radiant, in a nuclear blast, because the mushroom with a "fleshy cap" might always be "poisonous or magical" (*U* 466), or maybe even a little of both, nature itself being the first inventor of contraband and contrabanded opposites.

> Death and magic, that's the mushroom. Or death and immortal life. Psilocybin is a compound obtained from a Mexican mushroom that can turn your soul into fissionable material, according to scholars of the phenomenon.
>
> (*U* 466–7)

Opposites come together and co-exist, or else collide, making for all the differences in the world, light and darkness, life and death, right and left—this latter a matter of life and death in its own right not only in Ratner's discourse of creation ("the point expanded so that darkness took up the left, light the right") but in the deliberations of, for example, the Texas highway serial killer in *Underworld* as he is trying to work out the logistics of shooting another driver with his left hand versus his right while he himself is driving, with things like the distance the bullet would have to travel in either case and through how many windows opened or closed factoring into the calculations (*U* 267–8; see also *U* 265 and *RS* 407).

Opposites thus attract in DeLillo, though sometimes only in order to repel one another just as soon. It is thus always well worth following them in DeLillo's narratives. For just as day follows night, and night day, they are the things—the first and last things—of everyday life, as well as the things at the center of most of the world's religions and philosophies. What all this means for DeLillo's writing is that things are always accompanied in some way by their opposite, creation being always shadowed by destruction, the sun always casting shadows, except when it is itself eclipsed by the moon or an umbrella, every lifesaving consumer product (those little plastic tubes of sunscreen, for example) being haunted by their uselessness or their dangerous afterlife in the landfill. It means that the fall of the American empire—and the accompanying question "What comes after America?" (*FM* 192), a question that appears explicitly only in 2007, in *Falling Man*, a novel about 9–11, but one that has been animating DeLillo's work from the very start—is an attempt not to presage an end or an apocalypse on the horizon but, rather, to give voice to the end or the apocalypse that has in some sense *already* happened, that is *already* the shadow or the underside of the American empire, the end that was already there in the beginning, pitting America against what is outside it and against it, juxtaposing it, in short, with what it never was or what it no longer is. The fact is that the end of America, or that which comes after America, will have been casting its shadow over America from the very beginning of DeLillo's work. For creation and destruction, the thing and its shadow, band and contraband, world and underworld, do not cancel one another out here. As with the two parts of *Ratner's Star*, the first titled "Adventures: Field Experiment Number One" and the second "Reflections: Logicon Project Minus-One," one and minus-one add up not to zero but to a literature of last things.

Though the many short sections of *Apocalyptic Ruin and Everyday Wonder in Don DeLillo's America* can be read more or less independently of one another, they have been grouped together into seven chapters that take us roughly from things in America to global concerns to—after a detour through the personal—cosmic last things. The first chapter thus looks at the place of place—and particularly that place called America—in DeLillo's work. It begins by considering the central role of New York City in almost all of DeLillo's works and the way in which DeLillo tends to play New York off of—in a movement of contraband, precisely—the United States more generally (of which New York both is and is not a part), but then also the American West, the desert, and, who could forget it, California. This trip across the states leads to a consideration of travel, and the means of travel, in DeLillo, which always tend to create a relationship—by car or by plane—between these disparate, separated, or contrasting places, including places not only inside America but beyond it.

Chapter 2 looks at various countercurrents or even countercultures in American life, from the place of sports and games in American culture to the role played by the university and its disciplines, beginning with philosophy and science. The chapter concludes with a consideration of the various technologies of "life and death" that are always on display in DeLillo's novels, conflicting values that are commonly woven into DeLillo's narratives or, more often than not, set off within them. The same can be said for the themes of Chapter 3, where we turn to production and the shadow of counterproduction that always hangs over it, to economic systems and symmetries and the inevitable collapses and asymmetries that always attend them. Hence the role of empire, capitalism, and the corporation, as well as DeLillo's decades-long exploration of the themes of advertising, money, consumerism, and, as its contraband, waste.

Chapter 4, "Counterhistories," looks at themes for which DeLillo is, perhaps, best known, his recontextualizing or retelling of historical events such as the Kennedy assassination in *Libra*, the rise of global terrorism in the 1970s and 1980s in *Mao II*, and the attacks on the World Trade Center on 9-11 in *Falling Man*—including the strangely prescient place the twin towers will have always played in DeLillo's work, their looming presence and, already from the beginning, their anticipated fall. All this is followed by a consideration of the themes of destruction and war in DeLillo, wars real and imagined, historical and counterfactual, wars lived live or through images, all the wars and threats of war that haunt our twentieth and twenty-first-century consciousnesses and imaginaries.

From the political and geopolitical we turn in Chapter 5 to creation and destruction on a smaller scale, to micro-dramas lived by individual selves in their relationship to other selves, whether just one or two or a handful of people in a room—as in DeLillo's most recent work *The Silence*—or else individuals in a crowd, that seemingly contemporary phenomenon that DeLillo appears to argue is our future. We thus see in this chapter the various countermeasures taken by individuals to protect themselves from being absorbed or swallowed up by the crowd, or more simply contaminated by others in it, or more simply still polluted by themselves, overcome by the network of secretions and excretions that they are, by the dank underworld that subtends their lives. We thus look here at DeLillo's emphasis on prophylactics and purifying rituals of various kinds, some exceptional, as a preparation for death or transformation, and some very common, like the daily shit, shower, and shave. For the earth-shaking and the everyday, the exceptional and the quotidian, are always contrabanded in DeLillo's work as well, intertwined, which is why a simple haircut, as we will also see in this chapter, is always more than just a simple grooming ritual but a sign that something momentous is about to happen to that person in the mirror.

In Chapter 6 we turn, finally, to what are usually meant by "last things," that is, to the serious themes of life, death, and mourning, along with the always amusing topic of the afterlife, at once on an individual scale and writ large in the form of the apocalypse, the end of the world, and the ends times that anticipate it. Once again, we see how, in the works of DeLillo, life is always haunted by the fear of death, the birth of a nation always accompanied by its decline, the sun always shadowed by its eventual eclipse. We thus return by the end of this chapter to the political and the geopolitical, even the cosmological, that is, to the threat of future wars that promise to hasten these end times, and, finally, to the thought that it is not we humans who really control any of this inasmuch as everything seems to be driven by a kind of suicidal impulse or death drive, by an omega point that seems to be pulling us and everything else in the cosmos toward it.

So it is that the micro and the macro, the big and the small, the geopolitical and the hyper-personal, are so often juxtaposed and combined in the works of DeLillo, set right next to one another. From the world or the cosmos, then, we often come back—as in DeLillo's plays, and as in *The Silence*, as we will see—to the simplest of scenes or premises: a couple of people together in a room, as all the great themes of war and peace, love and desire, hope and despair, become focused on these individuals or, even more elementary, on the light and darkness, the time and space, between and around them. As we will see in Chapter 7, DeLillo is ultimately a writer not just of geopolitical issues of war and peace, not just of momentous events in US history, but also of time and space, the basic elements of all our experience, and the ones that will ultimately wear us down or do us in—always, everyone, without exception, which is why their eclipse or their end is always there, looming or threatening, in every DeLillo work.

But that is not where DeLillo usually leaves us. He does not simply suggest that we as individuals, or that we as a nation, this American nation, or we as a world, this world called earth, third planet from the sun, are simply doomed to apocalyptic ruin, even if we clearly are. For DeLillo is, if I may risk these terms, too irreverent and too religious for such simple despair, despite all the despair in his works and the skepticism or deeply contrarian ways that always mark them. That is why there is always in a DeLillo work, usually near the end, a moment of enlightenment or, better, of radiance, one associated almost always with language, with words coming to shine—the ultimate contrabanding—through the things they name. Each time, in novel after novel, there is a moment when, to speak here in trinities, something of earth, moon, or sun comes to be seen differently or comes to shine miraculously—a rising moon, a setting sun, a part of the earth being excavated to reveal some treasure. Each time, there is not so much hope but surprise or wonder, almost always associated with some miraculous Trinitarian object like a tricycle or a coat hanger or a boomerang or the Ballantine beer logo (intertwining "Purity, Body and Flavor" in one great taste (*U* 631)). Each time, and each time in conjunction, as always, with language, with the event of language or with language as an event. Each time, it might be said, up until *The Silence*.

In the conclusion, "Silent Mode (The Future of Contraband)," everything that has come before is put to the test of a reading of DeLillo's 2020 novel or novella *The Silence*, everything from the role played by those contrabanded forms of living epitomized by sports, academia, air travel, and tourism to contemporary questions of religion, philosophy, and physics to the promises of modern technology and the ruin—the end of the American empire or an even more global apocalypse—that is portended when all that technology breaks down. Everything will be there from the relationship between self and others to crowds, mirrors, even the need for a ritual shave, along with a challenge to the claims made in the final chapter of this work that DeLillo's novels and plays typically end with a sort of signature miracle or moment of radiance, a rule of thumb that seems to find a stunning exception in *The Silence*. In the end, it will perhaps all come down to how we read or receive the language and the gestures at the end of that work, and what they might tell us about the kinds of reception DeLillo's contrabanded narratives are likely to receive in the future, whether here on earth, near Ratner's Star, or in the hereafter.

1

Countermovements

America

I've come to think of Europe as a hardcover book, America as the paperback version.

N 23

The American mystery deepens.

WN 60

Don DeLillo is a decidedly *American* writer—an assignation that is made here on the basis not of his biography or Wikipedia page ("Donald Richard DeLillo (born November 20, 1936) is an American novelist… born in New York City") but of his work. For while DeLillo has written about places other than America, and while he writes about themes that are universal in scope, his idiom is decidedly American and, more often than not, the setting of his narratives is America. DeLillo's first novel is, after all, titled *Americana*, and it attempts to explore what it means for the young TV executive David Bell to grow up in America and try to become an American writer or artist of some kind. To play on that opening line of *Underworld*, "he speaks in your voice, American" (*U* 11), DeLillo does, and he speaks of things that matter to America.

But what exactly is America for DeLillo? It is, first of all—cue up Sinatra and strike up the band, or, better, Jay-Z and Alicia Keys in contraband—

New York, New York

We're talking about New York, New York. It's so awesome we say it twice. It's like the tail end of a prayer. The priest turns to the congregation and he spreads his arms out wide and says, "New York." And the congregation answers, "New York." And then everybody gets up and goes home because there's obviously nothing left to say.

AZ 6–7

Lenny Bruce: "New York, New York. We say it twice. Once to entice them to leave Kansas. And once more over their grave."

U 624

"Who's your hero? Tell us and we'll get him."
"People from the Bronx don't have heroes."

RS 247

If America is the setting, the word-scape, for most of DeLillo's works, it is more often than not a very particular America within America that takes center stage—namely, New York City, an America that is often at odds with the greater America in which it is apparently located, that is, an America that is either a lot less American than the rest of the nation or a whole lot more. From beginning to end, most of the action in many of DeLillo's most important works takes place in NYC, the creation as well as the destruction, the miracles along with the catastrophes. A few take place almost exclusively there, for example, *Great Jones Street*, which gets its name from a small street in the East Village connecting East 3rd St. to West 3rd St., *Cosmopolis*, another name, of course, for New York itself as a "world city" (*C* 88), *Falling Man*, which takes place—with the exception of just a couple of sequences in Germany—in New York City in the days and weeks after 9–11, and, of course, *The Silence*. And then there are many other novels in which New York City, without being the sole setting, figures prominently, from *Americana*, *Players*, and *Mao II*, to *Underworld*, *Point Omega*, and *Zero K*.

We are thus treated in DeLillo's novels to a portrait of New York City from the 1950s into the twenty-first century, from the rough and tumble New York of the 1950s and 1960s to the struggling New York of the 1970s, the rundown New York of the 1980s, the New York of the mega-rich at the center of the financial boom of the 1990s, the New York of 9-11, and then, most recently, the New York of the twenty-first century, where all kinds of things can happen, from spectacular art exhibits and miraculous sunsets between high-rises to airplane crashes and technological disasters.

There are thus many different faces to New York City, or many different New Yorks, in DeLillo's novels, but New York seems to be, first of all, a place of the many, of people in crowds, a city where the crowd is "essential to the individual" (*A* 29; see *P* 206), where one can experience on a daily basis "the surge of the noontime crowd" (*M* 103; see 146), the vast sea "of overflowing faces" (*M* 148). It is also a place where kids play games in the street (*RS* 328; see 363), or at least used to, as well as a place with neighborhoods you wouldn't want to go to after dark (*RD* 3); it is a place where people don't own but rent, "like people in the Middle Ages" (*FM* 68; see *DR* 11), where you know a good neighborhood by the presence of "Jewish doctors" and "delivery boys without needle tracks in their arms" (*AZ* 35), a place where people take a walk in the park just for "the palpable relief of being in unmetered space for a time" (*ZK* 196), a place where people will not, contrary to the lore, "walk right past victims of cardiac arrest and other misfortunes." No, "they will inspect to see if it is someone they know," and "if he is dead and has a nice apartment, they will try to sublet his apartment until the lease expires and the rent goes up" (*AZ* 375). And by "nice apartment" what is often meant is an apartment with all the amenities that only a world-class city can offer:

> I'm moving into a brand new high-rise. The kind of building I've always hated. Doormen around the clock. A package room. A swimming pool. Laundry rooms. A barber shop. Endless carpeted hallways. A twenty-four hour gynecologist.
>
> (*AZ* 301)

New York is also a place where one is expected to "learn how to express dissatisfaction in an interesting way" (*WN* 65), and where one's status is measured by the notoriety of one's doctors and the hospitals with which they are associated. Just ask Alfonse "Fast Food" Stompanato from *White Noise*:

> In New York, people ask if you have a good internist. This is where true power lies. The inner organs. Liver, kidneys, stomach, intestines, pancreas. Internal medicine is the magic brew. You acquire strength and charisma from a good internist totally aside from the treatment he provides.
>
> (*WN* 217)

New York City is also, or at least used to be before ride-sharing became a thing, a place of "jouncing yellow cabs with their slender Ethiopians at the wheel" (*M* 185) and buses that go by "in packs, lit up like operating rooms" (*A* 46). It is a place of power and affluence, of fame and fortune, but also, in the 1970s, a place of "ragpickers and bottle-savers, those evolutionary masters of survival" (*A* 46), a place where homeless people come out to wash your windshield at intersections (*GJ* 159), and, in the 1980s in *Mao II*, a city where thousands of people live on the streets, bag people (*M* 145, see 148–9), people talking to themselves "in profound and troubled monologues like saints in the depths of temptation" (*M* 88), "soot-faced people pushing shopping carts filled with bundled things … like holy pilgrims marching on endlessly" (*M* 148–9), the "hobbling man" in *The Silence*, for example, "pushing a battered cart that probably contained everything he owned" (*S* 63).

New York is thus the contraband city par excellence, a city of the mega-rich and the down-and-out, a city with two levels, a superstructure and an underground, a city of skyscrapers—the kind billionaires like Eric Packer live in, luxury towers that loom over everything—and a city of undergrounds: "This is the subway. You don't know about this. Nobody looks at anybody else" (*LL* 7). It could all seem rather unreal, but DeLillo seems to insist on it being the most real place in an otherwise surreal world. While bus tours are organized in *Underworld* to visit "*South Bronx Surreal*" (*U* 247; "AE" 84–5), Gracie the nun, the side-kick of Sister Edgar, insists for DeLillo himself, it seems, that "Brussels is surreal. Milan is surreal. This is real. The Bronx is real" (*U* 247; see "AE" 86). Indeed as someone already argues in *Great Jones Street*, "New York is too real. It's just about the realest thing there is in the observable universe" (*GJ* 174). It is thus often the rest of the country that's a bit unreal or surreal or too real to believe, a strange place where people shout—

"USA! USA! USA!"

We were a town then, American in our outlook, plain and meat-eating, relatively unhurried, willing to die for our country, or for photographs of our country.

A 132

He watches them at dinner in the officers' mess and he thinks he knows why they look so satisfied with themselves. They have begun to feel the bond of being American. They almost glow with self-awareness.

L 133

So there is New York City and then there is everywhere else. As someone suggests in *Great Jones Street*, everything beyond the George Washington Bridge is "America. The whole big thing. Popcorn and killer drugs" (*GJ* 144; see 153, *A* 159, *P* 147). As with the famous cover of *The New Yorker* featuring a map of the United States where everything west of the Hudson River is unchartered territory, New York City is something apart, exceptionally American and yet an exception to America as such, that is, to America with a capital "A," to all those places—like Olympic games or political rallies—where people might chant in gleeful satisfaction "USA!...," etc. etc.

In DeLillo's novels there is thus almost always New York City and then some counterplace, either far outside the city or just beyond its five boroughs. For one does not have to go all that far outside the city, maybe just as far as Old Holly, David Bell's hometown, to find people living "squarely in the American tradition" (*A* 107), in "all-American" places that DeLillo can treat with as much cynicism and humor as anyone but that his characters sometimes cannot help but love: "I tried to imagine, to remember really, what it was like to live without the terminal fears of the city, for I had loved a town once without knowing it, and the love would not release me" (*A* 124; see 60, 130). Years after leaving Old Holly, Bell would look back on his all-American childhood with genuine affection: "I was happy there as a child… I filled my room with fishing rods, college pennants, baseballs and model planes" (*A* 132).

There is, then, a tension or a contradiction, at the very least a contrast or a back-and-forth, between the city and what lies outside it, David Bell's Old Holly or Bill Gray's undisclosed retreat, "about two hundred miles outside the gates of the medieval city" (*M* 59), or else, further away still, upstate New York, where the mountains are, since, as we know from *White Noise*, that's where the mountains are always placed, in the north of a state (*WN* 235). That is where they put the Adirondacks, for example, where Gary Harkness is from (*EZ* 8), and where Bucky Wunderlick had his "spectacular mountain retreat" (*GJ* 115), and the Champlain islands, near the Green Mountains, where James Axton, Kathryn, and Tap in *The Names* lived for a time when they were a family. One retreats upstate in order to get away from it all, or else one gets sent there in order to be gotten away from it all, to state prison, for example, as in "Hammer and Sickle," or the correctional facility in Staatsburg where Nick Shay was sent at the age of seventeen after pleading guilty to "criminally negligent homicide" (*U* 502). This latter is not that far from the city, not even a hundred miles, but it is already a different world. And then there is, of course, somewhere in DeLillo's fictional geography, Blacksmith, the city in upstate New York where *White Noise* takes place, with its college and its malls, its "abandoned car district" and its "uncollected garbage district," its "sniper-fire district," its "districts of smoldering sofas and broken glass" (*WN* 303). It's a small college town with some big city appeal.

The contraband effect is thus created in DeLillo's works by means of a movement in the narrative, a back-and-forth, between New York City and somewhere outside the city, be it upstate, or New Jersey (often the object of a joke, but not always, since that is where the inimitable Marvin Lundy lives (*U* 172; see also *A* 313)), or Maine (often Deer Island) in *Players* and *The Body Artist*. And then there's flyover country, places closer to the center of the country that occasionally appear in DeLillo's work but are rarely central to it, Chicago, for example (see *A* 256–65; *AZ* 200, 332; *L* 344), or Pittsburgh (*RS* 219), Seattle (*BA* 106), Minneapolis (*M* 51), White Cloud, Kansas (*M* 83), Yankton, South Dakota (*U* 549), or Madison, Wisconsin, where Marian Shay grew up, "in her Big Ten town, raised safely, protected from the swarm of street life and feeling deprived because of it—privileged and deprived, an American sort of thing" (*U* 344).

Finally, in *Americana* there is Fort Curtis, nowhere or anywhere USA, Fort Curtis in whatever state Fort Curtis is in, a town that was "simply the sum of its unfilmed monotonies" (*A* 334), distinct only in its indistinction: "Any description of the main street of Fort Curtis can begin and end inside this very sentence. Beyond that I find only redundancy. The same six words identify the thing to be described and serve to describe it. The main street of Fort Curtis" (*A* 301). If it has a road leading out of it, you can be certain that that road has "the sadness of all roads leading out of town" (*A* 224). Fort Curtis is thus the prototype for other small towns, like Cleo Birdwell's hometown of Badger, Ohio, an all-American, "literal-minded place": "The school was on School Street, the bank was on Bank Street, the river ran by River Road" (*AZ* 38). It's a good place to be born and raised and it gives you a point of reference for all future travels and experiences: "the odors from the kitchen were pungent and sort of ethnic beyond belief. If an odor like this ever wafted down Bank Street in Badger, they would have called out the National Guard" (*AZ* 123; see 163-4). And the theology of Badger is about as wholesome as its tastes in food. For example, "Easter was pretty big in Badger. Forget Good Friday. That's not a Badger kind of day. Badger doesn't have the kind of temperament that really digs in and enjoys a day like that" (*AZ* 163).

There is, to be sure, something poetic, even lovable and charming, about this America, something that allows DeLillo's characters to discover something about themselves. But the other side or the underside of this more poetic America is an America that is often all too self-satisfied or certain of itself, an America whose patriotism and chauvinism might be greeted with a smile until we learn about the war-mongering to which they give rise. Early on in *Americana* the narrator is able to explain that he got out of serving in Vietnam because of "my trick knee and chronic cyst at the base of my spine," and because "the action was really just beginning then and they were fairly selective about the young men they tapped for immortality" (*A* 35). Here is another example of the same war cynicism, this one from *End Zone* in the form of a good old-fashioned rant:

> Let me just simply mention flag-waving and the insane repetitive ritualizing that goes on every time a flag is hiked up a pole or some veterans of Gettysburg come hobbling along with their medals, their stickpins, their poppies, their flags, their hats, their banners, their bumper stickers, or some simple sports event where ... three hundred and eighty-five high school girls dressed in red, white and blue ... are

prostrating themselves on the cold earth as they assume the shape of an American flag... and off to the side there's some crippled television personality in a wheelchair and pulleys singing the national anthem as the cystic fibrosis child of the month poses in the nude for the cover of *Life*. I tend to worry about such spectacles.

(*EZ* 164–5; see *AZ* 39)

To put it in a more succinct, less ranty form, "A nation is never more ridiculous than in its patriotic manifestations" (*EZ* 161; see *A* 226 and "HM" 41). Murray Siskind begins filling out the picture of this patriotism in *White Noise*:

Picture a state funeral, Jack. It is all precision, detail, order, design. The nation holds its breath. The efforts of a huge and powerful government are brought to bear on a ceremony that will shed the last trace of chaos.... The nation is delivered from anxiety, the deceased's life is redeemed, life itself is strengthened, reaffirmed.

(*WN* 292)

It's a patriotism that is often related to religion in America (see *A* 179), though just as often to media and advertising, speculation and consumerism (*A* 270-1). There is thus often right alongside a certain celebration of America this searing critique of it, celebration and critique in the same breath and words. Already in DeLillo's first novel America is the land of both the junk food jingle and giants like Kirk Douglas or Burt Lancaster in "From Here to Eternity."

There is, therefore, New York City and then everything one flies over or, preferably, drives through, the America of the open plain, the one that David Bell wants to discover, to film, the America of "lost roads" and "lost towns" (*A* 49, 125). It is here that we encounter America as a place of travel and adventure, America as the land of the automobile, from *Americana* to *Cosmopolis*, a place where the outer journey makes possible an inner adventure, that is, for David Bell, a "great seeking leap into the depths of America, wilderness dream of all poets and scout-masters, westward to our manifest destiny,... westward to match the shadows of my image and my self" (*A* 341). America as a place of the journey, then—and of a certain literature. As David Bell confesses, with words that sound as if they come as much from DeLillo as from Bell: "what I was engaged in was merely a literary venture, an attempt to find pattern and motive, to make of something wild a squeamish thesis on the essence of the nation's soul. To formulate. To seek links" (*A* 349).

To seek links: this is the stuff of conspiracies and plots, though also of plots and characters, of writing and cinema. As David Bell again testifies, "once again I felt it was literature I had been confronting these past days, the archetypes of the dismal mystery, sons and daughters of the archetypes... I drove at insane speeds" (*A* 377). Of course, in the end it is less a question of Bell trying to find himself or his voice than it is of him, as he says, trying to "outrun" himself, even if these things might not be so different in the end (*A* 360).

The trip out West is thus always a pilgrimage of sorts, a religious ritual, "a sacramental journey" (*A* 204), even when it is incomplete, as in *Americana* (*A* 348), or when it ends in death, out in the desert at Marathon Mines, as in *Running Dog* (*RD* 179–81). "I'd like to do something more religious," says David Bell, "Explore America in the screaming night. You know, Yin and yang in Kansas. That scene" (*A* 10). In the end, "there is nothing more thrilling than the first days of a long journey on wheels into the slavering mouth of an incredible and restless country" (*A* 111). It is this journey— which is supposed to culminate in Bell's Navaho documentary out west—that will provide Bell with a pretty much endless detour, allowing him to make a more personal film than the documentary he had planned, even though it will cause him to get fired in the process (see *A* 10).

There's Texas too, of course, and especially Dallas—the Dallas of 1963— where "everybody has two first names" (*RD* 201), starting with Lee Harvey, "the city that proves that God is really dead" (*L* 234). The description is obviously colored because of what happened there, those "seven seconds that broke the back of the American century" (*L* 181), unless what happened there happened there because it was Dallas. In either case, it is America itself that will change so radically as a result of those seven seconds.

By the mid-eighties, America had developed in DeLillo a somewhat different persona, less wholesome or earnest, maybe, but also more looney and absurd. *White Noise* is famous for its depiction of this America, an America of TV and advertising and the American supermarket with its endless array of consumer products: "shiny bags of potato chips, bowls of pasty substances covered with plastic wrap, flip-top rings and twist ties, individually wrapped slices of orange cheese," bold-colored packages containing no less "brightly colored foods" (*WN* 7; see 20). It's a happy, postwar America that, in *Underworld*, is already prefigured in the late 1950s refrigerator of the Demings:

> He went into the kitchen and opened the fridge, just to see what was going on in there. The bright colors, the product names and logos, the array of familiar shapes, the tinsel glitter of things in foil wrap, the

general sense of benevolent gleam, or eyeball surprise, the sense of a tiny holiday taking place on the shelves and in the slots, a world unspoiled and ever renewable.

(*U* 517–18)

And, of course, America is unthinkable without its malls, like the Mid-Village Mall in *White Noise* where an elderly couple, the Treadwells, wander about and tread not so well for "two days, lost, confused and frightened, before taking refuge" in "an abandoned cookie shack" (*WN* 59). Because, in the end, "nothing is too absurd to happen in America" (*EZ* 69).

The West, the Desert, and, Inevitably, California

The west is death, the setting sun. You will bury the dead on the west bank.... Put the house in the east, put the tomb in the west. Between there will be the river.

N 148–9

Let's just say the desert is an impulse.

U 63

Words, pictures, numbers, facts, graphics, statistics, specks, waves, particles, motes. Only a catastrophe gets our attention. We want them, we need them, we depend on them. As long as they happen somewhere else. This is where California comes in.

WN 66

If DeLillo's novels almost always have two places, at least two, in a relationship of contraband, New York and Elsewhere (Maine, Fort Curtis, etc.), one other name for this Elsewhere is the Desert. It was said during the student protests of May 1968 in Paris that beneath the paving stones there was the beach. One could say that, in DeLillo's novels, beneath the city there is the desert. In the American imaginary, the desert is, of course, the place of native Americans—steelworkers and visionaries, holy men with names like Black Knife (*A* 66, 117–21; see 336, 349, 355–6). It is also, and by the same token, the place of a culture and people about which the average American knows next to nothing, which is why it is such a surprise when one of David Bell's colleagues seems to know so much about the Navaho reservation David proposes to focus his film on: "It's out around Arizona, New Mexico, Utah and/or Colorado. I happen to know that for a fact" (*A* 69).

The American desert is the great Elsewhere of DeLillo's novels. *Point Omega*, for example, takes place between NYC and Richard Elster's house, his "spiritual retreat," out in this Desert Elsewhere, "out beyond cities and scattered towns" (*PO* 23, 18; see 54). For the desert is, above all else, the place for another thinking of place and another experience of time. It is, as someone puts it in *The Names*, a sort of preemptive answer to all human progress:

> Let me tell you what I like about the desert. The desert is a solution. Simple, inevitable. It's like a mathematical solution applied to the affairs of the planet. Oceans are the subconscious of the world. Deserts are the waking awareness, the simple and clear solution.
>
> (*N* 294)

In the desert, out beyond the vertical city, where the horizon is blocked at almost every turn (except, as we will later say, on those days of miraculous sunsets), there is nothing but distance: "Everything here was in the distance. Distance was the salient fact" (*RD* 190). That is what Elster liked most about living in the desert: "there was the house and then nothing but distances" (*PO* 18).

The desert offers not only a counter-space but a counter-time. In cities, says Elster, who is talking about not just any city but, again, NYC, "It's all embedded, the hours and minutes, words and numbers everywhere... train stations, bus routes, taxi meters, surveillance cameras. It's all about time, dimwit time, inferior time, people checking watches and other devices, other reminders. This is time draining out of our lives" (*PO* 44–5). The city seems in fact to have been "built to measure time, in Elster's formulation, the slinking time of watches, calendars, minutes left to live" (*PO* 59). As Bill Gray observes before Elster, "The city is a device for measuring time" (*M* 27), sometimes irritating and life-draining, sometimes energizing and invigorating, as in *Zero K*: "I like to dash across the street with the red seconds on the crossing light down to 3 or 4 .... It makes me feel true to the system, knowing that unnecessary risk is integral to the code of urban pathology" (*ZK* 189).

In the desert, another kind of time imposes itself; as opposed to the human time of the city, there is animal time, rock time, earth time. Alex in *Love-Lies-Bleeding* knows how to feel it: "I can sit and watch a hawk in a tree for unnumbered hours. I'm on his time. He don't move, I don't move" (*LL* 52). In the desert, says Elster, "time becomes slowly older. Enormously old. Not day by day. This is deep time, epochal time" (*PO* 72).

The time of the desert, this hawk time, this epochal time, is often a source of contentment for DeLillo's character, a relief or an escape. But because the other-banded, watch-band time of cities is almost always there as well in the form of the past or of memories, the desert can also become a place of great solitude and despair, a place to encounter death or else to lend one's hand to it. In *Point Omega* Elster's daughter Jessica seems to succumb to that solitude, wandering off one night to what seems to be her death (*PO* 82). As Alex in *Love-Lies-Bleeding* says, people think he has retreated to the desert "to find peace of mind" (*LL* 52), but, he says, "There's no safety here. It's all one thing. The art, the artist, the landscape, the sky" (*LL* 63). This is where the memories come in, the memory of being in New York, that other band, on the subway, below the surface: "Do you know what I miss? I miss the subway," he says (*LL* 57; see *ZK* 57).

A place of counter-times and counter-spaces, the desert is thus surely not for everyone. Matt Shay's wife Janet in *Underworld* does not know "how to look at the desert. She seemed to resent it in some obscure personal way. It was too big, too empty, it had the audacity to be real" (*U* 449). Jim Finley has a similar reaction: "The desert was outside my range, it was an alien being, it was science fiction, both saturating and remote" (*PO* 20). A science fiction place indeed, which no doubt explains why *Ratner's Star* and *Zero K*, both science fictions of a sort, take place there (see also *A* 361). It is thus in a desert, not an American desert but a desert nonetheless, this one in Kazakhstan, that the Convergence of *Zero K* is located: "We have remade this wasteland, this secluded desert shithole, in order to separate ourselves from reasonableness, from this burden of what is called responsible thinking" (*ZK* 71).

The desert is a place to travel to, to be sure (*U* 420), a place to do art (*LL* 61), a place of revelation for mystics and psychics of various kinds (*U* 451), but it is also a place where people—sometimes entire peoples—tend to go missing (*U* 343). From *Americana* to *Point Omega*, it is a place of barrenness and ritual death. When the sheriff comes to investigate the disappearance of Elster's daughter in this latter work he "lists a few categories of people in distress, ending with those who come to the desert to commit suicide" (*PO* 82; see 89). That is no doubt because of "the heartbreaking beauty of it, the indifference of it" (*PO* 93). It is not for nothing that Glen Selvy in *Running Dog* goes into the desert to get himself killed, to commit suicide, in effect, at the hands of his assassins: "Glen used to talk about pure landscape. He loved the desert. When you leave the earth-plane, there's a right place and a right way" (*RD* 245). The desert appears to be that right place, from *Running Dog* right up through *Zero K*. "Is the desert where miracles happen? Are we here to repeat the ancient pieties and superstitions?" (*ZK* 128).

In DeLillo the young men almost always go west—Bell, Selvy, the Shays— and some older men as well, Richard Elster, Alex Macklin. They go there to renew or reinvent themselves, though they inevitably take the east along with them. East and west, city and desert, band and contraband: DeLillo does not just give us both of these but, in novels such as *Americana*, *Falling Man*, and *Point Omega*, and plays such as *Love-Lies-Bleeding*, goes back and forth between them. Keith Neudecker in *Falling Man* goes to the desert—assuming that Las Vegas is still in the desert—to reinvent himself as a professional poker player in the wake of 9-11, though New York and what happened there are always just a memory or a stray perception away.

East and west, then, NYC and the desert: in *Zero K* the narrator's father, Ross Lockhart, was from New York, and his mother, Madeline Siebert, from the desert, "a small town in southern Arizona. A cactus on a postage stamp, she called it" (*ZK* 58). Sounds like a marriage made in DeLillo heaven, though it didn't really work out—not even close. Perhaps the point is that one cannot easily combine what is supposed to remain in tension, in juxtaposition, in contraband. It's like the New York Giants playing in San Francisco, or the Brooklyn Dodgers in LA.

From east to west, New York City to the desert, band to contraband: that is the trajectory of DeLillo's characters either in the short term or, like Nick Shay, the long. Born and raised in the Bronx up until that fateful day when, at the age of seventeen, he kills George the Waiter, Nick goes from New York to Staatsburg to Minneapolis to Palo Alto and other sundry places, before winding up in the desert. As he says to Klara Sax, "I live a quiet life in an unassuming house in a suburb of Phoenix. Pause. Like someone in the Witness Protection Program" (*U* 66). The joke is canned and well rehearsed, but in Nick's case it still has some bite, not just because of his own actions but because of his fantasies about what happened to his low-level mobster father "back east."

From east to west, NYC to the desert: if one wants a single image with which to mark the contradiction, a single image divided against itself in counterpoint, one could find none better than this one: Nick driving out into the desert to see Klara Sax for the first time in forty years and encountering a vehicle, "but not your everyday average all-terrain vehicle…. It seemed to be, it clearly was a New York taxi, impossible but true, yellower than egg yolk and coming fast" (*U* 64–5). Turns out to be an art project of some kind, not a "real" taxi, not one you could actually flag down, but a quote unquote "New York City Taxi Cab."

Of course, not even the desert is singular or unique; it too is doubled, double-banded, the desert in the American West already the shadow or double of all the deserts in the Middle East, in Iraq, in India, and so on. It is a place of blazing sunlight but then also, and this too will need to be thought in terms of contraband, a privileged place for the sun's eclipse. It is the place of ritual and renewal, the place of what came *before* America, though also, as

Matt Shay well knows, the place of the most sophisticated weapons research and tests, the place where one can glimpse what might come *after*. And that too is an integral part of "the desert experience" (*U* 211), the invention of that ungridded space, that "white space on the map" (*U* 529; see 404 and 451). It is as if "the desert was clairvoyant," a "landscape [that] unravels and reveals," that "knows future as well as past" (*PO* 87). As Owen Brademas confesses near the end of *The Names*: "I was afraid of the desert but drawn to it, drawn to the contradiction" (*N* 296). For no one today can even imagine the desert, and especially the American desert, a place of stunning beauty and clarity, without flashing on that blinding white light spreading out across it and then the mushroom cloud rising gloriously above it.

But then, after New York and the East Coast, after Middle America, the prairie states and the desert—there is, inevitably, California, "at the shallow end of the continent" (*A* 150), where David Bell might have stayed after college were it not for his father back east. For those born and raised back east, California can be either a destination of choice or the object of good and sometimes not-so-good hearted humor.

> I found southern California too interesting. The experimental aircraft, the fault systems, the inferno of cars and smog, the women from nowhere, even the street gangs that were coming into prominence at the time, adopting varsity colors.
>
> (*U* 340)

Just the thought, just the name, seems to call for a jab: "California. I need to tone up my orgasm" (*N* 245; see 165). Or else: "Californians invented the concept of life-style. This alone warrants their doom" (*WN* 66).

New York, the Mid-West, California, the desert, America is all these things in DeLillo, internally divided, self-absorbed and yet inevitably open to what is beyond or outside it. America the beautiful: land of contrasts, of contradictions, and, of course, of contraband. In the end, America seems always in the works of DeLillo to be in conversation with what lies beyond it, beyond it and after it. In *Falling Man*, for example, there is a long conversation or debate about the place of America in the world after 9-11:

> We're all sick of America and Americans. The subject nauseates us…. There is a word in German. *Gedankenübertragung*. This is the broadcasting of thoughts. We are all beginning to have this thought, of American irrelevance. It's a little like telepathy. Soon the day is coming when nobody has to think about America except for the danger it brings.
>
> (*FM* 191)

It's an interesting theory—and we see this sort of telepathy return in *The Silence*—the idea being that "there's an empty space where America used to be" (*FM* 193). It's a bit like losing a loved one, a mother or a father perhaps, and not knowing where to look for them any more: when Jeffrey Lockhart tries to imagine the time he and his parents were all together, he says he "came up with nothing…. All I felt was a shattered space where my father used to be" (*ZK* 26). Maybe America is now like that to the rest of the world.

Land of secrets and discoveries, conquests and contrasts, America suggests already, all by itself, both itself and its others. Perhaps that is what was meant, already back in *Americana*, by this provocative, enigmatic, but perhaps also prophetic statement: "America can be saved only by what it's trying to destroy" (*A* 256).

Automobiles

"It's a Cadillac all right." "The Rolls-Royce of automobiles."

RS 14

He sat hunched by the radio listening for hints of total global collapse in the news of a flipped vehicle on the inbound Gowanus.

"*S*" 191

He didn't want me to drive, he didn't trust other drivers, other drivers were not him.

PO 74

"I drove at insane speeds" (*A* 377): that's David Bell, as we already heard, near the end of *Americana*. He says this because the spiritual journey out west, the trip from east to west that is so central to the bi-coastal DeLillo, is something that had to happen, at least early on, *by car*. For "cars are religious," as Bell says, in a way that planes are not, and some cars are more religious than others, for example a "red Mustang, an infinitely more religious vehicle than the T-Bird [Bell] owned in college" (*A* 111). Near the end of the novel, we see Clevenger, who has picked up Bell hitchhiking near the end of his pilgrimage, "doubly screened behind stained windshield and sunglasses, bowed low in his cool church, and I knew this was why I was with him, to search out the final extreme" (*A* 362).

The road-trip car is just the first in a long line of cars in DeLillo, cars more or less alone on the open road (recall the video-feed of a road in Finland that Lauren watches in *The Body Artist*) or else involved in races (*U* 529–30), or highway shootings, or burnt out and abandoned, like the cars located by sisters Edgar and Gracie and then "cannibalized" for parts by Ismael and his crew (*U* 241–3). There is also, of course—and this too is a ritual in America—one's "first car," the car that the young (male) adolescent saves up for, buys, and then "simonizes... once a month," because, among other things, "the car gets him laid" (*L* 9). DeLillo's characters look back upon such cars with fondness: "He missed his shit-heap Chevy, no plates, no insurance, no license to drive it, transmission shot to hell, the door on the passenger side opening up unannounced every time he made a left turn" (*U* 705; *U* 686–7, 691–3). It's a piece of junk, but that's the car Nick thinks of and misses, not the 1950 Merc we see him driving later on (*U* 549) or the Lexus—the perfect car for upper management—he has decades later in Phoenix (*U* 63). In America our cars define us, both in life and in death: "The dead have faces, automobiles....'He drove an orange Mazda'" (*WN* 38).

With all these cars driving around there are, inevitably, traffic jams, and so traffic reports on those jams (*ZK* 81, 84), reports "on the routine havoc out there" ("S" 184). It's often an absolute nightmare, but sometimes a source of sheer wonder:

> I watched the cars speed below me.... I watched and listened, unaware of passing time, thinking of the order and discipline of the traffic.... This is civilization, I thought, the thrust of social and material advancement, people in motion, testing the limits of time and space.
>
> ("HS" 179)

There can be something mystical about all those cars going by at such insane speeds, as not only Jack and the family know in *White Noise* but Jerold Bradway in "Hammer and Sickle," watching the traffic and "breathing the fumes of free enterprise" ("HS" 181). "Why don't they crash all the time?" ("HS" 180), the watcher of traffic is bound to ask himself. But of course they do crash, occasionally, and people do die, to the tune of some 30+ thousand a year, and some of those accidents come to feed and haunt our national or personal imaginations, from the deaths of Jimmy Dean (*WN* 68) or Jayne Mansfield—"Ho-rrific car crash" (*U* 484)—to the car accident of *Valparaiso*, which, as we progressively learn, seriously injured a son and effectively destroyed a family (*V* 74).

As with guns and knives and tools, it is the names and the language of cars that are, for DeLillo, just as essential as the moving vehicles themselves. In *Libra* alone there is a whole fleet of cars—each affectionately named and often dated—a '55 green Chevy (*L* 337), a Bel Air, a '57 Merc (*L* 379), a Galaxie convertible (*L* 288), and a Rambler (*L* 169), all of them, the whole cortege, leading up to President Kennedy's limousine, a deep blue "Lincoln," as comparative assassination buffs well know (*L* 392). *Underworld* too has some beauties, a lime-sherbet Chevrolet, a '57 Bel Air convertible (*U* 165), the Demings's two-tone Ford Fairlane convertible (*U* 515), J. Edgar Hoover's "bulletproof black Cadillac" (*U* 568), a VW "bug"—suspicious to the germophobic Hoover just because of the name (*U* 578–9)—and on and on. Sometimes, we see these classic American cars in foreign places, sometimes decades after they were present on American streets, in Istanbul, for example, where the taxis are all Olds 88s, Buick Roadmasters, Chrysler limousines, and DeSotos (*N* 93; see *AZ* 253, 312). (If anyone is looking for DeLillo's most hilarious depiction of driving in traffic, one will find it in a description not of New York, Boston, or LA, but of Tehran in *The Names*, where drivers are apparently taught to drive as quickly in reverse as going forward (*N* 65; see *AZ* 191–3).)

There is Bell's red Mustang, then, and JFK's blue Lincoln, and the thirty-six stretch limos in the funeral procession for Brutha Fez in *Cosmopolis*, but then also, and especially—since a good part of the novel actually takes place *in* it—the stretch limo that Eric Packer gets driven around in as he slowly makes his way from the upper East Side in New York to the lower West Side. It is not the first car used as an office or workspace in DeLillo—Lomax basically works out of his car in *Running Dog* (a limousine as well, see *RD* 26, 86)—but nobody lives out of their car quite like Packer does (not quite Packard, but close (see *AZ* 252–3)). Up until the final pages of the narrative Packer appears more or less inseparable from his car, the ultimate prosthesis for his mega-rich body. His stretch limousine is quite literally a metaphor, that is, a means of conveyance, a moving image of supposed autonomy and self-sufficiency, of an ego on the go. Self-enclosing and self-enclosed, the limo's tinted glass allows Packer to see without being seen, the whole world incorporated into the automobile through innumerable "visual display units," computer monitors, TV screens, and video feeds (*C* 13). "Oh and this car, which I love. The glow of the screens. I love the screens. The glow of cyber-capital" (*C* 78). It is the ultimate work "cubicle," but designed for the captain of industry rather than the underling (see *C* 75). And it's "Prousted" to boot, that is, "cork-line[d] against street noise" (*C* 70), cut off from the world, like Proust's room on Boulevard Haussmann—even better than the armored car of *Ratner's Star*: "Is this thing bulletproof?" "Absolutely, top to bottom" (*RS* 15; see *N* 65).

Cosmopolis is in many ways an extended reflection on the way in which those of us who love our automobiles, especially in America, are sold a certain image of freedom and independence, an image of solitude and a certain way of achieving—or not—some community if not communion with others. At issue throughout the novel is precisely America's "auto industry," its promise, in short, of autonomy, which is no doubt why politicians have tried so hard to save that industry. It is thus perfectly appropriate that this quintessential late twentieth-century American novel in the quintessential cosmopolitan city should revolve around an automobile, for what would America be, what would the modernity and postmodernity of America be, without the automobile?

Packer's limousine is, in many ways, a response to life in the city, and especially New York City, where "eye contact was a delicate matter. A quarter second of a shared glance was a violation of agreements that made the city operational. Who steps aside for whom, who looks or does not look at whom" (*C* 66). One has to be careful with looking, and even more so with touching: "No one wanted to be touched. There was a pact of untouchability" (*C* 66), which is why Packer, at least initially, crosses the city in his stretch limo, seemingly safe and protected from the outside, not yet realizing that, in the end, no one is immune. For just hours into his contemporary odyssey Packer will be extruded from his car, absorbed into a crowd of extras being filmed naked on a New York City street: "people unlike each other who were now alike, amassed, heaped in a way, alive and dead together" (*C* 174). Just as Packer's wife, Elise Shifrin, loses her auto at the beginning of the day (*C* 177), so, by night fall, Eric Packer will lose his—his automobile, his fortune, his supposed autonomy, and, shortly thereafter, his life.

By the time of *Zero K* and *The Silence* there will still be motor vehicles, mostly vans, SUVs, to shuttle characters to and from the airport, but it is planes that will do most of the heavy lifting. The transition is already presaged in *Americana*: "This is a religious journey.... Planes aren't religious yet. Cars are religious. Maybe planes will be next." "Planes are sexy" (*A* 49).

Airplanes

The sooner we get them in the air, the better. Like swimming or ice skating. You have to start them young.

WN 93

Only the sense of leaving earth. This always seems slightly disallowable.

V 19

Was there ever a moment on the foggy tarmac / When you thought that nothing mattered.

V 70

> *A stewardess came along and asked him to extinguish his smoking materials, and the pilot on the intercom said we would be landing real soon, the Good Lord willing.*
>
> AZ 173

And so elsewhere in DeLillo it is the plane rather than the car that is the means of contraband, the plane and not the car that brings us elsewhere, and that proves that "the point of our century is people move" (*L* 49). Much of the play *Valparaiso* is about a plane flight to Valparaiso, the one in Chile, though the flyer thought he was going to Indiana. *Players* begins in the lounge of a luxury liner with an in-flight movie playing in the background, while *Ratner's Star* opens with "Little Billy Twillig," fourteen-year-old math prodigy and Nobel Laureate from the Bronx, aboard a "Sony 747, labeled as such" (*RS* 3; see 97), *en route* to a secret location to work on a super-secret project. *Zero K* opens in a similar way, with Jeffrey Lockhart following the flight itinerary planned by his father Ross to bring him to Kyrgyzstan (*ZK* 27). And, of course, *The Silence* begins aboard a plane, with Jim Kripps and Tessa Berens returning from their two week vacation in Paris on that fateful Super Bowl Sunday 2022.

Given DeLillo's interest in movement, in travel, it is no surprise that there should be so many reflections on air travel, and, first of all, on all those holding areas or counter-spaces called airports. For there's the whole process of just getting to and onto the plane, which is described here in *Zero K* with a series of eight paratactic *ands* to mark the mind-numbing march:

> Those blanked-out eternities at the airport. Getting there, waiting there, standing shoeless in long lines. Think about it. We take off our shoes and remove our metal objects and then enter a stall and raise our arms and get body-scanned and sprayed with radiation and reduced to nakedness on a screen somewhere and then how totally helpless we are all over again as we wait on the tarmac, belted in, our plane eighteenth in line, and it's all ordinary, it's routine, we make ourselves forget it. That's the thing.
>
> (ZK 172)

But once we've made it through all the screening, we begin to feel the power of these strange, nowhere spaces—they are called "terminals" for a reason—that connect nations, link continents, and contraband lives:

> In this vast space, which seems like nothing so much as a container for emptiness, we sit with our documents always ready, wondering if

someone will appear and demand to know who we are, someone in authority, and to be unprepared is to risk serious things.

(*N* 253)

Nothing would seem to be more alienating, more inimical to our sense of self, and yet DeLillo seems to suggest that this is precisely who we are or who we have become: "Air travel reminds us who we are. It's the means by which we recognize ourselves as modern" (*N* 254). We recognize ourselves, in short, as contrabanded creatures—at once up there (or here), in the air, and down here (or there), able only to imagine ourselves down here when up there and vice versa. Up there, 36,000 feet above sea level, we live another kind of life, separate from the one we live on the ground: "I believe in death-in-life. One flows through the other. I mean what else is the meaning of a long plane trip spanning continents? What is a three- or four-thousand-mile journey on a 747 except an example of death-in-life?" (*GJ* 43)

Life in the air is thus a sort of counter-life, with its own language, gestures, and codes: "We're strangers on a plane. We're having a friendly talk about this and that. Calls for smiles, don't you think? That's what travel's all about. Supposed to release all that pent-up friendliness" (*RS* 6). But, of course, "people are polite on airplanes" for another reason: "We sense the presence of death …. The hush of death" (*DR* 7). "You don't push and shove when you're moving down the aisle of a giant, gleaming death machine" (*AZ* 169).

> And this is why the airplane is the perfect laboratory for a study of fear. You are cut off from the earth, from all the things that console you or support you. Your fear is pure. It is pure fear. It is naked and isolated and pure. You are there helpless and practically shining in the purity of your fear. It is a kind of sainthood. It is that pure.
>
> (*AZ* 171)

There is death in the air when you are in the air, but there are also small wonders, brief returns to childhood, as this frequent flier testifies in *Amazons*:

> I've never outgrown the thrill of getting a window seat…. Window seats may be the only way that remains for adults to stay in direct touch with their own childhoods…. When I don't get a window seat, I feel a tiny, crushing sensation deep inside. It would not be overdramatizing the matter to say it is a spiritual loss.
>
> (*AZ* 189)

DeLillo reserves a number of his reflections for the world's large and ever-growing traveler class, people who travel for a living, as it were, circling the globe in the air rather than walking across it as their ancestors used to do. They are today a readily identifiable species, "a subculture, business people in transit, growing old in planes and airports" (*N* 6; see *AZ* 24). They are the ones, we realize in retrospect, who didn't "exchange wild looks when the oxygen masks dropped during touchdown" (*N* 7), the ones the other passengers look to when there are no crew members around "for some indication that the aircraft is *supposed* to be flying sideways" (*AZ* 168), the ones who know how "to appear crisp and businesslike in the face of burnt-out engines, jagged streaks of lightning, and ski-masked, religious-fanatical hijackers with explosives strapped to their chests. You need people like this on a rough flight" (*AZ* 170).

But, of course, these are the same people who would see right through the euphemisms of airline personnel trying to convince passengers that what they are about to experience is not a "crash" but a "crash *landing*" (the kind Jim and Tessa will survive, by the way, in *The Silence*):

> "Crash landing, crash landing." They saw how easy it was, by adding one word, to maintain a grip on the future, to extend it in consciousness if not in actual fact.
>
> (*WN* 91)

But the wise are also the weary, as in those members of a new race of people who live a life of contraband, a life in the contrails, as it were, disconnected from life on the ground. "People who travel a great deal lose their souls at some point.... There's a soul belt up there. People who travel talk about nothing but travel. Before, during and after" (*GJ* 54).

And then there's tourism. If travel belongs to a kind of counter-life, a life away from life, then tourism is the logical extension of all travel. It's travel not to places you really want to see, exactly, but to "the kind of place you were glad you'd seen, like Edwards Air Force Base, just to know you'd seen it" (*AZ* 132). It's a life without responsibility or consequence, a life without "accountability." When you are a tourist, says the narrator of *The Names*,

> errors and failings don't cling to you the way they do back home. You're able to drift across continents and languages, suspending the operation of sound thought. Tourism is the march of stupidity. You're expected to be stupid.... Being stupid is the pattern, the level and the norm. You can exist on this level for weeks and months without reprimand

or dire consequence.... There is nothing to think about but the next shapeless event.

(*N* 43–4)

There is thus a resistance to tourism of this kind throughout *The Names*. Axton's sort-of-friend Volterra says: "I never understood the lure of fabulous places. Or the idea of losing yourself in a place.... I'm the place, I guess that's the reason. I'm the only place I need" (*N* 143). Axton himself seems to share this view of famous places, at least initially. At the beginning of the novel he still has not visited the Acropolis, even though he lives in Athens. "Beauty, dignity, order, proportion. There are obligations attached to such a visit" (*N* 3). By the end of the novel, however, he does visit, and comes to understand "that the Parthenon was not a thing to study but to feel."

> I hadn't expected a human feeling to emerge from the stones but this is what I found, deeper than the art and mathematics embodied in the structure, the optical exactitudes. I found a cry for pity. This is what remains to the mauled stones in their blue surround, this open cry, this voice we know as our own.
>
> (*N* 330)

This is what the visit to the Acropolis brings James Axton—a cry, a voice, the very thing, it turns out, that we bring to it: "This is what we bring to the temple, not prayer or chant or slaughtered rams. Our offering is language" (*N* 331). In other words, what we bring to the *things* of the world are the *words* we use to speak of or to say them. That, it seems, is our offering, our contraband, the kind we do not need to check in or pick up upon arrival at our destination.

Beyond America

> *I was wary of pressure groups and I foresaw the remark from someone in such a group saying "cradle of whose civilization," for there is always this prejudice against Western civilization having its own cradle and calling it the cradle when other peoples have their own ideas of where the cradle is and even whether or not there is a cradle as we employ the term...*
>
> RS 215

> *That's one of the things about living abroad. It takes a while to find out who the madmen are.*
>
> N 132

I go everywhere twice. Once to get the wrong impression, once to strengthen it.

N 255

Don DeLillo is, as we have seen, an American writer who writes mostly about America. But the rest of the world is hardly absent from his work. In early novels, characters sometimes travel to places just outside the United States, places like Toronto (*P* 191–2; see *N* 49), or else very far away, like some undisclosed or unidentifiable region of China, where *Ratner's Star* appears to take place. But there are no novels before *The Names* in 1982 where most of the action takes place abroad or where there are serious reflections upon life abroad. *The Names* thus takes this movement into the foreign, this contrabanding of America, to another level, with a narrator, an American, James Axton, living in Athens while his son and estranged wife live on the Greek island of Kouros (see *N* 3, 7–8). As Axton says, "Americans used to come to places like this to write and paint and study, to find deeper textures" (*N* 6). But Axton, who has previously lived in California, Vermont, and Ontario (*N* 8), takes his family to Greece not because he is a writer or painter trying to find these deeper textures— even if he will unwittingly find them and, by the end of the novel, seems poised to become a writer—but because he was sent there as a risk analyst for major corporations, if not, perhaps, and unbeknownst to him, the "Corporation" itself, that is, just in case it needs spelling out, the CIA. As part of his job, Axton regularly visits Turkey and Pakistan (*N* 11), Istanbul and Lahore, as well as Cairo (*N* 94, see *DR* 72). It's quite a change, and Axton—like DeLillo himself, it seems, if we simply follow the references— really takes to it. "It's an interesting part of the world," he says, "I feel I'm involved in events" (*N* 12).

So it is that Athens, and the Aegean more generally, became a favorite place for DeLillo, whether to locate a story or a character. This is no doubt due in part to the Aegean's unique light, the way spaces are illuminated there, "Euclidean rigor in quantum space" (*FM* 130), and, of course, the layers of history, the one on top of or sometimes right next to the other, concealing or juxtaposed with one another in contraband. That helps explain as well why archeology is such a favorite discipline for DeLillo—from *The Body Artist* (where Lauren Hartke's father was a classical scholar studying in the Aegean (*BA* 104)), to *Falling Man* (Lianne's parents met "on a small island in the northeast Aegean" (*FM* 130)) and *Zero K* (where Artis Martineau, Ross Lockhart's second wife, is an archaeologist (*ZK* 3, 13; see *PO* 90)). *The Names* itself actually revolves around an archeological dig that Axton's wife Kathryn works on: "It had struck her with the pure light of a major saint's vision. She would sift dirt on an island in the Aegean" (*N* 16).

The Names might therefore seem to be an exception to DeLillo's penchant for having his protagonists travel from east to west, for we actually go further east as the narrative progresses (to Jordan, then Pakistan and India), but the real tension at the end of the novel revolves around what is happening in an eastern place (the desert of India—a desert, once again) and what happened long ago to Owen Brademas, the head of the archaeological dig, in a small town in the west, on the American Prairie. It's not the desert, but it seems to serve a similar purpose. As Brademas says, "We were in the middle. Everything was around us, somehow equidistant. Everything was space, extremes of weather" (*N* 78). *The Names* thus moves, just like other DeLillo novels, from the city (in this case Athens) with its buildings and its people to places bereft of both: "Wherever you will find empty land, there are men who try to get closer to God" (*N* 149).

From east to west and then from the West (the United States) to the East, with Europe being more or less, with just a few exceptions, a flyover zone: that appears to be the flight plan or the plot line of most DeLillo works. In fact, with the exception of Greece (in *The Names* and "The Ivory Acrobat"), there are very few extended sequences in or even about Europe. There are references to France and to French, which start off well enough with David Bell in *Americana* fantasizing about impressing his girlfriend "by speaking French to the waiter with the warmth and intimacy of a hero of the Resistance greeting an old comrade-in-arms" (*A* 7), but the references are soon not quite so positive. Just a hundred pages later in the same novel a Sioux mystic speaks of future senators in Washington spending "eight hours a day in their identical offices, chained to radiators, being flogged by French tarts. This is known as the philosophy lesson, the wisdom of the old world, the culture we so badly lack" (*A* 119).

France is a decent place to live, it seems, but it is especially noteworthy as a place to die, like "those fabled khans and their nymphomaniacs who are always crashing into trees somewhere between Paris and Nice" (*A* 172). It is also, of course, a place of art and architecture (*A* 260, *S* 13), of literature (*A* 181; see *RS* 78), of fashion and of culture (see *U* 437, 445, 688), or at least the appearance thereof. Take, for example, the couple in *Point Omega* visiting the exhibit at the MOMA, first identified as "French or Italian, intelligent-looking, standing in the faint light near the sliding door" (*PO* 108), but then simply as French, a couple that would "talk about the experience for hours afterward," "talking through dinner in a restaurant recommended by friends, an Indian place, a Vietnamese place, Brooklyn, remote, the harder to get to, the better the food" (*PO* 111). You get the type.

France is also the land of intellectuals and philosophers (*A* 291) and Gauloises (*A* 226), and, often, a "particularly dramatic" way of smoking them, even when the smoker is not a French existentialist but a French-Canadian hockey coach:

> He was a passionate smoker of cigarettes. You've seen these people. It is a performance. The way they light up. They way they inhale. The way they *hold* their cigarette. Every time [he] blew out smoke, it was the French Resistance all over again. It was that dramatic. I thought the German tanks were making a left turn past his mother's house.
>
> (*AZ* 172)

It's dramatic, historic, even political, and it can fog up a narrative like nobody's business:

> He talked with smoke coming out of his mouth and the cigarette in his hand, with the cigarette in his mouth and smoke in his face, with smoke coming out of his nose and tobacco on his tongue, with his hand in the air and smoke in my face, with the cigarette in his hand, tobacco on his tongue, smoke in his face and my hand in the air.
>
> (*AZ* 185)

There is in the end no wide-eyed enthusiasm in any of DeLillo's characters for either France or Europe more generally, despite the poetry of certain descriptions of them (see *A* 265). Notice how, in *The Day Room*, Budge begins his praise of foreign cultures with Western Europe before then suggesting that the most important things—like talk, like language—become more intense the further east one goes:

> I admire the European experience. Cafés, cigarette smoke. Talk becomes more passionate as you travel east. Paris, Rome, Athens. An intensity enters the voice. Words take on deeper meaning. There is a life-force in the simplest greeting.... Look at the Arab experience. People dress for conversation. Flowing garments, sandals, dark beards.
>
> (*DR* 8; see 28; *AZ* 268)

When writer Bill Gray thus leaves the United States in *Mao II*, it is not to Rome, Paris, or Brussels but Cyprus, via Athens (*M* 50, 169, 196), and then Beirut (*M* 214, 238, see *RS* 379).

There are plenty of foreign places in *Libra*, though these are programmed, to a large extent, by Oswald's life, by the historical record, which could not be rewritten. There is, for example, Cuba, endless talk in 1963 about Cuba, right off America's southern coast, living in America's shadow, though also, precisely, America's shadow and nightmare since at least April 1961 (see *L* 187, 337). But then there are even more exotic places, such as Atsugi, Japan (*L* 83), where Oswald was stationed in the service, and then Moscow and Minsk in the Soviet Union, to which he seems to have tried to defect. DeLillo didn't choose any of these places for Oswald, but the places did give him a chance to consider what Americans might think about such foreign places and what people in those places might think about America and Americans, even if Oswald, well before the assassination, was not your typical American.

> He was someone interesting, an American, a stranger with a story. America was a rumor down the street, a gleaming place people didn't quite believe in, and they wanted to hear what he had to say.
>
> (*L* 190)

There is the Soviet Union, therefore, and Eastern Europe, and former Soviet states—Ukraine, where *Konstantinovka* is, a place with two *k*'s inside a place with one, and the place where, in *Zero K*, Stak (with one *k*), the adopted son of Emma, Jeffrey's companion, is killed (*ZK* 264, 272). And then there are all the -stans. The Convergence in this same novel is located near Bishkek, the capital of Kyrgyzstan. As Ross says to his son, and we too would do well to heed the advice: "Once you know the local names and how to spell them, you'll feel less detached" (*ZK* 29).

Near the end of *Underworld* Brian and Nick travel to Sheremetyevo, in Kazakhstan (*U* 787), to witness a nuclear blast designed to destroy nuclear waste. It is already an echo, an aftershock, as it were, because Kazakhstan is also the place where, as we recalled in the preface when we were talking about opposites and mushrooms, the Soviet Union in 1951 conducted a nuclear test on the same day as Bobby Thomson's shot heard 'round the world. Shot and counter-shot, then, half a world away, band and contraband. Perhaps that is why DeLillo, a decidedly American writer who is well steeped in American and European literature, tends to locate his contraband not in Western Europe but rather in Lebanon or Kazakhstan or China, the latter being the setting, it seems, for most of *Ratner's Star*, as well as the place where Artis had once worked as an archeologist, well in advance of the Convergence (*ZK* 30–1). The place is evoked already with some admiration—at least by one of his characters—in *Americana*: "Did you know that China had mastered most of the arts and sciences at a time when the Europeans were still combing fleas out of each other's hair?" (*A* 72).

Life lived elsewhere or seen from afar, on an island in the Caribbean ("Creation") waiting to return to the United States, in Greece as an expat

("The Ivory Acrobat"), in space contemplating a planet at war ("Human Moments in World War III"), or in Kazakhstan (also with two *k*'s), thinking about or juxtaposed with New York, New York—this is the stuff of DeLillo contraband. And it will have been there from the beginning, that is, from that very first novel with America in its title. For if the entire story of *Americana* takes place in America, the writing seems to take place, precisely, elsewhere, on an island—perhaps the Mediterranean already—since there is a narrative frame that appears to be outside or beyond America, as if the narrator, David Bell, had to leave America, to get some distance on it, in order to speak of it. Though there are only a few references to this narrative frame, the effect of this double-banded narration is striking:

> From this window I can see the ocean, far out.... Later I'll walk on the beach for an hour or so. If the weather has cleared by then I'll be able to see the coast of Africa.... But right now it is a pleasure to anticipate slipping once again (a paragraph hence) into a much more filmworthy period of my life.
>
> (*A* 347; see 129)

It's not exactly clear where Bell is writing; the reference to the coast of Africa might suggest the Mediterranean, as in *The Names* and *Mao II*, but the narrator speaks of the "ocean" rather than the "sea," so it is unclear where that leaves us. What is important to note is that, already from the beginning, DeLillo's narration is double-banded, not only at the level of what is narrated (New York City + Elsewhere) but at the level of the narration. That is perhaps why *Americana* ends with a flight and a signature, with a reference to an American credit card if not to America itself, along with everything that lies beyond or after it: "Then, with my American Express credit card, I booked a seat on the first flight to New York. Ten minutes after we were airborne a woman asked for my autograph" (*A* 377). If *Americana* is a sort of "Portrait of the Artist as a Young American Man," it, like its Joycean counterpart, seemed to require some sort of exile in order to get the contraband narrative off the ground, in order for Bell/DeLillo to write or to sign—there in place of his name, there aboard a plane—the closing word "autograph."

2

Countercurrents

Sports, Games, Sports Gaming

Some teams are named for places they don't play in. Other teams are named for places that don't even exist anymore. Still other teams are named for entire regions. And still other teams are named for lofty descriptions of cities, states, or regions. Some places have names but no teams. Some places have teams but no names. Some places have names and teams but don't exist in people minds as the places that have these teams because the teams are named for different places. That's why bus drivers get lost going to arenas. It's like some secret geography. Anaheim, Inglewood, Landover, Bloomington, Uniondale, Irving.

AZ 320

I've never seen a good football player who wanted to learn a foreign language.

EZ 199

I told [the coach] I knew all the plays; there was no reason to practice them over and over; the endless repetition might be spiritually disastrous.

EZ 19

I reject the notion of football as warfare. Warfare is warfare. We don't need substitutes because we've got the real thing.

EZ 111; see 164

"How has the team been going?"
"Tie some, lose some."

AZ 267

Throughout DeLillo's novels, sports and games—particularly American sports and more or less universal games—provide a sort of counterpart or foil to everyday life, a contraband life to the life one usually lives. Early on in *Americana* we see David Bell playing basketball with crumpled pieces of paper in the office (*A* 91), a half ironic nod, perhaps, in this first novel, to Updike's Rabbit Angstrom. Later we see him trying to keep up with a kid in Fort Curtis whom he has filmed playing basketball (*A* 253). As Bell says, "Basketball has always seemed to me the most American of sports, a small town thing, two kids in a driveway and daddy-built backboard" (*A* 91). Though baseball seems to take the place of basketball in *Underworld*, even there Nick, like Bell, plays basketball in the correctional facility in upstate New York with "members of a street gang named the Alhambras," who play the game with their "customary combat skills, hacking the shooter, wheeling off the boards with elbows jutting" (*U* 501, 503; see *RS* 135).

But basketball is just the first sport, the headliner, of DeLillo's many sports pages, which also feature hockey, in *Amazons* (*AZ* 2, 10), tennis, in *Zero K*, with a reference to that "Latvian woman who groaned erotically with each fierce return" (*ZK* 196; see *A* 151, *RD* 38, *AZ* 14), boxing—with nods to Sugar Ray Robinson (*A* 190) and Jack Dempsey (*U* 15-16)— that "spiritual effort" called "long-distance running" (*FM* 233), lacrosse (*WN* 226), fencing (*AZ* 330-2), even golf, "that anal round of scrupulous caution and petty griefs" (*P* 9, 178), "the puritan ethic" incarnate, only "landscaped," with "it's eighteen anal openings with waving flags" (*AZ* 261, see *GJ* 170), and soccer, with its wild, writhing crowds on TV (*M* 33), a game that, were it "an American invention," would surely be criticized by "some European intellectual" as "a game structured on anti-masturbatory principles" in accordance with America's "historically puritanical nature" ("HS" 158).

But then there is, as the title *End Zone* announces, football. Coach Creed characterizes the ethos just perfectly, "It's only a game, but it's the only game" (*EZ* 15). For it has a simplicity to it that most games lack: "hit and get hit" (*EZ* 4). It is a sport of epic confrontation that also strives for unity, for that intangible something that turns forty-five unique individuals into a thing with "one body, a thing of ninety legs" (*EZ* 56). And in addition to the game itself, there are all the pregame rituals, the repetitive grunts, the prayers and obscenities, "the chant or urgent breathing of men in preparation for ritual danger" (*EZ* 106). Though steeped in satire, these passages are not unserious. It is funny, to be sure, to hear footfall compared to "ancient warriorship," to "cults devoted to pagan forms of technology" (*EZ* 36), or to hear of players "painting [themselves] in barbaric manner before going forth to battle in mud" (*EZ* 41), football players who then take up their "frozen insect pose" just before the battle is joined (*EZ* 140). But the satire works only because of the seriousness with which these things are treated. Same thing with the little game dubbed by Gary Harkness "Bang You're Dead," a game whose motto seems to be: "To kill with impunity. To die in the celebration of ancient ways" (*EZ* 33).

There is a simplicity to these sports, though there is also the temptation to compare them to any number of other things, like war, or the cosmic violence of the universe, a comparison that is particularly tempting when one is stoned on pot, not your typical drug of choice for football players but the one Gary Harkness chooses in *End Zone*:

> "Listen to those noises out there. Pop, pop, pop. Ving, ving. Existence without anxiety. Happiness. Knowing your body. Understanding the real needs of man.... The universe was born in violence. Stars die violently. Elements are created out of cosmic violence."
> "Gary, this is football."
>
> (*EZ* 121)

It is not too long thereafter that Gary has to leave the game—complaining of hunger pangs (*EZ* 176).

So there's basketball, golf, soccer, football, and then, and especially, and from *Americana* on, baseball. David Bell plays catch with a kid on the Indian reservation out west (*A* 359; see 138), as does Keith with Justin in *Falling Man* (*FM* 59), and thinks: "Baseball is so beautiful and lazy. It's our version of the café life. You sit there and nothing happens. I really love it. The season's underway now. If this were 1955 I could be sitting in the bleachers at the old Polo Grounds, watching the Giants play the Cubs" (*A* 361). Bell thus takes us out to the ballgame at the Polo Grounds (and against the Cubs, no less) decades before *Underworld*, which famously begins with a fifty-page Prologue that recounts blow by blow, or pitch by pitch, the closing moments of the famous baseball game in the Polo Grounds between the New York Giants and the Brooklyn Dodgers on October 3, 1951, to determine who would win the National League Pennant and go on to face the New York Yankees in the World Series, the game that ends, of course, with the homerun by the Giants' Bobby Thomson that came to be known as "the shot heard 'round the world."

There are the gestures of sports, the body moves and body memories that take one back to childhood. David Bell has such memories when shagging fly balls in his late twenties: "I was nobody. I was instinct and speed and a memory that extended back for no more than seconds" (*A* 199). Billy Twillig's father, named Babe, would actually imitate the stances of famous baseball players (*RS* 26).

But more than places and gestures and the games themselves, it is the language of these games that seems to be most important. We see throughout DeLillo's work the role played by announcers, radio announcers, for instance, in *Underworld*, and TV announcers in *The Silence*, though that is just the most mediatized edge of the whole language of sports, which includes telling stories from the past, rattling off statistics, HRs, ERAs, RBIs, the whole mathematics and poetry of baseball. As *End Zone* puts it, "much of the appeal of sport derives from its dependence on elegant gibberish" (*EZ* 113). The language of the thing—the chants and gibberish and jargon— seems to count more than the thing itself. David Bell says in *Americana*: "The best part of prep school was suiting up for a baseball or basketball game. I loved that phrase—*suiting up*" (*A* 158). It's quite a claim: the best part of prep school would have been not prep school itself (that's understandable), and not playing some sport after school, or even suiting up for the games. The best part seems to have been the phrase *suiting up*. That's the power of words, of place-names like "the Polo Grounds" or "Yankee Stadium," or the simple word "baseball": "The word has resonance if you're American, a sense of shared heart and untranslatable lore" (*M* 8–9). And then there are all the little phrases, like "batting first," or "playing second base," that alone can take you back, back to the voice of Russ Hodges, for example, doing the play-by-play of that famous 1951 baseball game in the Polo Grounds. That is in fact how Bill Gray would calm his mind and put himself to sleep at night, not by prayer or counting sheep but by remembering players' names: "In his sleeplessness he went down the batting order of the 1938 Cleveland Indians.... The names of those ballplayers were his night prayer, his reverent petition to God, with wording that remained eternally the same" (*M* 136). It's hardly surprising that Alfonse Stompanato, respected professor at the College-on-the-Hill, would have sewn on his academic gown not the insignia of his alma mater but "a Brooklyn Dodger emblem" (*WN* 214). Or that Selvy would say to Moll: "You have a third baseman's walk.... Like you've been spending a whole career too close to home plate, expecting the hitter to bunt but always suspicious, ready to dart one way or the other" (*RD* 59). Or that someone known for his anti-American politics would nonetheless appeal to the language of America's national pastime: "They recalled how Fidel used baseball terms when he talked about operations. We'll get them in a rundown. We'll shut the bastards out" (*L* 185).

And so speaking of Cuba, a word should be said here about those games known as "gaming," gambling, whether legal or illegal, everything from horse-racing (*LL* 92) to, especially in *Falling Man*, cards, poker. Since this latter is a game played with "intuition and cold-war risk analysis" worthy of the world's great game theorists or economists (*FM* 97), the line between it and investing, or between it and the calculations of insurance companies and risk analysts, becomes all the more difficult to discern, especially when someone like Ross Lockhart began making his fortune by "analyzing the profit impact of natural disasters" (*ZK* 13–14), or when teenage kids like Emma's son Stak can frequent "online wagering sites" in order to bet "on plane crashes, real ones, various odds, posted depending on the airline, the country, the time frame, other factors," or "on drone strikes. Where, when, how many dead" (*ZK* 193-4).

Games engage us because, more than anything else, they have a language of their own, a legend and a lexicon, an order and a logic all their own, with rules, rituals, and routines, all seemingly implacable and yet all absolutely arbitrary. In short, every game, like every sport, is "a benign illusion, the illusion that order is possible" (*EZ* 112; see 190, 199). Some of the most hilarious passages in all of DeLillo's work expose the arbitrariness of such order and of the rules behind it, passages that thereby expose the arbitrariness of all rules in general. There are, for example, all the rule changes during a pickup tag-football game in the snow in *End Zone*—"After two plays it was decided, by unanimous consent, to replace tagging with tackling" (*EZ* 195)— or the invention of "halfball" in *Ratner's Star*, with its own language and elaborate set of rules (*RS* 332-5), or the soccer game in a state penitentiary in "Hammer and Sickle," where rules are "invented, broken and abridged" until a huge fight breaks out with "the game going on around it" ("HS" 158). But the most uproarious of all such passages—with the possible exception of an enthusiastic game of strip Monopoly in *Amazons* (*AZ* 278-84)—is the extended description in *Falling Man* of Keith Neudecker's weekly poker game. We there hear of how the rules of the game were solemnly decreed, initially adhered to and refined over weeks and months, and then brutally changed pretty much over night. Once again, what is significant is less the game itself, whatever that might mean, than the name and language of the game, the ritual of announcing it, and the formulas exchanged during it. The weekly poker game is recalled only retrospectively, after 9-11, when the game no longer has the same appeal with "two players dead, one badly injured" (*FM* 27). With time to reflect, Keith recalls the evolution of their game, the wild proliferation and then sudden suspension of the rules governing their play. To follow the changes, one has to know the names of the guys around the table: "Three of the cardplayers were called by last name only, Dockery, Rumsey, Hovanis, and two by first name, Demetrius and Keith. Terry Cheng was Terry Cheng" (*FM* 149).

It all started out innocent enough—with a call to order, the imperative "to announce the name of the game, five-card stud." Though it became "the only game they now played... the words became a proud ritual, formal and indispensable" (*FM* 99). Then came the call for rigor and focus: "How disciplined can we be, Demetrius said, if we are taking time to leave the table and stuff our jaws with chemically treated breads, meats and cheeses" (*FM* 97). So that's how the purge began: "No food. Food was out. No gin or vodka. No beer that was not dark. They issued a mandate against all beer that was not dark and against all dark beer that was not Beck's Dark" (*FM* 98)—this last amendment voted on and passed because of a touching story one of them brought to the table about poker players in Germany who drank Beck's Dark and were later buried together in a mausoleum for four. It was all a way of creating order out of chaos, a way of "creating a structure out of willful trivia" (*FM* 98). But then one day, all of sudden, "they rescinded the ban on food and demanded Polish vodka…. They bet and raised, ate and drank, and from that point on resumed playing such games as high-low, acey-deucy, Chicago, Omaha, Texas hold'em, anaconda and a couple of other deviant strains in poker's line of ancestry" (*FM* 100). It's surprising just how funny the invention of such rules can be, rules in contraband games that then cast a particularly revealing light upon all the rules and prohibitions of what some might be tempted to call the "the game of life."

In addition to sports—what are commonly called sports, for the lines between these categories are, admittedly, rather porous—there are, simply, games, especially childhood games, as we will soon see, but also more adult games, like chess. We see chess being played by everyone from Lee Oswald (*L* 39) to Eddie Robles, New York City Subway worker, "with a miniature chess set practicing moves at two in the morning in his token booth," "and don't think people didn't pop their faces in the slot and challenge him to a game" (*U* 226). Chess in the subway, then, but then also chess by correspondence, with Jack Gladney's son Heinrich, for example, working "well into the night, plotting chess moves in a game he plays by mail with a convicted killer in the penitentiary" (*WN* 25). "Still playing with the fellow in prison? How's it going?" asks Jack "Pretty good. I think I got him cornered" (*WN* 43). Then there is Nick Shay's brother Matt, who was something of a chess prodigy as a kid (*U* 199, 211), and who first took an interest in the game when he found a book of chess problems belonging to his father (*U* 212)—the same father who, as a local bookie, was reputed to have used his prodigious memory for that other kind of gaming. As Father Paulus knows and tries to teach Matt:

> The game is location, situation and memory. And a need to win. The psychology is in the player, not the game. He must enjoy the company of danger. He must have a killer instinct. He must be prideful, arrogant, aggressive, contemptuous and dominating. Willful in the extreme. All the sins of the noncarnal type.
>
> (*U* 674; see 707–8)

But this is what Matt ultimately rejects about the game. While he initially "loved winning at chess and loved hearing the loser declare himself dead"

(*U* 707), he eventually came "to hate the language," the whole idea of trying to "crush your opponent" (*U* 212). It's for similar reasons that he will give up his job doing weapons research to protect us from the Russians. And yet what brought him back to chess as an adult, you might ask? "It was Fischer-Spassky that brought him back" (*U* 457)—the *Queen's Gambit* of its time.

And then there is *Underworld* again, which, in addition to being a long paean to baseball, is a big loud shout in the street to all the childhood street games of the 1930s–1990s in America, games that offer a sort of counterlife within urban life, and perhaps especially in New York City. Once again, what is most interesting seems to be less the moves than the language, "the smatter language of old street games and the rhythms of a thousand street-corner conversations, adolescent and raw" ("PH"). There are more adult games, like pool, usually played in a bar, something Nick often did with George Manza, George the Waiter (*U* 690; see 686, 760), while Matt was playing chess with Bronzini, but there are especially kids games, "girls playing jacks and jumping double dutch. Boys at boxball, marbles and ringolievio," a "kid who is *it*" and a kid "wondering about being *it*" (*U* 677), a kid who stands "at the center of the circle with a ball in his hand and slowly chants the warning words: *I declare a-war u-pon*" (*U* 662, 677; see 675, 678, 747), or "a boy playing handball against himself, hitting Chinese killers" (*U* 666), and then kids playing "hango seek" (*U* 726)—a game few of us born in America have ever known how to spell—and all kinds of "nickel-and-dime dice games" (*U* 726). There is even a brief reference in *Underworld* to Bruegel's *Kinderspiele*, a painting that depicts "dozens of children playing games in some town square" (*U* 682)—a sixteenth-century version of what Bronzini sees and describes in the streets of the Bronx. It is the inventiveness and innovation, the pure art of these games, that makes Bronzini think that part of a New York sidewalk should be sent to a museum in California—because, as we have seen, the west coast has nothing like this: "*Street drawing, hopscotch, chalk on paved asphalt, Bronx, 1951*" (*U* 662). And then there are the card games: *scopa* (*U* 380), gin rummy (*U* 761–2), knock rummy (*U* 711), shots on knucks (*U* 743), pinochle (*U* 766), *briscola* (U 722), "*sett' e mezz'*, for pennies," which Matt won regularly because "he memorized the cards coming out of the dealer's hand" (*U* 605). And the scavenger games, "bottle caps ... cork, rubber bands, tin cans" (*U* 663), and the sadistic games, recalled by the good-hearted Bronzini: "We put the fly in a cage .... It buzzed until it died. If it took too long to die, somebody lit a match. Then we put the match in the cage. My god what terror" (*U* 664).

As Bronzini says, "The thing about these games. They mean so much while you're playing. All your inventive skills. All your energies. But when you get a little older and stop playing, the games escape the mind completely" (*U* 663). You stop playing and soon the only thing left is an "old boccie court grown over with weeds" (*U* 213). That and the language: "He recalled the word do-it-over," or else: "Cheeky chose always goes. That's what the kid said when he got a second chance and did the same thing he'd done before the interruption. Hit a homer, kicked the can, shot a marble on target through the gutter dust" (*U* 235). (Never heard that? Cheeky chose always goes? Me neither, and without a novel like *Underworld* it could have been lost forever.)

There is something about these games, their innocence or their earnestness, or the way in which they engage you for a time in a completely other time, in a contraband time, a lost time that elicits some of the most melancholic or nostalgic words from DeLillo's characters. From Nick, our narrator in *Underworld*: "I'll tell you what I long for, the days of disarray, when I didn't give a damn or a fuck or a farthing" (*U* 806), "the days of disarray when I walked real streets and did things slap-bang and felt angry and ready all the time, a danger to others and a distant mystery to myself" (*U* 810). Nick can talk like this because he knows that one day, for all of us, it all just simply ends—the whole slap-bang thing, a life of play on the streets, childhood itself, everything except, if one is lucky, a sound or a word or a song from a children's game:

> What a wound to overcome, this passage out of childhood, but a beautiful injury too, he thought, pure and unrepeatable. Only the scab remains, barely seen, the exuded substance. / Ringolievio coca-cola one two three.
>
> (*U* 675–6)

This memory of childhood games continues right up to the very end of *Underworld*. On its final page, in fact, the narrator looks out his window and sees kids "playing a made-up game in a neighbor's yard, some kind of kickball maybe, and they speak in your voice"—a phrase that recalls that opening line of the novel, "He speaks in your voice, American" (*U* 11)—"or piggy-back races on the weedy lawn" (*U* 827). The novel begins with a game, a historic sporting event in New York City, and it concludes with the narrator looking at children playing a game in someone's backyard, maybe it's Phoenix, where Nick lives, but it could be Anywhere, USA.

There are thus all these (relatively) innocent games of childhood and then the far less innocent games of early adulthood, the game "Bang, you're dead" in *End Zone*, for instance, reminiscent of the macabre game of "godsave" in *Americana* or "*ab-orrrt that feetusss!*" in *Ratner's Star* (*RS* 32). And then, finally, a game that should look as innocent as all those childhood games played in the Bronx but that is tinged by other more grotesque pastimes. It's a children's game being played somewhere in the Ukraine by kids handicapped or deformed, victims of radiation poisoning from nuclear test blasts: "The kids are playing follow the leader. A boy falls down, gets up. They all fall down, get up" (*U* 802). It's a strange game, a contrapuntal game that combines purity and deformity, childhood innocence and corruption, and it leads to the narrator noting the contrast—the contraband—between the deformed faces and their backdrop: "Something about the juxtaposition deepened the moment, faces against the landscape" (*U* 802). It is reminiscent of children in *Ratner's Star* playing an odd game during a solar eclipse, "a shadow game in last light ... the players safe when they make their shadows disappear" (*RS* 431), which means safe only at the moment the moon eclipses or contrabands the sun. We will see the play of other children and other eclipses later, other children in the sun and other meteorological wonders.

Academia

> *I was acquiring meaningless degrees, teaching a freshman course in the dynamics of reality TV.... I used my index and middle fingers to place quote marks around certain ironic comments.*
>
> "HS" 154–5

> *You're brilliant but not savagely brilliant. I miss the killer instinct of the liberal arts major.*
>
> RS 164

> "What else do you teach?"
> "Greek, Latin, ocean sailing."
>
> WN 55

Like the wide world of sports that we just saw, academia is also a place outside society that is somehow lodged within, a counterculture within the culture, a counterplace that at once studies and reflects the place and culture in which it is uncomfortably situated. As such, the American university is fodder for endless amounts of goodhearted fun and derision from *Americana* right on through *Zero K*. The former contains DeLillo's first portrait of an American liberal arts college, Leighton Gage in southern California, which David Bell attends contrary to his parents' wishes, "a small, expensive and very modern liberal arts college," the kind of school where they offered "theology of despair in a palm grove" (*A* 32), where "the faculty was good but somewhat lazy," while "the reverse could be said of the students" (*A* 143; see 314), where the faculty fraternize with their students in various healthy and unhealthy ways (*A* 146), a place where a class in English poetry is "the best kind of class to have in the afternoon, an exercise in almost pure language, demanding nothing more than fractional consciousness" (*A* 173), where the most memorable thing about a class on Zen is a student eating D. T. Susuki's book on the subject right in front of the professor, Professor Oh—like the exclamation—who didn't mind because "one must become a book before one can know what is inside it" (*A* 175; see *U* 141). This is the same Oh who encourages his students to enjoy it all while they can, warning them with "a whisper of the eyes, down, my child, this is your last chance, tomorrow the corporations come calling" (*A* 177). It's enlightened, maybe even enlightening, but it is not quite what Bell's parents had in mind for him: "Your father and I have been arguing over Princeton and Virginia for three years now. Suddenly you come waltzing into the house and announce that you plan to attend some unheard-of school in California" (*A* 178; see *AZ* 1 and 352).

For better and for worse, then, college tends to leave its mark on those who pass through it. It was at Leighton Gage that David Bell began taking film seriously, the film he had hoped to make while in college finally getting made, in effect, years later as Bell effectively goes AWOL from his TV job in New York. During the making of his film Bell even calls his former film professor at Leighton Gage, Simmons St. Jean (*A* 247), for advice or encouragement, though he follows up that call just a few pages later to ask his old girlfriend, Wendy Judd: "Did you ever go to bed with Simmons St. Jean back in the old days at Leighton Gage?" (*A* 251)

DeLillo pokes fun at the entire system, from America's elite universities to its small liberal arts, technical, and religious institutions (see *WN* 142 and *L* 86). In *End Zone*, which features schools with good Christian names like Logos College, or names that sound like weapons or pharmaceutical manufacturers, like West Centrix Biotechnical (*EZ* 53), we see the perverse hold that sports have on American institutions of higher learning. For it is not just at Logos, obviously, that Black athletes such as Taft Robinson are recruited for the sole purpose of winning football games, or that the only person on campus referred to as "scholarly" is an assistant football coach who earns the distinction simply because "he smoked a pipe and did not use profanity" (*EZ* 27; 73).

But colleges and universities are not all bad or laughable in DeLillo's novels. At least there are professors like Alan Zapalac at Logos College (*EZ* 91, 163), zany, paranoid, phobic, but interesting, able to take a joke (*EZ* 210), and able to deliver one with a Woody Allen sense of timing: "My wife-to-be is a white Protestant fencepost.... A Zurich theologian lives inside her" (*EZ* 211). And at least there's a bit of excitement in the college, sex in the library stacks, pickup football games in the snow, beer parties, and dorm room banter.

In *Great Jones Street* there is the delightfully ridiculous pipe-smoking Professor of Latent History (turns out to be the elusive Dr. Pepper in disguise) who studies events that could have happened but did not or that did happen but no one knew it. As he says, "It's axiomatic that history is a record of events. But what of latent history? We all think we know what happened. But did it really happen? Or did something else happen? Or did nothing happen?" (*GJ* 74; see also *RS* 387). The professor in question was involved in gathering evidence to show that during the French Revolution a "dissident faction of the sans-culottes used to assemble secretly under cover of dark for the sole purpose of wearing culottes" (*GJ* 75). It's pretty ridiculous, to be sure, but there is a serious underside to it all, for a latent history is also a kind of contraband history or, more precisely, a counterfactual history, even a kind of literary or fictional history: what if X had happened instead of Y? For example, what if a rogue element of the CIA had planned an attempt on the president's life in 1963 and used a disaffected Lee Harvey Oswald as their patsy, and what if the attempt went all wrong and the president was actually assassinated? That's the kind of question a historian, or the author of *Libra*, might one day want to ask.

Then there's the university's cozy (and therefore uncomfortable) relationship with big business. In *The Names*, for example, we learn that James Axton had once worked for the "Institute of Risk Analysis at American University" (*N* 48), before transferring his unique skill set to the private sector, a consortium of insurance companies, perhaps a front for the CIA. This helps explain elsewhere the protests at the University of Wisconsin when Dow Chemical comes on campus to recruit (*U* 599–601) and the reason why CIA agents like Win Everett, the mastermind behind that JFK assassination attempt, are asked to teach at places like Texas Woman's University, to "check out promising students," "foreign girls in particular": "If there's a future prime minister here, the idea is we recruit her now, while she's still a virgin" (*L* 19; see 146, 382; see *AZ* 356).

Even Nick Shay taught for a time. Well before his career in waste management he was "doing some vague consulting work and teaching Latin once a week at a junior college" (*U* 447). That will not quite make him an advocate for the academy, however. Indeed Nick will hardly be impressed when, having himself become an expert in waste, he hears a trash archaeologist speak about garbage or waste and civilization, his thesis being that, between the two, "garbage comes first, then we build a system to deal with it" (*U* 288), in other words, garbage is not the result of civilization but civilization the result, the response, to garbage. When asked whether he really believes this stuff, the expert answers, "Bet your ass I believe it. I teach it at UCLA. I take my students into garbage dumps and make them understand the civilization they live in. Consume or die. That's the mandate of the culture" (*U* 287).

Finally, there is the College-on-the-Hill, the best known of all of DeLillo's institutions of higher learning, tuition (we're talking 1985) "fourteen thousand dollars, Sunday brunch included" (*WN* 41), and Jack Gladney, the best known of all DeLillo academicians, "Chairman of the department of Hitler studies," a discipline he himself invented "in North America in March of 1968" (*WN* 4). The college had itself become "internationally known" thanks to Gladney's Hitler studies brainchild (*WN* 11), with many "Hitler majors" and a full slate of classes ranging from Intro to Nazism to "Advanced Nazism, three hours a week, restricted to qualified seniors" (*WN* 25). Had Eldred Peck from *Americana* known about Jack's program, he may well have attended College-on-the-Hill. Instead he "went to some obscure college down South where he wrote his master's thesis on the swastika in history" (*A* 280).

The rest of the teaching staff at College-on-the-Hill is "composed almost solely of New York émigrés, smart, thuggish, movie-mad, trivia-crazed... an Aristotelianism of bubble gum wrappers and detergent jingles.... Together they look like teamster officials assembled to identify the body of a mutilated colleague" (*WN* 9). If their faculty lunch room conversation more or less takes over where the dorm room repartee of *End Zone* leaves off, at least it's still entertaining and the food fights are almost as good. The banter usually revolves around such pressing societal questions as: "Did you ever spit in your soda bottle so you wouldn't have to share your drink with the other kids?" or "Did you ever get an erection from a dental hygienist rubbing against your arm while she cleaned your teeth?" or "When you bite dead skin off your thumb, do you eat it or spit it out?" (*WN* 215). But then there's this: "How much pleasure did you take as a kid in imagining yourself dead?" (*WN* 216). It's a question that, for Jack, who suspects he has contracted something deadly during the airborne toxic event, cuts a bit too close to the bone: "I didn't want to listen to this. I had my own dying to dwell upon, independent of fantasies" (*WN* 216).

Among the elite group of émigrés is Alfonse (Fast Food) Stompanato, who, when he "talked about popular culture... exercised the closed logic of a religious zealot, one who kills for his beliefs" (*WN* 65; see *U* 323). He is just one among the many professors at College-on-the-Hill who "read nothing but cereal boxes" (*WN* 10), or who teach "the cinema of car crashes" (*WN* 40; see *U* 484), or Elvis. First among these others is Jack's colleague Murray Jay Siskind, "an ex-sportswriter" (whose first appearance was in *Amazons*) and "visiting lecturer on living icons" (*WN* 9–10). His plan in going to College-on-the-Hill was to do for Elvis what Jack did for Hitler. As he says in admiration for his older colleague: "I marvel at the effort. It was masterful, shrewd and stunningly preemptive. It's what I want to do with Elvis" (*WN* 12). The relationship between Jack and Murray leads to a mock epic confrontation where the two square off like sartorial warriors to debate the relative influences of Hitler's and Elvis's mothers on their sons, a debate Jack kindly indulges in order to bestow some of his academic celebrity upon Murray:

> I had been generous with the power and madness at my disposal, allowing my subject to be associated with an infinitely lesser figure, a fellow who sat in La-Z-Boy chairs and shot out TVs. It was not a small matter. We all had an aura to maintain, and in sharing mine with a friend I was risking the very things that made me untouchable.
>
> (*WN* 74)

Later, the two esteemed scholars can be seen strolling across campus like peripatetics or Oxford dons (or, skipping ahead a few decades to *The Silence*, like Martin Dekker and Albert Einstein at Princeton):

> Murray and I walked across campus in our European manner, a serenely reflective pace, heads lowered as we conversed. Sometimes one of us gripped the other near the elbow, a gesture of intimacy and physical support. Other times we walked slightly apart, Murray's hands clasped behind his back, Gladney's folded monkishly at the abdomen, a somewhat worried touch.
>
> (*WN* 237)

The College-on-the-Hill provides sufficient proof of the well-known maxim that in academia petty rivalries have a way of becoming bitter fights because the stakes are so low. Here's how Murray Siskind responds to the news of the death of a colleague when he sees Jack in the supermarket: "Cotsakis, my rival, is no longer among the living.... Lost in the surf off Malibu. During the term break. I found out an hour ago. Came right here" (*WN* 168).

Being a faculty member at the College-on-the-Hill means that one can analyze society from a safe distance, protected from the sorts of infirmities or disasters that strike the commoners dwelling squarely within it. As Jack says, "People in low-lying areas get the floods, people in shanties get the hurricanes and tornados. I'm a college professor. Did you ever see a college professor rowing a boat down his own street in one of those TV floods?" (*WN* 114). Actually, Jack is more than just your run-of-the-mill professor, and so deserves even greater protections from nature and chance: "I'm not just a college professor. I'm the head of a department. I don't see myself fleeing an airborne toxic event. That's for people who live in mobile homes out in the scrubby parts of the county, where the fish hatcheries are" (*WN* 117).

Not surprisingly, colleges and universities—the whole college experience, if you will—are represented more in earlier novels than later ones: Leighton Gage in *Americana*, Logos College in *End Zone*, College-on-the-Hill in *White Noise*. But even in later novels, the academy, and particularly the American academic, continues to be a target of DeLillo's humor and irony. In *Point Omega*, for example, the man watching *24 Hour Psycho* speculates that two men who enter the exhibit—they turn out to be Richard Elster and Jim Finley—are a "professor emeritus" of film theory and an "assistant professor" of the same, the younger scholar being forced "to follow the traditional theorist with the braided hair or risk damaging his academic future" (*PO* 11; see *WN* 197). Elster will turn out to be not an academic but, not too far removed from the clan, a public intellectual whose braided hair "gave him a kind of cultural identity, a flair of distinction, the intellectual as tribal elder" (*PO* 23), sought out by the Pentagon for his "interdisciplinary range" (*PO* 35). All the way up to *Zero K* the life of the academic is a sort of counter-life that is either forthrightly mocked or accorded a certain degree of cultural capital that it does not merit. When we meet Jeffrey Lockhart, aged thirty-four (*ZK* 49), we know that he is not going to follow in his billionaire father's entrepreneurial footsteps, but it is not clear exactly what, as they say, he will "do with his life": "Would I write poetry, live in a basement room, study philosophy, become a professor of transfinite mathematics at an obscure college in west-central somewhere" (*ZK* 54). In the end, he will become a "compliance and ethics officer for a college in western Connecticut" (*ZK* 221; 226), learning "to perform the requisite duties and conform to the indigenous language" (*ZK* 266). It's not quite as prestigious as Cyril in *Ratner's Star*, who "taught transitional logic at universities on four continents" (*RS* 29), or even Sean in *Love-Lies-Bleeding*, who teaches "geophysics" (*LL* 77) at a "private academy for rich kids who deal drugs" (*LL* 57), but it's a living—and it's about as far as you can get from what his father did.

Finally—or nearly—there is DeLillo's vision for the future of university education. It is laid out quite clearly in *Americana*, already in 1971, as an Indian sage, a Sioux mystic, describes what sounds like the new American university, a kind of University of Phoenix decades before the fact, or else the old American university in the age of Zoom and the Coronavirus:

> It would work this way. At the beginning of each semester the entire student body—which would have to number at least five hundred

thousand in order to give the computers enough to do—would assemble in a large open space in front of a TV camera. They would be televised and put on videotape. In a separate operation the instructors would also be videotaped, individually. Then two TV sets would be placed in the single room which represented the university. The room would be in a small blockhouse at the edge of a thirty-six-lane freeway; this proximity would help facilitate transmission of electronic equipment. Oh, there might be some banners on the wall and maybe a plaque or two, but aside from these the only things in the room would be the TV sets. At nine o'clock in the morning of the first day of classes, a computer would turn on the two television sets, which would be facing each other. The videotape of the students would then watch the videotape of the instructors. Eventually the system could be refined so that there would be only one university in the whole country.

(*A* 119–20)

There are, then, a lot of teachers in DeLillo. Seems like "everybody's a teacher. Half the world is teaching the other half" (*U* 688). They can be pompous and ridiculous or else, sometimes, inspiring and inspired, with serious ambitions—like murder. Because there's not just Jack Gladney but also Benno Levin, a former "assistant professor of computer applications... in a community college" turned assassin, a man who left the academy to work for Eric Packer and "make [his] million" (*C* 56). It turns out, of course, that he will fail at this too, because, like so many others in DeLillo, Levin seems to confirm the age-old adage—but in contraband: those who teach, can't.

Philosophy

He spent a year in college in his late twenties, working nights at the main post office on Eighth Avenue, and he took a course in philosophy that he looked forward to, week by week, page by page, mining even the footnotes in the text. Then it got hard and he stopped.

"*S*" 191

I watched the coffee bubble up through the center tube and perforated basket into the small pale globe. A marvelous and sad invention, so roundabout, ingenious, human. It was like a philosophical argument rendered in terms of the things of the world—water, metal, brown beans. I had never looked at coffee before.

WN 103

> It occurred to Wayne that for some time now he was always arriving or departing. He was never anywhere you could actually call a place. He wasn't here and wasn't there. It was like a problem in philosophy.
>
> L 143
>
> Let's not have metaphysics this evening. I'm a plain girl from a mill town.
>
> N 57

Philosophy literally is and/or is not everywhere in DeLillo. Like the academy, it too is more often than not spoken of with a certain ironic distance, as one of those airy, highbrowed things people take up in their late teens and twenties in a place like Leighton Gage, Logos College, or College-on-the-Hill before getting wise to the thing and dropping it. But there is also always a serious underside to the general mirth. In *Americana* David Bell has colleagues at the TV network who spice up their conversation with "German philosophical terms" (*A* 12) and one colleague, Warburton (aka Trotsky), who goes so far as to send out an office memo citing Augustine: "And never can a man be more disastrously in death than when death itself shall be deathless. I've committed it to memory. It overwhelms me. I'm not sure why but it just hits me. It knocks me out" (*A* 99; see 21). In other words, as it gets parsed, "We are endlessly dying. We begin dying when we are born. A short time later we die. By universal consent, more or less, this is known as death" (*A* 100). Just to prove that these things can stay with you, the phrase itself returns in DeLillo some forty-five years later, in *Zero K*: "Saint Augustine. Let me tell you what he said. Goes like this.... 'And never can a man be more disastrously in death than when death itself shall be deathless'" (*ZK* 240). Two pages later it gets reduced to a fragment that reads like an epigraph to the novel as a whole: "A man in a room, where death shall be deathless" (*ZK* 243).

Again in *Americana* there are philosophical claims every bit as profound as Bill Clinton's ontology, "The whole thing can be brought down to a question of metaphysics and first principles. Whatever is, is" (*A* 157) and questions "as old as Plato" regarding (though I'm not sure what dialogue) a tree falling in the forest with no one to hear it (*A* 158). As a radio rant already phrases it in the same novel, "There is but one truly philosophical problem and that is the station break. The clock crows. It's all numbers. Numbers and Deuteronomy. I'm losing my edge but stay with me. It's your only hope" (*A* 233). Such references are thus never without irony or playfulness, but also never without another more serious side. Here is a passage in which philosophy is identified with solitude and, as if responding to the very definition or etymology of philosophy, with the love or the pursuit—though not the attainment—of wisdom:

> Men on small islands would do well to avoid the pursuit of philosophy. The island illusion, that solitude and wisdom invented each other, is a very convincing one. Day by day I seem to grow more profound. Often I feel I am on the verge of some great philosophical discovery. Man. War. Truth. Time. Fortunately, I always return to myself. I look beyond the white lace of the surf to my own unassembled past and I decide to let others stitch together the systems.
>
> (*A* 129)

In *End Zone* Professor Zapalac would be one of those "stitchers" of systems, with talks of love, salvation, and immortality, of wanting "to stir up ecstasy" in his soul and "ascend to the world of forms" (*EZ* 212). That has Plato written all over it, though DeLillo is much more prone to go with enigma and provocation. In "Midnight in Dostoevsky," for example, there is a logic class with Professor Ilgauskas that is every bit as inspiring as the class on Zen with Professor Oh at Leighton Gage: "'The causal nexus,' he said, and stared into the wall" ("MD" 122). "'Imagine a surface of no color whatsoever,' he said. / We sat there and imagined" ("MD" 131; see 132, 138-9). And then there is the poster of Wittgenstein on Taft's dormitory wall—Wittgenstein, who will have famously said, in what could well be the untyped epigraph to *The Silence*, "Whereof one cannot speak, thereof one must be silent."

> I took a moment to scan the walls for tape-remnants. Poster of Wittgenstein, I thought. Maybe that's what he'd had up there, or almost had. Dollar ninety-eight poster of philosopher surrounded by Vienna Circle. Two parts to that man's work. What is written. What is not written. The man himself seemed to favor second part. Perhaps Taft was a student of that part.
>
> (*EZ* 233)

If the reference to Wittgenstein is a bit too heady for a novel ostensibly about college football, this one about phenomenology brings it all down to earth: "My roommate wets the bed. It's a little hard for me to evolve any kind of genuine stasis under the circumstances. Somehow pee is inimical to stasis. Although I wouldn't want to have to prove it phenomenologically, if that's the word I want" (*EZ* 240).

There are thus references to philosophy throughout DeLillo (see *N* 291, *P* 58, *GJ* 225 and 228), *Existenzphilosophie*, for example, spoken in a foreign accent, of course, to give it the proper *Eigentlichkeit* (*RS* 149), and set theory: "Take my advice. If you go out there ten times, you'll never come back once for each time you go out. This is called set theory" (*DR* 54). There is even a reference to the Kantian end in itself, though it is put to an end that would have surely surprised Kant: "Nothing has been an end in itself since Garbo in *Camille*. You can't expect to find ends in themselves in contemporary life" (*AZ* 145). Among Oswald's books in *Libra* we find Jean-Paul Sartre's *Ideology and Revolution* (*L* 179) and, in *Players*, we have something like a philosophico-ideological justification for terrorism in the person of Rafael and his "doctor of philosophy approach to bombing" (*P* 107). And then there's the *image* of philosophy and philosophers: "We faced each other, propped on elbows, like a sculpture of lounging philosophers in a classical academy" (*WN* 196; see "HM" 26, "S" 188).

There are thus in DeLillo references to philosophers as recent as Wittgenstein and as old as Lao Tse (*WN* 150), or Plato and Socrates (*WN* 282). There are even pre-Socratics, "He wanted to be a dry wise soul (Heraclitus), less slipshod and indecisive, more willing to see into the core of a complicated matter" (*U* 768; see 73, 282), and even a little debate over who was the Greeker, Thales, who said "All things are water," or Heraclitus, who said "All things flow" (*RS* 31). And then there is Endor, Billy Twillig's former teacher, who, having seemingly solved the mystery of the Ratnerian code before anyone else, reconciling past and present, up and down, also seems to have ended the debate as "the wizened child of Thales and Heraclitus" (*RS* 21–2). This is the world of opposites philosophy-style.

Such ironic or at least playful references to philosophy will become less frequent in later novels, though they will never wholly disappear. In *The Body Artist* Lauren Hartke is said to have been "twisted enough to major in the subject until she dropped out of school to join a troupe of street performers in Seattle" (*BA* 106). *Cosmopolis* and *Falling Man* could both be described as great philosophical novels about finitude and death, or about the leap, the ethical leap or leap of faith, that might be identified with both terrorists and their victims (*C* 57). In the latter, the ideology that convinces one of the 9-11 terrorists that the deaths of innocent people can be justified is derided as a kind of philosophy: "Those who will die have no claim to their lives outside the useful fact of their dying. / Hammad was impressed by this. It sounded like philosophy" (*FM* 176). Moreover, the novel revolves around Keith Neudecker (a name with two *k*'s) in the days after the attack, with several nods, most implicit but some explicit, to Kierkegaard—his thought as well as his name, his belief that belief or faith always involves a teleological suspension of the ethical, that is, a suspension of all the ethical rules or dogmas by which we usually live. As always, however, DeLillo is careful not to hit us over the head with these references. Lianne invokes Kierkegaard in reference not to those who leapt out of the burning World Trade Towers or the performance artist who imitates their fall but to poker players on television:

> She watched the players, they drew her in, deadpan, drowsy, slouched, men in misfortune, she thought, making a leap to Kierkegaard, somehow, and recalling the long nights she'd spent with her head in a text.
> (*FM* 117)

Watching people play high stakes poker on TV thus reminds Lianne of Kierkegaard, which brings her back to her college days—a recollection that, however ironic, is not without its own existential angst (and, perhaps, regret, since it may well have been Kierkegaard who first attracted her to Keith).

> She loved Kierkegaard in his antiqueness, in the glaring drama of the translation she owned... she used to love Kierkegaard right down to the spelling of his name. The hard Scandian *k*'s and lovely doubled *a*.... Kierkegaard gave her a danger, a sense of spiritual brink. *The whole of existence frightens me*, he wrote. She saw herself in this sentence.
> (*FM* 118)

The philosophy of Kierkegaard, or at least the notion of the leap, the leap of faith, is thus at the center of *Falling Man*, linked implicitly to the leap of the falling man at the World Trade Center or the leaps of Mohammed Atta or Keith Neudecker. But Kierkegaard was also already in DeLillo as early as *White Noise*, in the anguished words of the wife of the Chairman of the Hitler Studies Program at College-on-the-Hill: "You mean am I sick unto death?" (*WN* 263)

From thoughts of human death we then arrive at thoughts of an even more general or generalizable death, Teilhard de Chardin's "omega point," as we will look at in more detail later, and then at inanimate or inorganic things, things like stone or rock—the latter inspired by Heidegger in *Zero K*:

> I looked at him intently and said in the most deliberate voice I could manage, "Rocks are, but they do not exist." / After a pause I said, "I came across this statement when I was in college and forgot it until very recently. 'Man alone exists. Rocks are, but they do not exist. Trees

are, but they do not exist. Horses are, but they do not exist.... God is, but he does not exist." What I did not tell him was that these ideas belong to Martin Heidegger. I hadn't known until fairly recently that this was a philosopher who'd maintained a firm fellowship with Nazi principles and ideologies. History everywhere, in black notebooks, and even the most innocent words, *tree, horse, rock*, gone dark in the process.

(ZK 213–14)

Once again, philosophy is one of those things we remember from college, one of those things, however frivolous or meaningless at the time, that leaves its mark:

He watched her and thought of something he'd heard or read years earlier, in philosophy class. / *All existence is a trick of light.* / He tried to recall the context of the remark. Was it about the universe and our remote and fleeting place as earthlings? Or was it something much more intimate, people in rooms, what we see and what we miss, how we pass through each other, year by year, second by second?

("S" 195)

Finally, there is the philosophical joke of *Love-Lies-Bleeding*, more or less the same philosophical joke that David Foster Wallace tells, and at more or less the same time, in his famous graduation address of 2005 at Kenyon College:

All right, here's a joke. It's a philosophical joke. I told it to my seniors in geophysics. Goes like this. Two tiny young fish are swimming in the sea. They come upon an older fish. He says to them, Hey, fellas, how's the water? The two young fish swim on past. They swim for many miles. Finally one fish says to the other. What the fuck is water?

(LL 77)

The point, it seems, is that some second perspective, some contraband, if you will, is always required in order to see the band in which we live. Earlier on in DeLillo's corpus, that thought is identified with the wit and wisdom of Wadi Assad: "Why does the fish know nothing of the sea?" "Because the sea is all there is" (*AZ* 59). Metaphysics would thus perhaps be the ultimate contraband, the contrabanding of one world by another, the one more real than the other. The problem would then be trying to determine which is which—a problem that maybe only a graduate seminar in deconstruction would be able to solve.

Technologies of Life and Death

Technology is crucial to civilization why? Because it helps us make our fate. We don't need God or miracles or the flight of the bumble bee. But it is also crouched and undecidable. It can go either way.

C 95

No definition of science is complete without a reference to terror.

RS 36

Science fiction is just beginning to catch up with the Old Testament…. See carbon dioxide melt the polar ice caps. See the world's mineral reserves dwindle. See war, famine and plague. See barbaric hordes defile the temple of the virgins…. I said science fiction but I guess I meant science. Anyway there's some kind of mythical and/or historic circle-thing being completed here.

EZ 160

"Study the planet. Observe the solar system. Listen to the universe. Know thyself" (*RS* 21). That would be a pretty good motto, or series of mottos, Delphic and otherwise, to inscribe over the lintel of *Ratner's Star*, the DeLillo novel that includes the greatest number of reflections on science. But what is science exactly? Well, in the same novel, just a few pages after those incentivizing words, we learn that in Field Experiment Number One a whole committee had been formed to answer just this question. The task was simply to define "science," but the committee—because we all know how committees can be—was having a tough time of it and, as the novel begins, "the definition at present ran some five hundred pages" (*RS* 30), including things that many would claim are the opposite of science. For as someone argues quite reasonably, "we've got to admit the possibility that what we think of as obscure ritual and superstition may be perfectly legitimate scientific enterprises" (*RS* 35-6). In other words, there may be a much closer kinship than we tend to think between "Eastern mysticism and Western science" (*RS* 35). The combination is treated ironically early on in the work, but Ratner's discourse at the center of the novel regarding the relationship between science and Kabbalah seems to affirm this kinship (see *RS* 215-22).

But the first thing to be said about science is that, instead of answering most of our unknowns, it has vastly expanded the field of unknowns, and that has been precisely the source of its power:

It used to be thought that the work of science would be completed in the very near future. This was, oh, the seventeenth century. It was just a matter of time before all knowledge was integrated and made available, all the inmost secrets pried open.... But the thing continues to expand.... Every time we make a breakthrough we think this is it: the breakthrough. But the thing keeps pushing out. It breaks through the breakthrough.

(*RS* 65)

In the end, there is something mystical if not religious about science—and maybe even science teachers, from Bronzini in *Underworld* to Professor Zapalac in *End Zone*. Here's the latter trying to make that connection between religion and science—complete with a signature DeLillo non-sequitur, that is, a signature moment of contraband:

Science is religion, did you know that? Consider what it is we're talking about. Earthly origins, meteorites dropping from the heavens, creation of solar system ... unforeseen procedures which completely wipe out so-and-so in what other discipline. Let me tell you about my childhood in Oregon.

(*EZ* 92)

DeLillo is a thinker of science, of all kinds of science, and especially of astronomy, in *Ratner's Star* and elsewhere. But he is much more frequently a thinker or writer of technology. For there is something quasi-magical if not mystical about certain technologies as well. This was already clear back in *White Noise*, where grocery store doors open with the same magical power as the gates of heaven in Homer: "The large doors slide open, they close unbidden" (*WN* 37; see *Iliad* 5, line 800). Such technologies are magical if not mystical, as if drawing upon some ancient power, and they seem to be accompanied by an equally ancient fear or foreboding. "I feel they're working on the superstitious part of my nature. Every advance is worse than the one before because it makes me more scared" (*WN* 161). In other words, "the greater the scientific advance, the more primitive the fear" (*WN* 161). And this faith in technology and fear of it, this belief in its magic and the recognition of our total dependence upon it, all need to be understood in relation to the average person's almost complete inability to explain how any of it works. Though Heinrich's remarks in *White Noise* are an Oedipal-inspired attack on his father's presumed omnipotence, it is hard for the reader, who might have thought himself safe on the sidelines, not to feel implicated. The quotation here is drawn out at some length in order to show just how deep Heinrich is willing to drive the patricidal knife:

Can we make a refrigerator? Can we even explain how it works? What is electricity? What is light? We experience these things every day of our lives but what good does it do if we find ourselves hurled back in time and we can't even tell people the basic principles much less actually make something that would improve conditions. Name one thing you could make. Could you make a simple wooden match that you could strike on a rock to make a flame? We think we're so great and modern. Moon landings, artificial hearts. But what if you were hurled into a time warp and came face to face with the ancient Greeks. The Greeks invented trigonometry. They did autopsies and dissections. What could you tell an ancient Greek that he couldn't say, "Big deal." Could you tell him about the atom? Atom is a Greek word. The Greeks knew that the major events in the universe can't be seen by the eye of man. It's waves, it's rays, it's particles.... If a Stoner Ager asked you what a nucleotide is, could you tell him? How do we make carbon paper? What is glass? .... Could you tell those people one little crucial thing that might save a million and a half lives? .... What is a radio? What is the principle of a radio? Go ahead, explain. You're sitting in the middle of this circle of people. They use pebble tools. They eat grubs. Explain a radio.

(*WN* 147–8)

When Jack, the dad, makes a good faith effort to answer this last challenge—"There's no mystery. Powerful transmitters send signals. They travel through the air, to be picked up by receivers." (*WN* 148)—his explanation just leads to more follow-up questions:

They travel through the air. What, like birds? Why not tell them magic? They travel through the air in magic waves. What is a nucleotide? You don't know, do you? Yet these are the building blocks of life. What good is knowledge if it just floats in the air?

(*WN* 148)

Unable to explain most of the things we use on a daily basis, the things on which our lives today all nonetheless fully depend, we have become the pliant or compliant objects of technology, the docile servants of it. DeLillo often insists on the way technology molds us to it, makes us willing, flexible, and compliant. For example, in *Libra*: "Devices make us pliant. We want to please them" (*L* 362; see 77, *U* 466). Or in *Running Dog*: "Banks, insurance companies, credit organizations, tax examiners, passport offices, reporting services, police agencies, intelligence gatherers.... Devices make us pliant" (*RD* 93).

If the devices and machines themselves make us pliant, then we become absolute putty in the hands of those who control them. Take Michael in *Valparaiso*, perfectly compliant aboard an aircraft (yet another reason why air travel is so central to DeLillo's work): "I said nothing. I was intimidated by the systems. The enormous sense of power all around me. Heaving and breathing. How could I impose myself against this force?" (*V* 86; see 55). So powerful are these systems that when Michael, in the act of committing suicide in the airplane lavatory, hears an announcement from the pilot asking people to return to their seats because of turbulence, he dutifully complies and puts his suicide off to a later time: "I became a docile traveler again. I had to submit to the systems. They were designed to save my life. And I complied gratefully. Returned to my seat. Fastened my seatbelt" (*V* 101).

It is the technology that makes us comply, as well as the authority of those who wield it, and that authority can sometimes be produced by something so simple as a uniform. It's a lesson that even the wackiest of wack jobs, in this case David Ferrie of *Libra*, knew well and used to his advantage:

> You wear a uniform, it makes all the difference. Look at me. I put on my captain's jacket, all this bleary shit just falls away. I become a captain for Eastern. I talk like a captain. I instill confidence in anxious travelers. I actually fly the goddamn plane.
>
> (*L* 45)

It's one of the things that pilots share with medical personnel: they both wear uniforms, and much of our willingness to let them hold our lives in their hands seems to stem from that simple fact. As Nurse Baker says in *The Day Room*, "I'm wearing a uniform, you are not. I have authority, you do not… it's the uniform that matters. The person in the uniform controls the facts. That's what uniforms are for. They prove that truth is possible" (*DR* 53). So it's having the right uniform or, sometimes, just the right stamp, seal, or letterhead that gives one authority. That's what Oswald realized when he was told he couldn't open a local chapter of a pro-Cuba group in New Orleans:

> He didn't need New York's backing to open an office. He had his rubber stamping kit. All he had to do was stamp the committee's initials on a handbill or piece of literature. Stamp some numbers and letters. This makes it true.
>
> (*L* 313)

It has become easier and easier, it seems, for individuals to manipulate the signs of power—and thus have power itself—regardless of competence or training or genuine worth. As for larger structures like governments and corporations, capital and military force, there, too, being able to "project power" seems to be the precondition not simply for maintaining power but for getting it in the first place.

There is, to be sure, in all this compliance a desire to reduce risk, to save ourselves, to keep ourselves safe and sound, but also the equally great desire to lower or efface ourselves, to give ourselves over to some higher power. For there is, in addition to all these advances in science, along with the authority that science and technology have given us, or given some, the sheer awesome power of it all, as when a pair of F-4 Phantoms goes screeching overhead, leaving one "speechless in the wake of a power and thrust snatched from nature's own greatness," speechless before the way "men bend heaven to their methods" (*U* 468; see 289). For better or for worse, for better and for worse, "technology is our fate," wrote DeLillo just weeks after 9–11:

> Technology is our fate, our truth. It is what we mean when we call ourselves the only superpower on the planet. The materials and methods we devise make it possible for us to claim our future. We don't have to depend on God or the prophets or other astonishments. We are the astonishment. The miracle is what we ourselves produce, the systems and networks that change the way we live and think.
> But whatever great skeins of technology lie ahead, ever more complex, connective, precise, micro-fractional, the future has yielded, for now, to medieval experience, to the old slow furies of cut-throat religion.
> It is their technology that marks our moments, the small, lethal devices, the remote-control detonators they fashion out of radios, or the larger technology they borrow from us, passenger jets that become manned missiles.
> Maybe this is a grim subtext of their enterprise. They see something innately destructive in the nature of technology.
>
> ("RF")

Zero K, published some fifteen years later, says something similar about a technology that seems to have gotten away from us and taken on a life of its own: "Technology has become a force of nature. We can't control it" (*ZK* 245). This force of nature that has escaped the control of the science that produced it thus seems to return us to rudimentary fears and the forebodings of religion:

> Apocalypse is inherent in the structure of time and long-range climate and cosmic upheaval.... And are we counting the days before advanced

nations, or not so advanced, begin to deploy the most hellish weapons? Isn't it inevitable?

(*ZK* 243)

In short, technology has taken on a life of its own and that life seems to have a death drive, "a death wish" (*ZK* 70). It can be seen in Eric Packer's day-long drive across Manhattan in *Cosmopolis*, and it is the thesis that Murray Siskind in *White Noise* advances in his upper-level course on car crashes in American culture:

> We've looked at hundreds of crash sequences. Cars with cars. Cars with trucks. Trucks with buses. Motorcycles with cars. Cars with helicopters. Trucks with trucks. My students think these movies are prophetic. They mark the suicide wish of technology. The drive to suicide, the hurtling rush to suicide.
>
> (*WN* 217–18)

It is thus no coincidence that *Zero K* will set side by side the newest technologies of communication used by everyday people in their everyday lives and the technologies being dreamt up by the super-rich to live forever or at least for a time beyond their so-called natural deaths. We read of the Convergence, the place where bodies are cryogenically preserved for the future: "Here was science awash in irrepressible fantasy. I could not stifle my admiration" (*ZK* 257). DeLillo moves back and forth here between these dramatic, exceptional kinds of technology and the kind used by billions of people around the world everyday—which is itself exceptional, as we will see, in its own way. Jeffrey Lockhart, the narrator of *Zero K*, speaks of "the puppet drug of personal technology" (*ZK* 55), palm pilots and iPhones and tablets, and of being connected through those devices "instant by instant, in the numbing raptures of the Web" (*ZK* 167). It's all about "the loss of autonomy. The sense of being virtualized. The devices you use, the ones you carry everywhere, room to room, minute to minute, inescapably" (*ZK* 239). All these things that connect us and extend us into the world also seem to empty us out, to make us "unfleshed" (*ZK* 239). As someone remarks in *Zero K*: "The thinness of contemporary life. I can poke my finger through it" (*ZK* 89). In *The Silence*, as we will see, someone apparently does just that, silencing all these devices that tell us who we are.

If all technologies—even those that promise to help and enhance life—have a death wish, if they are all technologies of both life and death, then we should not be surprised to find technologies explicitly related to life and death—medical technologies, for example—at the center of DeLillo's theater of operations (see, e.g., *AZ* 100, 108–22, 227). If technology in general makes us pliant, medical technology makes us super-pliant, about as firm as one of Erica Demings's Jell-O mold creations. While there can be something brutally frank and aggressive, even medieval, about medicine—Matt's girlfriend Janet Urbaniak, working in an emergency room in Boston, "described scenes that were like paintings of the European masters, the ones who did miracles and wars" (*U* 414)—it can also be so high-tech that it gleams, and it is that gleaming that makes us comply. Even Jack Gladney will submit to it, despite his moments of insight and resistance:

> I will send you to Glassboro for further tests. Would you like that? There is a brand-new facility called Autumn Harvest Farms. They have gleaming new equipment. You won't be disappointed, wait and see. It gleams, absolutely.
>
> (*WN* 261; see 276)

Jack will thus submit to the tests, or at least to some of them, until he pulls away, afraid "of the imaging block," "afraid of its magnetic fields, its computerized nuclear pulse. Afraid of what it knows about me" (*WN* 325).

For the technology that tries to monitor death also seems to announce it: "No startling numbers on the printout. This death was still too deep to be glimpsed" (*WN* 204). During the airborne toxic event, "men in bright yellow Mylex suits and respirator masks" walk around "through the luminous haze, carrying death-measuring instruments" (*WN* 116), instruments that can detect the truth of who we are not from our words or our thoughts but from the print-outs analyzing our bodily fluids and secretions, which we therefore need to harvest and preserve for medical analysis, a bit of excrement, for example, "reverently enclosed in three interlocking Baggies, successively twist-tied ... certain to be looked upon by the technicians on duty with the mingled deference, awe and dread we have come to associate with exotic religions of the world" (*WN* 275). It is those instruments, then, not the doctors who use them, that tell us our fate, that announce who will live and who will die, that allow us to become spectators to our own dying.

> Death has entered. It is inside you. You are said to be dying and yet are separate from the dying, can ponder it at your leisure, literally see on the X-ray photograph or computer screen the horrible alien logic of it all. It is when death is rendered graphically, is televised so to speak, that you sense an eerie separation between your condition and yourself.... It makes you feel like a stranger in your own dying.
>
> (*WN* 141–2)

It's a powerful passage, immediately followed by this contrabanding thought, this gesture of self-protection: "I wanted my academic gown and dark glasses" (*WN* 142). It takes someone with Marvin Lundy's dry cleaner humor to take the bad news medical science has to offer with the requisite distance and equanimity:

> I'm in the category myself where I'm undergoing tests. This means I have cancer recurring in so many parts of my body the doctor gives me group rates.... The doctor calls it a fungating mass.... It's not in the dictionary because I looked in two dictionaries When they get their terms outside the dictionary, it means they're telling you goodbye.
>
> (*U* 191–2)

Here he is again, just because one can never get enough of Marvin Lundy:

> They have stools you can buy in surgical supply outlets that you place in your shower so you can sit and do the far-flung parts of your body without falling and breaking a hip, which he saw one day on the hip replacement channel, with molded seats and nonskid legs. They have a channel for every body part.
>
> (*U* 191)

So technology makes us pliant, and it itself seems to have a mind if not a life of its own, and that life seems oriented toward death as much as life (*N* 114–15). It can initially look like technology is in a struggle against death, that it wards off death and grants more life. The drug Dylar in *White Noise* was designed, after all, to rid us of our life-draining fear of death. It was supposed to be "technology with a human face" (*WN* 211), a technology serving us and our interests, the first of which would be, presumably, life:

> It prolongs life, it provides new organs for those that wear out. New devices, new techniques every day. Lasers, masers, ultrasound. Give yourself up to it, Jack. Believe in it. They'll insert you in a gleaming tube, irradiate your body with the basic stuff of the universe. Light, energy, dreams. God's own goodness.
>
> (*WN* 285)

But there is another, less human face to this technology, or else another, more ominous side to our human face: "It creates an appetite for immortality on the one hand. It threatens universal extinction on the other" (*WN* 285). Technology is thus also, essentially, about death; it is about preventing it and producing it. It both promises life and threatens death. And the two sides are not equal, for if it cannot yet deliver on immortality (*Zero K* not withstanding) it is more than capable of bringing on death—either on a massive and now almost universal scale or one little catastrophic failure at a time. As someone says of the Challenger space shuttle disaster of January 28, 1986: "He wasn't sure people wanted to see this. Willing to see the systems failure and the human suffering. But the beauty, the high faith of space, how could such qualities be linked to death?" (*U* 227). And then there are all those waves and rays in the air, not to mention the chemicals (see *WN* 175).

Technology at once threatens the planet with destruction and, with the Convergence, promises to preserve some of its inhabitants for some future, immortal life. We already get a foretaste of this latter in *White Noise*, in the freezer compartment of the Gladney family refrigerator:

> I opened the refrigerator, peered into the freezer compartment. A strange crackling sound came off the plastic food wrap, the snug covering for half eaten things, the Ziploc sacks of livers and ribs, all gleaming with sleety crystals. A cold dry sizzle. A sound like some element breaking down, resolving itself into Freon vapors. An eerie static, insistent but near subliminal, that made me think of wintering souls, some form of dormant life approaching the threshold of perception.
>
> (*WN* 258)

It's a vision of capitalism in America, though already of the Convergence, the dream—the nightmare—of a dead, desolate planet with the machines still whirring below the surface, everyone dead above ground and a select few below in a state of suspended animation, the machines around them still heaving and pulsating with the only life left.

The danger—the possibility of apocalypse—thus comes from multiple directions, from the nuclear weapons that would appear to be the culmination of this scientific or technological drive to self-destruction, the most advanced outpost of the Omega Point, to those little devices we hold in the palm of our hand. The ultimate danger seems to come either when the first of these get deployed or the second all stop working or suddenly go silent or blank. As someone says in *Cosmopolis*, it is "crouched and undecidable," technology is, and "it can go either way" (*C* 95). The problem is that we can already see which way it's leaning.

3

Counterproductions

Empire, Capital, the Corporation

"What are you training for?"
"Night drop into Iran. The bank's determined to be the first ones back in. I'll be leading a small elite group. Credit officers with blackened faces."
N 131

He took off his glasses, revealing clear, gray, flinty eyes. The eyes of a man who billed three hundred million worldwide.
AZ 317

They're all part of the same motherfucking thing.... The state, the nation, the corporation, the power structure, the system, the establishment.
U 575

"There ought to be something higher than the corporation."
"There's the orgasm."
N 12

In the world of Don DeLillo, where the question of language is usually the first and last question to be asked, being able to speak more than one language is often a sign of worldliness and sophistication, of education and openness, the sign of a certain progress. But *having* to speak different languages is also sometimes a sign of the opposite, that is, a sign of subjection or domination, in a word, a sign of empire. This is something that, in *The Names*, James Axton, stationed in Athens, learns from Eliades, a Greek militant:

> How is it so many people know three, four, five languages? ... This is politics too ... the politics of occupation, the politics of dispersal, the politics of resettlement, the politics of military bases.
(N 57)

Axton is hardly naïve, but he gets pretty well schooled while living in Athens in the ways of global capital and US domination. And much of that schooling comes from the same Eliades, who, despite the colossal chip on his Greek shoulder, could not be more spot on in his analysis of the way America develops and protects its interests abroad:

> It is very interesting how Americans can learn geography and world history as their interests are damaged in one country after another. This is interesting.... I think it's only in a crisis that Americans see other people. It has to be an American crisis, of course.... The whole world takes an interest in this curious way Americans educate themselves. T.V. Look, this is Iran, this is Iraq. Let us pronounce the word correctly. E-ron. E-ronians. This is a Sunni, this is a Shi'ite. Very good. Next year we do the Philippine Islands, okay?
>
> (*N* 58)

When *The Names* opens Axton is posted in Athens, working for a company that sells insurance policies, "political risk insurance," to companies trying to protect themselves financially from the kidnapping of their employees (*N* 46). It's a good business because "companies don't want to be caught short" (*N* 215) and, well, "somebody had to tell us what our chances were" (*N* 46). He is thus charged with doing risk assessment and analysis for a number of Middle Eastern countries. It's insurance but with a geopolitical bent:

> Policy updates, we call them. In effect I review the political and economic situation of the country in question.... Prison statistics weighed against the number of foreign workers. How many young males unemployed. Have the generals' salaries been doubled recently.... Together we analyze the figures in the light of recent events. What seems likely? Collapse, overthrow, nationalization?
>
> (*N* 33–4)

For Axton, the Middle East in the late 1970s was not just the place to be for his job but the place to be to learn about the world in general: "We're right in the middle.... Analysts of risk.... The world is here. Don't you feel that? In some of these places, things have enormous power. They have impact, they're mysterious. Events have weight" (*N* 98; see 101, 264). Axton is, again, hardly naïve, but it slowly dawns on him that his real employer is not some international insurance provider but the CIA, which is just as interested as large corporations in the political and economic stability of foreign nations.

All this leads to reflections about America and Americans abroad in the global economy, who were on the winning side—at least for the time—of empire.

From very early on in *The Names* there is the sense that Americans are far from innocent in their interactions abroad and that—the flip side of their mono-linguistic confidence and arrogance—they have come to know it: "Wasn't there a sense, we Americans felt, in which we had it coming?" (*N* 41) It goes well beyond Americans "with the prayer rugs they'd bargained for in the souk and bought as investments," since, as every savvy ex-pat knows, "they seem to go together, carpet-weaving and political instability" (*N* 176), or Americans who are able to avoid being punished or attacked in foreign countries "for the crimes of drinking whiskey, making money, jogging in shiny suits along the boulevards at dusk" (*N* 41; 218). When an American banker survives what seems to be an assassination attempt in Athens, Axton is reminded of the last of the thirty-seven "depravities" or accusations against him from his estranged Canadian wife: "*American*" (*N* 328). Indeed who better than a Canadian to see the true colors of the American empire? Who better to understand "the colonialism theme, the theme of exploitation"? Who better to see all our depravities?

> They are right next to us, sending their contaminants, their pollutants, their noxious industrial waste into our rivers, lakes and air. The theme of power's ignorance and blindness and contempt. We are in the path of their television programs, their movies and music, the whole enormous rot and glut and blare of their culture.
>
> (*N* 266)

While the themes of American empire, capitalism, and global domination are central to *The Names*, they really run throughout all of DeLillo's works. In *Ratner's Star* there is the appropriately named multinational corporation ACRONYM (*RS* 413) and, in *White Noise*, the unnamed "multinational giant" trying to develop Dylar, "operating in the deepest secrecy in an unmarked building just outside Iron City" (*WN* 299). You could pick either one to illustrate this immemorial truth from *Underworld*: "Corporations are great and appalling things" (*U* 282). And it is these great and appalling things and the systems of capital that support them that have led to this equally true claim in *Zero K*: "Half the world is redoing its kitchens, the other half is starving" (*ZK* 70).

Of course, as the counterpart or contraband to capitalism there is in DeLillo's work of the 1980s, just as there was still in the world at the time, the possibility and promise of communism. George Haddad—who has certain sympathies for the Maoist organization in Beirut that has taken a UN worker hostage—seems to see communism as the way out of our contemporary economic and social dilemma and its staggering inequalities. George says to Bill Gray, novelist:

> "You could have been a Maoist, Bill.... I can easily see you blending into that great mass of blue-and-white cotton.... And you would have seen the need for an absolute being, a way out of weakness and confusion. This is what I want to see reborn in the rat warrens of Beirut."
>
> (*M* 163)

But Bill's not buying it. Instead of some utopian future for workers united in a common vision of man, he sees death and terror in the prospect of a new closed society:

> "The point of every closed state is now you know how to hide your dead. This is the setup. You predict many dead if your vision of the truth isn't realized. Then you kill them. Then you hide the fact of the killing and the bodies themselves. This is why the closed state was invented. And it begins with a single hostage, doesn't it? The hostage is the miniaturized form. Her first tentative rehearsal for mass terror." "Some coffee," George said.
>
> (*M* 163)

In *Libra* we see the teenage Lee Harvey Oswald trying to school himself in a related Marxist ideology through books at the local library, books that, he says, "showed me the key to my environment," that "capitalism is beginning to die. It is taking desperate measures" (*L* 110). Later, we find him "in his room reading about the conversion of surplus value into capital, following the text with his index finger, word by word by word" (*L* 49; see 38–9, 41). This was the beginning of his education, his "radicalization," as one would say today.

Returning from Russia to the United States, Oswald will come to identify with Trotsky, seeing what he saw "near the end of his second foreign exile, 1917, the skyline of the New World" (*L* 214). For Leon Harvey, "Trotsky is the pure form" (*L* 312; see 317, 358), since it was Trotsky who had written that "revolution leads us out of the dark night of the isolated self" (*L* 101). The conflict between capitalism and communism is a struggle over different conceptions of the self—and, as we will see, different ways of thinking crowds. "He could see the capitalists, he could see the masses. They were right here, all around him, every day" (*L* 35; see *C* 41). What attracts Oswald to the cause is what attracts most people to causes: a counternarrative to oppose to the prevailing narrative, in this case, one to brandish before the ruling class:

> He was the product of a sweeping history, he and his mother, locked into a process, a system of money and property that diminished their human worth every day, as if by scientific law. The books made him part of something. Something led up to his presence in this room, in this particular skin, and something would follow.
>
> (*L* 41)

There are thus protests and attacks against the system in each of these works about the system, as if—in a kind of death drive—the one always led to the other, the forces against capitalism being spawned automatically by it or from within it. The anti-globalization demonstration in *Cosmopolis* is only the most theatrical of these protests.

Written in the late 1990s, *Cosmopolis* is no doubt DeLillo's most speculative and prescient narrative about what is happening to money and capital in the age of globalization. The main character, Eric Packer, seems to be the very embodiment of the global capitalist, acting without care or conscience: "I've never liked thinking back, going back in time, reviewing the day or the week or the life. To crush and gut. To eviscerate. Power works best when there's no memory attached" (*C* 184). But it cannot last forever. Just after Vija Kinski, Packer's "chief of theory" (*C* 77), has sung the praises of cyber-capital, its beauty, its speed, its glow, Kinski goes on to suggest that this runaway system sometimes calls for its own correction, for a crash, a revolt or a revolution.

> "Time is a corporate asset now. It belongs to the free market system…. The future becomes insistent. This is why something will happen soon, maybe today," she said, looking slyly into her hands. "To correct the acceleration of time. Bring nature back to normal, more or less."
>
> (*C* 79)

That something begins to happen to those who represent the system as well as to those who protest against it. While Packer had always been infallible at detecting the latent patterns of currency movements, he cannot crack the code on this one day. Though he continues to believe that "there's an order at some deep level," "a pattern that wants to be seen," "a common surface, an affinity between market movements and the natural world," an "aesthetics of interaction," as Vija Kinski suggests, he begins to doubt his ability to read it (*C* 86; see 63). As he confesses to Levin near the very end of the novel: "The yen eluded me. This had never happened. I became halfhearted" (*C* 190). But Packer's reaction is in fact anything but halfhearted. Against the advice of everyone, including his currency analyst, "He borrowed yen in dumbfounding amounts. He wanted all the yen there was" (*C* 97), his yearning for yen, his yen for yen, becoming insatiable. As a result of his misguided investments, the portfolio of Packer Capital is "reduced to near nothingness in the course of the day" (*C* 121), and Packer's unpredictable, irrational behavior—his irrational exuberance, as a former Fed chair might have said—is almost enough to bring the whole system down:

> His actions regarding the yen were causing storms of disorder. He was so leveraged, his firm's portfolio large and sprawling, linked crucially to the affairs of so many key institutions, all reciprocally vulnerable, that the whole system was in danger.
>
> (*C* 116)

Eric will thus lose his own fortune and then that of his wife, Elise, born into an old world banking fortune, her marriage to Packer the perfect corporate merger of old and new money. As his 47-year-old mistress, Didi Francher, puts it, "Two great fortunes. Like one of the great arranged marriages of old empire Europe" (*C* 26). Having lost his own fortune earlier in the day, he "impersonates" his wife "algorithmically," hacking into her account and sinking her entire fortune, 735 million dollars, into leveraging even more yen. "He was making a gesture of his own, a sign of ironic final binding. Let it all come down" (*C* 123).

Only at the very end will we see Packer return, albeit only briefly, to his old capitalist self. When Benno Levin, an employee of Packer's who is threatening to kill him, tells Packer his name, Packer responds coldly, "Means nothing to me," and with this "he felt a trace of the old stale pleasure, dropping an offhand remark that makes a person feel worthless" (*C* 192). Levin had understood Packer completely: "The huge ambition. The contempt. I can list the things. I can name the appetites, the people. Mistreat some, ignore some, persecute others. The self-totality. The lack of remorse. These are your gifts" (*C* 191). What he probably did not see was Packer's own desire to bring the whole thing down upon himself. It is in this way that Packer begins to resemble less and less the self-absorbed cyber-capitalist he is when the day begins and more and more some great potlatch chief bent on losing or destroying more than anyone else.

Packer does his level best from the side of capital to bring the whole system down. But there is, of course, another side to capital, the forgotten side or the side of the forgotten, which has its own designs on the future of capital, and its own plans for bringing the system to its knees:

> The more visionary the idea, the more people it leaves behind. This is what the protest is all about. Visions of technology and wealth. The force of cyber-capital that will send people into the gutter to retch and die. What is the flaw of human rationality? ... It pretends not to see the horror and death at the end of the schemes it builds. This is a protest against the future. They want to hold off the future. They want to normalize it, keep it from overwhelming the present.
>
> (*C* 90–1)

Hence the anti-globalization protests that accompany Eric Packer's all-day limousine ride across Manhattan, first "a woman in gray spandex on the median strip holding a dead rat aloft" (*C* 38), then two men in full body rat suits walking into a mid-town restaurant holding rats by the tails and "shouting something about *a specter*" (*C* 74; see also *U* 601). It's a protest against him and his kind, of course, but, this time, the rat holds him "rapt": "He was held nearly spellbound. He admired this thing, whatever it was" (*C* 74). "Whatever it was" because it's unclear if it's a political protest, a performance piece, a movement in the Marxist dialectic, a terrorist assault on global capital, or the reenactment of some ancient ritual: "The threats sounded ancient and formulaic, one phrase eliciting the next, and even the remarks in English had an epic tenor, deathly and stretchable. He wanted to talk to the guy, ask him what the occasion was, the mission, the cause" (*C* 75). Whatever it is, Eric wants to see where it's going. "Let it express itself," he thinks—like the pimple he found earlier in the novel festering on his previously unblemished capitalist body (*C* 74).

Kinski and Packer discuss whether these really are protestors or "a fantasy generated by the market," another expression of the free market itself, with protesters who "don't exist outside the market" since "there is no outside" (*C* 90). It's a hypothesis that has to be taken seriously, the notion that there is no place completely outside the market, no anti-market force that cannot be incorporated into the system, the dialectic between capital and counter-capital taking place within capital itself:

> there was something theatrical about the protest, ingratiating, even, in the parachutes and skateboards, the styrofoam rat, in the tactical coup of reprogramming the stock tickers with poetry and Karl Marx. He thought Kinski was right when she said this was a market fantasy. There was a shadow of transaction between the demonstrators and the state.

The protest was a form of systematic hygiene, purging and lubricating. It attested again, for the ten thousandth time, to the market culture's innovative brilliance, its ability to shape itself to its own flexible ends, absorbing everything around it. (*C* 99)

Packer's fascination with the way monetary systems turn everything into code, into numbers and electrical impulses, into the energy and momentum of capitalism, ultimately turns into a corresponding fascination with the death and destruction that these very same systems seem to portend. As both the Tiresias-like Vija Kinski and the Creon- or Oedipus-like Packer seem to understand as they watch the anti-globalization demonstration, "The urge to destroy is a creative urge," and this urge is "also the hallmark of capitalist thought. Enforced destruction. Old industries have to be harshly eliminated. New markets have to be forcibly claimed.... Destroy the past, make the future" (*C* 92). Earlier, it was "cyber-capital that creates the future" (*C* 79). Now, it's the destruction of cyber-capital that seems to lay claim to that future. Between the capitalists and the anarchists, Packer and those who are trying to destroy him, there would be a sort of "aesthetics of interaction" (*C* 86), an unconscious accord, signed and sealed not by separate, autonomous, rational subjects, but by a kind of collective death drive. "Let it all come down," thinks Packer, like an American Oedipus where everything is revealed and everything is destroyed within a single circuit of the sun.

It is a similar notion of the market and of capital that, in *Players*, Rafael and his terrorist organization want to disrupt by bombing the New York Stock Exchange, "the idea of worldwide money," the system itself, its current and its currency (*P* 107), in a word, to "make it appear a little less inviolable" (*P* 183): "They have money. We have destruction" (*P* 107). The response, the riposte, is thus to take it down from the outside, or else from within, or else to be there to push it over the edge when the system itself is good and ready to take itself down, when "the instruments of world repression ... fall apart on their own" (*P* 107).

The first sign that something is wrong with this system is, thus, a sign, an old man near Wall Street "holding his sign up over his head—the banks, the tanks, the corporations" (*P* 27; see 13), and then, much later, a more detailed sign: "Recent History of the Workers of the World ... May 1886: Haymarket Riot, Chicago, protest police killings of workers, 10 dead" (*P* 151–2). In between these two signs, there is the recruitment of Lyle, a young partner in a Wall Street firm (*P* 26), into the terrorist group that carries out an assassination on the floor of the New York Stock Exchange (*P* 29). Once again, it is those inside the system who are best suited to turn against it or to turn it against itself. That might seem odd except that what ultimately interests Lyle about joining the terrorist organization is the same thing that attracted him to the exchange: "It was a test environment for extreme states of mind" (*P* 27). Like Packer, he had taken his status as capitalist overlord in stride: "It's not an easy matter, being an oppressor. A lot of work involved" (*P* 34). Like Packer, he had been successful because "he saw in the numbers and stock symbols an artful reduction of the external world to printed output, the machine's coded model of exactitude" (*P* 70). The assassination on the floor of the New York Stock Exchange in *Players* thus seems to be, in retrospect, a warm-up or rehearsal for the attacks on the Stock Exchange in *Cosmopolis* and the assassination of the head of the IMF.

Sometimes, then, it's a little deviation from the established order that make us feel like the whole thing is collapsing, that we are witnessing the first signs of what will be a total collapse: an "aberration" in a bank account in *Zero K*, "not even a bank mistake but something in the structure itself. Beyond the computers and grids and digital algorithms and intelligence agencies" (*ZK* 172), "deviations from the logic of the number concept" (*ZK* 198). Aberrations and deviations—like Eric Packer's festering pimple or asymmetrical prostate, which of themselves seem to forebode his own collapse and that of the worldwide monetary system.

It is, precisely—and this is DeLillo's word—a "counterforce" that seems to be revealed in the little asymmetry or deviation, the aberration or anomaly, that seems to portend the collapse of an entire system. In a world of supposed order, pattern, and symmetry, an asymmetrical prostate appears as the ominous sign of a world out of balance and the impending collapse of the whole damn system. When Packer's confidence in a rational order is compromised, his belief in himself and his autonomy has to follow suit. Instead of moving and shaking others, he understands that he must now himself be moved and shaken—and the strange thing is, he likes it, indeed he is elated by it, as if this breakdown of certainty and predictability meant that he could now devote himself not to business but to life, to the business, finally, of living.

Cosmopolis is something like a postmodern fable of auto-immunity, the fable of a world "in deconstruction." Packer's "asymmetrical" prostate was the first sign, the first manifestation, of a counterforce that he resists and, in resisting, is irresistibly drawn to (*C* 8; see 47):

> He liked to track answers to hard questions. This was his method, to attain mastery over ideas and people. But there was something about the idea of asymmetry. It was intriguing in the world outside the body, a counterforce to balance and calm, the riddling little twist, subatomic,

that made creation happen. There was the serpentine word itself, slightly off kilter, with the single additional letter that changes everything.

(*C* 52; see *RS* 38, 300, 302, 376, for some asymmetrical testicles, a deviation from their everyday "bilateral symmetry")

It is the subatomic twist, the veer, the swerve, that is of interest, that gives life its zest, its particularly, that, as Lucretius already knew, is at the origin of the world—and, no doubt, at its end.

But there are, perhaps, just perhaps, things that resist consumption and capital, or at least things that mark its limits and suggest an end that is more than just sheer destruction. As Eric Packer's limo traverses Manhattan and Packer loses more and more of his colossal fortune, he runs through a whole series of art forms, from poetry, the bad poetry of Elise Shifrin, his wife of twenty-two days (see also *C* 66), to art, music, and so on—things that, perhaps, just perhaps, to some extent at least, resist the appropriation of capital, that are, even if it sounds hokey, worth more than all the money in the world. Things like art or, better, as we will see, a haircut from Anthony the Barber.

Money

All my money's tied up in cash.

RD 50

The wrist watch, or chronometer, was the sole outward sign of Richie's wealth, excluding his DC-9.

RD 143

"I have trouble imagining death at that income level," she said. "Maybe there is no death as we know it. Just documents changing hands."

WN 6

Money makes you live longer. It seeps into the bloodstream, into the veins and capillaries. I talked to my primary-care physician about this. He said he had an inkling I could be right.

"*HS*" 170

Empire and capitalism are, as we have just seen, central themes in DeLillo, the monetary system as a whole, along with the banks, corporations, and markets that support it. But a special word has to be reserved for money itself. For while it might be thought that money is simply the other side, the contraband, of all the things money can buy, money—not unlike the technology we spoke of a little earlier—comes to have in DeLillo a life and a logic of its own, independent of all those things to which good common sense would relate it, disconnected from all the things into which it can be supposedly translated. In the end, money too becomes self-referring. Already in *Great Jones Street* DeLillo expresses the whole idea and ideology of money: "It's tied up, the money. It's being used to make more money" (*GJ* 145). Though this idea of money is countered in the novel by another "idea of the value of money," namely, that money is simply that for which one works rather than that which does all the work, this other, older, quainter idea really doesn't have a chance today: "While I work and sweat, I want to think of my money resting in a cool steel-paneled room.... I don't like to think of money working. I'm the one who works" (*GJ* 44–5; see *C* 58). But the real capitalist understands that it is money that does all the work, and for that to happen it must be hot and liquid, which is to say, electronic, as virtual as possible (see *GJ* 234 and *ZK* 205).

Already in *Players*, there are reflections upon "money moving, shrinking as it moved, beginning to elude visualization," passing "from a paper existence to electronic sequences, its meaning increasingly complex, harder to name.... money not as a medium of exchange but as something to be consigned to data storage, traceable only through magnetic flashes" (*P* 110). Monetary transactions are, then, "nothing but waves and currents talking to each other" (*P* 109), "waves, systems, invisibility, power. He thought: *bip-bip-bip-bip*" (*P* 157). It is all, in short, "an occult theology of money" (*P* 132).

There are thus things, goods, products, and then there is money, "separable from the things it bought, money the coded impulse, ideational, a kind of discreet erection known only to the man whose pants are on fire" ("HS" 155). But then, as everything becomes more and more "ideational," there is "the concept-idée of money," even "more powerful than money itself" (*RS* 146; see 325), more powerful and, perhaps, more lucrative, a concept of money to produce money itself—a sort of bitcoin *avant la lettre* or *avant le dollar*. That's why, in *Ratner's Star*, the Honduran cartel tries to recruit math prodigy Billy Twillig to help them influence "the money curve," that is, to "manipulate abstract levels of all theoretical monies in the world today" (*RS* 145–6). While selling cocaine is a good and lucrative business venture, it cannot compare, as the cartel had learned, to the business of money.

Cosmopolis is the natural or theoretical extension of this interest in money. As Eric Packer says early on in the novel, "there's only one thing in the world worth pursuing professionally and intellectually.... The interaction between technology and capital. The inseparability" (*C* 23). Packer was not the only one in the late 1990s to be attracted by this interaction, as so many bankrupt day-traders can today attest. But Packer does not trade stocks and bonds—which would, in theory, be attached to some company, and that company to some product or service. He trades currency itself.

If secrets are, in DeLillo, the stock and trade of governmental and nongovernmental organizations trafficking in contraband of every kind, if they underlie every coded system of exchange, it should come as little surprise that secrets are also at the heart of every monetary system, the secret patterns and latent codes within systems, the kind Eric Packer used to be able to detect in the market before a wholly unexpected turn in the yen. Packer became mega-rich by seeing the "beauty and precision" of the "hidden rhythms in the fluctuations of a given currency" (*C* 76). Looking at the monitors in his limo and at the little world of binaries contained therein that had made him so rich, he thinks:

> Data itself was soulful and glowing, a dynamic aspect of the life process. This was the eloquence of alphabets and numeric systems, now fully realized in electronic form, in the zero-oneness of the world, the digital imperative that defined every breath of the planet's living billions. Here was the heave of the biosphere. Our bodies and oceans were here, knowable and whole.
>
> (*C* 24)

For Packer, the flow of capital had become less "the flow of information" than "pure spectacle, or information made sacred, ritually unreadable. The small monitors of the office, home and car become a kind of idolatry" (*C* 80). If the old world capitalist thinks that "time is money," and the countercultural folk artist sings that "money doesn't talk, it swears," it is the cyber-capitalist who knows that "money is talking to itself" (*C* 77). Old money money and old money ideas about money are, of course, still visible in New York, as Packer's limo makes its way through Manhattan's diamond district—"Cash for gold and diamonds. Rings, coins, pearls, wholesale jewelry, antique jewelry" (*C* 65)—but that is the life of "the souk, the shtetl" (*C* 65), light years and blips away from these new markets of cyber-capital and this new notion of money. In Packer's new world economy, money needs no justification, or, rather, it is its own justification. The higher the ticket price, that is, the bigger the number, the better the thing, or really, the better the number.

> The only thing that matters is the price you pay.... You paid the money for the number itself. One hundred and four million. This is what you bought. And it's worth it. The number justifies itself.
>
> (*C* 77–8)

It is cyber-capital, as Vija Kinski theorizes for Packer, that has changed everything. Or, rather, cyber-capital has revealed what capital has always longed to be. "Look at those numbers running. Money makes time. It used to be the other way around" (*C* 79). "It's cyber-capital that creates the future" (*C* 79). "All wave and codes," that's what cyber-capital is: "A higher kind of intelligence. Travels at the speed of light" (*U* 386). Everything that is truly cyber about capital can perhaps today be summarized in another single word, this one unhyphenated, as we will see in the conclusion when we turn to *The Silence*, a single word that should be uttered with the same reverence that "plastics" was once uttered in *The Graduate*: "Cryptocurrencies."

Advertising

Better living through chemistry. The Sears, Roebuck catalog. Aunt Jemima. All the impulses of all the media were fed into the circuitry of my dreams. One thinks of echoes. One thinks of an image made in the image and likeness of images. It was that complex.

A 130

Babette went to the pantry and began gathering tins and jars with familiar life-enhancing labels.

WN 119

There is only one truth. Whoever controls your eyeballs runs the world.

U 530

No look at DeLillo's incorporation of the corporation or capital or the market into his fiction would be complete without a pitch for the importance of advertising. *White Noise*, for example, is just as notorious for its seemingly incongruous or disjunctive, in short, its contrabanded use of advertising as it is for its integration of radio, film, or TV. Such intrusions are about as ubiquitous in the novel as they are in our lives. Most often, of course, they appear through these very same media, which we encounter at home, at work, or in our cars going from one to the other. Here, for example, is a nice juxtaposition of nature and American consumer culture, occasioned, it seems, by Jack and his family seeing a billboard on the side of the road as they attempt to escape the airborne toxic event: "The snow came more thickly, the traffic moved in fits and starts. There was a life-style sale at a home furnishing mart" (*WN* 120). We pass by these advertisements in our travels; they mark our landscape and thereby infiltrate our minds.

Sometimes we thus go to the advertisement—on the road or in the supermarket, where we might hear "a voice on the loudspeaker say 'Kleenex Softique'" (*WN* 36)—and sometimes, most times, it comes to us, through some medium like radio or television that is piped into our homes, and so into our lives, in the form of a slogan or jingle, or simply through one of the many brand names that give depth and meaning to our lives. Here are three counterband or counterbrand moments from *White Noise*, each made up of three names engraved or engrained in our collective consumer consciousness:

> She is afraid I will die unexpectedly, sneakily, slipping away in the night. It isn't that she doesn't cherish life; it's being left alone that frightens her. The emptiness, the sense of cosmic darkness.
>
> MasterCard, Visa, American Express.
>
> I tell her I want to die first.
>
> (*WN* 100)

> I watch light climb into the rounded summits of high-altitude clouds. Clorets, Velamints, Freedent.
>
> (*WN* 229)

> He helped an old man read the date on a loaf of raisin bread. Children sailed by in silver carts.
>
> Tegrin, Denorex, Selsun Blue.
>
> (*WN* 289)

The credit card, the breath freshener, the dandruff shampoo—but then there's this trio, not brand names but no less recognizable, three times three words that have become—whether acronymed or anacronymed—just as much a part of our identity as those brands:

> Ground glass crunched under the tires. I headed toward the foundry.
>
> Random Access Memory, Acquired Immune Deficiency Syndrome, Mutual Assured Destruction.
>
> (*WN* 303)

It can all be considered mere marketing or crass commercialism, but there is a certain genius to it, the way advertising takes language and reinvents it, makes it shine or glow, allowing it to become something far greater than itself:

> She uttered two clearly audible words, familiar and elusive at the same time, words that seemed to have a ritual meaning, part of a verbal spell or ecstatic chant.
>
> *Toyota Celica*
>
> The utterance was beautiful and mysterious, gold-shot with looming wonder. It was like the name of an ancient power in the sky, tablet-carved in cuneiform.... How could these near-nonsense words, murmured in a child's restless sleep, make me sense a meaning, a presence? She was only repeating some TV voice. Toyota Corolla, Toyota Celica, Toyota Cressida. Supranational names, computer-generated, more or less universally pronounceable. Part of every child's brain noise, the substatic regions too deep to probe. Whatever its source, the utterance struck me with the impact of a moment of splendid transcendence.
>
> (WN 155)

White Noise is itself often advertised and sold in literature classes as a postmodern novel that integrates American consumer culture and advertising in an innovative way. That is perfectly understandable and legitimate. I buy it. But one did not have to wait for *White Noise* for advertising to become a central theme in DeLillo. Already in *Americana* there are meditations on television, on advertising, and on the essential link between them: "A television set is an electronic form of packaging.... Who in America would want to watch TV without commercials?" (*A* 270). Who indeed. One can even imagine someone like Lee Harvey Oswald staying up late one night in 1963 and watching *only* commercials: "Lee sat there after the movie ended, with loud late-night commercials coming one after another, fast-talking men demonstrating blenders, demonstrating miracle shampoo, and Marina next to him, asleep, softly breathing" (*L* 370).

And then there's this, again from *Americana*, which could have come out of a communications or marketing course of the 1970s, or else a Don Draper sales pitch from *Mad Men*:

> In this country there is a universal third person, the man we all want to be.... Advertising has discovered this man. It uses him to express the possibilities open to the consumer. To consume in America is not to buy;

it is to dream. Advertising is the suggestion that the dream of entering the third person singular might possibly be fulfilled.

(*A* 270; see 233, 369)

Later in *Americana*, one of the actors David Bell has put into his little home movie is asked, "What do you think of the war?" and he responds: "I've seen it on television. It's sponsored by instant coffee among other things" (*A* 284).

So there is advertising, lots of it, along with reflections upon it, but then there is the industry that produces it. David Bell's father was in advertising, after all, and spent his spare time watching reels of TV commercials in the family basement (*A* 84). And at age twenty-eight, David Bell himself has a good bit of the brash, young adman about him: "It was not enough to be the best; one had to be the youngest as well" (*A* 7). "I was an extremely handsome young man.... I was blue-eyed David Bell... six feet two inches tall" (*A* 11). It is hardly surprising, then, that when Bell makes his own movie it will borrow, in a conscious or unconscious homage to his father, some of the formatting of the commercial: "I used a single camera position and shot straight on from the foot of the bed for about twenty seconds, a popular commercial length" (*A* 241; see 207, 271). Filming in his room in the Fort Curtis hotel, he will even try to capture the background sounds of certain daytime TV shows and their commercials—a double-banded film from the get-go. He thus had to film "in the early afternoon in order to get the right kind of TV show and commercials" (*A* 269)—a game show with "young married contestants and a suavely gliding master of ceremonies," the whole thing liberally peppered with "commercials, the usual daytime spasms on behalf of detergents and oral hygiene" (*A* 270). In one of the final sequences of the film, an interview with someone playing his father, Bell asks: "What is the role of commercial television in the twentieth century and beyond?" And his "father"—reading the words Bell has prepared for him—responds: "In my blackest moods I feel it spells chaos for us all" (*A* 274; see 24, 115).

The theme of advertising—of hype and promotion—is continued in *End Zone*, where a PR firm is hired to promote Logos College's football team. "People want spectacle plus personality," says Wally Pippich, "formerly of Wally Pippich Creative Promotion Associates" (*EZ* 152, 150), who gets the bright idea of marketing players based on their names rather than their abilities: "Gary Harkness. Good name. Promotable. I like it. I even love it" (*EZ* 151). (And it's got a *k*, notice.) In *Players* Moll's father too was an adman, "an advertising immortal" (*RD* 39), and it is surely no coincidence that, in *Underworld*, the whole long lineage of the famous Bobby Thomson baseball began "with a man named Charles, let me think, Wainwright. An advertising executive" (*U* 181), who bought the ball from Manx Martin when he was working for a "medium-sized" ad agency in Manhattan, the kind where the men have serial affairs with their secretaries and tell one another office jokes of the sort: "Had a date with a Swedish model last night.... When I touched her Volvo, she Saabed" (*U* 528). You get the type, and you get it even better when you hear how Wainwright wants to pitch the Minute Maid account:

> You show the froth on a perky housewife's upper lip, like the hint of a blowjob before breakfast. Of course there is no pulp in concentrate. And there is only a microtrace of pulp in container juice. But you can suggest, you can make inferences, you can promise the consumer the experience of citrusy bits of real pulp—a glass of juice, a goblet brimming with particulate matter, like wondrous orange smog.... If the can or package can be orgasmically visual, so can the product inside.
>
> (*U* 532–3)

This is, of course, the same Minute Maid that will be advertised on the billboard where Esmeralda will miraculously appear at the end of the novel. One couldn't imagine two more different—or contrabanded—associations for orange juice.

But well before Esmeralda Lopez there was Cleo Birdwell, "the First Woman Ever to Play in the National Hockey League," whom the New York Rangers hockey team want to use in a series of advertising campaigns, first for "Primal Vortex," a maker of whirlpools (*AZ* 85), and the "Kelloid Company—of Battle Creek, Michigan" (*AZ* 86; see 311, 314–18), but then for the Amazon line of products, "a snack food for women," "Amazon Ringos, Amazon Discos, Amazon Nuggets, Amazon Noshes," yes, even "Amazon Noshes," because "a little ethnic never hurts" (*AZ* 315). All Cleo had to do was stand there looking pretty and athletic and say "it's so good to be back among the Amazons" (*AZ* 315).

Advertisements exercise their power over us through the images they imprint upon us, but also, and maybe especially, through their slogans and jingles, "coded messages and endless repetitions, like chants, like mantras. '*Coke is it, Coke is it, Coke is it.*' The medium practically overflows with sacred formulas" (*WN* 51; see *GJ* 148). Indeed, for DeLillo, Coke really *is* it. David Bell calls himself a "child of Godard and Coca-Cola" (*A* 269; see 309); in *Ratner's Star* one of the essential clues to deciphering the code that has supposedly been sent by extraterrestrials appears on a Coca-Cola wall clock (*RS* 380), and, in *Mao II*, there are "advertising placards" for Coke II even in war-torn Beirut (*M* 230). So prominent, so American, is Coke (*L* 279, 287, 371, 150, *U* 738) that Lee Harvey Oswald thinks of grabbing one as a sort of prop just after shooting the President, the idea being that it would make him look normal, natural, innocent, all-American, because someone sipping a Coke on a lazy afternoon in Dallas could not possibly be the type of person who would take a shot at the president (*L* 404, 407). So it's mostly Coke (with just one *k* but two *k*-sounds), though Diet Pepsi gets a bit of airplay (*WN* 66), as well as Dr. Pepper (*L* 306), the name of a character in *Great Jones Street*, and 7-Up, which Nick Shay gets a job delivering in *Underworld* thanks to George the Waiter, the guy he ends up killing (*U* 724, 759). But that is just the beginning of a long line of product placements in DeLillo. There's Sears, Roebuck, and Company, Aunt Jemima syrup, Marlboro cigarettes, Jantzen bathing suits (*A* 272), Lemon Pledge, Miracle White (*AZ* 155), Chicklets (*AZ* 199), and Sprite (*AZ* 388), embedded ads for chemical companies like DuPont and Dow—"Common Sense, Uncommon Chemistry," that was (and I think we are supposed to hear some irony) "Dow's catchy-ad slogan" (*U* 601). All these advertisements and brand names are, of course, a way of smuggling not illicit but perfectly legitimate, legally saleable consumer goods into fiction. In the opening scene of *Underworld*, fans in the upper decks of the Polo Grounds tear up a Life magazine issue and send the pages, the stories and the ads, floating down onto the spectators and the field below, the picture of a Brueghel painting in a feature story on the Prado Museum right beside an ad for a "Packard car," because in the end it's "all part of the same thing, Rubens and Titian and Playtex and Motorola," "a Budweiser ad," "Johnson & Johnson and Quaker State and RCA Victor and Burlington Mills and Bristol-Myers and General Motors" (*U* 39). It's all one big thing, the Longines clock of the Polo Grounds (*U* 15), Balantine beer (*U* 631), DeNobili cigars (*U* 759), Lava soap (*U* 442), Cinzano (*U* 373), the IBM Selectric (*U* 533), Wheaties—"War and treaties, eat your Wheaties" (*U* 141)—Oreo cookies and then those other ones, Hydrox they're called, which kids like Eric Deming prefer "because the name sounded like rocket fuel" (U 519), and if you wanted to sound positively "interplanetary" you could put the leftovers in "Saran Wrap" (*U* 581). We live our lives with and through these products and we even compare ourselves and our lives to them. In *Underworld*, once again, Nick compares his wife Marian to the Camay soap girl (*U* 114), while Nick himself is compared to the Aqua Velva man (*U* 292)—it's a marriage made in consumer heaven, which is to say, on Madison avenue or on TV. There are even cross-novel marketing campaigns in DeLillo: Jack Ruby in *Libra* uses a "Wilkinson sword blade for the name appeal" (*L* 435) and then, wouldn't you know it, Willie Mays in *Underworld* appears to use the very same blade because, right there in the middle of the game at the Polo Grounds, Mays is "thinking helplessly, Push-pull click-click, change blades that quick" (*U* 22). It's an earworm in center field, not unlike the line advertising hats in a Sears catalogue that gets repeated in at least two different novels (*M* 170; see *L* 360).

And then there's "Panasonic," supposedly the original title of *White Noise*, the original title in the form of a contrabanded brand name, a title that was ultimately abandoned because of objections from the Panasonic Corporation (their mistake). The brand name there appears just as Jack is thinking about Babette in bed with Mink—the gray sheet being contrasted, it seems, with the white sheet that Jack or DeLillo would have just fed into his typewriter:

> Then gloom moved in around the gray-sheeted bed, a circle slowly closing.
>
> Panasonic.
>
> (*WN* 241)

The name appears again a few years later in *Mao II* as George Haddad, talking to writer Bill Gray about terrorism, suddenly interrupts his own argument in order to give him some unsolicited advice on his writing: "There's a new model that Panasonic makes and I absolutely swear by it" (*M* 164).

Then there are cigarettes, that is, smokes, butts, fags, or whatever you want to call them. *Underworld* can itself be read as a case study in American smoking culture during the latter half of the twentieth century. Here is an example of how brand loyalty used to be won: "You know why I smoke Old Golds? I wouldn't tell this to just anybody.... That's the cigarette that used to sponsor the Dodgers on the radio. Old Gold" (*U* 751). And it doesn't hurt to have a radio announcer like Russ Hodges egging you on—though it's for another brand, since he does the play-by-play for another team: "light up a Chesterfield and stay right here" (*U* 32; see 11). So it could be the sponsorship that gets you or it could be the slogan: "He smoked Lucky Strikes. He smoked the brand where they said, Light up a Lucky—it's light-up time. Be happy—go Lucky" (*U* 805; see 304 and 809). By the 1990s, most of these 1950s brands—Chesterfields, Old Golds, Lucky Strikes—often accompanied by 1950s gestures, like "tapping" your shirt pocket for a cigarette (*L* 25)—have been replaced by other, designer brands and their own accompanying gestures, Klara Sax, for example, who "pulled a box of Nat Shermans out of her blazer and lit one up" (*U* 73). You know what decade you are in just by following the brands and their accompanying gestures.

Slogans, labels, and logos—we spend a lot of time thinking about them and getting consumed by them. Here is Nick Shay in three Lucky Strike moments:

> My father smoked Lucky Strikes. The pack has a design that could easily be called a target but then maybe not—there's no small central circle or bull's eye.... But I call it a target anyway and fuck the definitions.
>
> (*U* 87)

And, besides, if it's not a target, why did they name the brand Lucky Strike? True, there's a gold-rush connotation. But a strike is not only the discovery of some precious metal in the ground. It is also a penetrating hit from a weapon. And isn't there a connection between the name of the brand and the design of concentric circles on the package? This implies they were thinking target all along.

(*U* 90)

> I look at the Lucky Strike logotype and I think target.

(*U* 122)

There are, in addition to all of this, the claims of advertisers, and the healthy skepticism that should accompany them. Sunscreen, for example, has been the object of skepticism in DeLillo since at least *White Noise*: "It is all a corporate tie-in," says Babette, "The sunscreen, the marketing, the fear, the disease. You can't have one without the other" (*WN* 264). In *Underworld* Nick Shay will follow up on Babette's skepticism—even though, as we will see, the sun and its screening (in an eclipse, for example) will be the ultimate source of wonder in many DeLillo novels:

> I knew this subject well. I'd read up on this subject, seen the research studies, I'd compared the products and the claims. And I knew with total certainty that a protection factor of fifteen was the highest level of sunblock scientifically possible. Now they were selling me a thirty.

(*U* 84; see 120)

Here is a final advertising reference, one that perhaps demonstrates better than any other the contraband effect that we have been trying to develop, the way in which advertising no longer refers to a world outside it but—a bit like money, which was itself a bit like technology—refers only to itself, a self-referring world with no outside. This is the world Brian Glassic finds himself driving around in in *Underworld* as he goes to visit the Fresh Kills landfill on Staten Island:

> He saw billboards for Hertz and Avis and Chevy Blazer, for Marlboro, Continental and Goodyear, and he realized that all the things around him, the planes taking off and landing, the streaking cars, the tires on the cars, the cigarettes that the drivers of the cars were dousing in their ashtrays—all these were on the billboards around him, systematically linked in some self-referring relationship that had a kind of neurotic tightness, an inescapability, as if the billboards were generating reality.

(*U* 183)

It's a self-referring world, but not one that is completely closed to innovation or product development. On the contrary, any number of products can be invented and advertised in that world. In "Hammer and Sickle," someone wears a T-shirt that bears simply the word "INSCRIPTION" ("HM" 31). It's a bit like the Minute Maid billboard at the end of *Underworld* that simply reads—after the ad has been removed—"Space Available." In other words, go right ahead, invent some product and advertise it right *here*. That's the genius of the market. As they say, just watch this space.

Consumerism and Waste

I shopped with reckless abandon. I shopped for immediate needs and distant contingencies. I shopped for its own sake, looking and touching, inspecting merchandise I had no intention of buying, then buying it.

WN 84

Dying is an art in Tibet. A priest walks in, sits down, tells the weeping relatives to get out and has the room sealed.... He has serious business to see to. Chants, numerology, horoscopes, recitations. Here we don't die, we shop. But the difference is less marked than you think.

WN 38

The landfill showed him smack-on how the waste stream ended, where all the appetites and hankerings, the sodden second thoughts came runneling out, the thing you wanted ardently and then did not.

U 184–5

If corporations and the products they make and market are so omnipresent in DeLillo's work, then consumer culture has to be central as well. Such culture is, of course, global today, but if credit is to be given where credit is due it was first of all American, and it has left its mark everywhere from the mall to the supermarket to the home. Walk into a supermarket with Murray from *White Noise* and you will perhaps begin to see anew the beauty and genius, the magic and the miracle, of consumption and consumer culture in America: "We simply walk toward the sliding doors. Waves and radiation. Look how well-lighted everything is. The place is sealed off, self-contained. It is timeless" (*WN* 38). *White Noise* is punctuated by such trips to the mall (*WN* 83–4) or the supermarket (*WN* 167; see 220–3)—a field of dreams for kids like Jack's son Wilder, who sits inside the cart, "on the collapsible shelf, trying to grab items whose shape and radiance excited his system of sensory analysis" (*WN* 167), all of this, of course, by design, the result of innumerable marketing studies, psychological tests, and consumer surveys. As Charles Wainwright, advertising exec, reminds us in *Underworld*, "They secretly photograph women in supermarkets. They have sensitive cameras hidden on the shelves that record excitations of the inner eye…. These are orgasms, basically, of the eye, the brain and the nervous system" (*U* 531). And the mystery doesn't even end when you get to the checkout line: "The terminals are equipped with holographic scanners, which decode the binary secret of every item, infallibly" (*WN* 326). Indeed the mystery and celebration even follow you home, not from the farm right onto your plate but, better, from those supermarket shelves right into your refrigerator, the great American refrigerator, another place of mystery and awe (*U* 517–18).

And yet the joy and celebration of American consumer culture, its endless and infinitely renewed display of goods and products for longer lives and better living, is always juxtaposed in DeLillo with threats and dangers, with waves and radiation, with the death that is always lurking behind these promises of a better life. In *Underworld* there is a short section in which a typical American home—the Demings, in Arizona—combines in counterpoint a paean to American consumer products, everything from the new refrigerators with crispers to two-tone station wagons and Jell-O molds, with the warning labels attached to everyday household products, things like, "May cause discoloration of urine or feces" (*U* 517), "To avoid suffocation keep out of reach of children" (*U* 517). The point, it seems, is that you cannot turn around or open a cabinet in an American kitchen and not be at once totally amazed and absolutely terrorized—or both, in contraband.

In the epilogue of *Underworld*, entitled "Das Kapital," Nick and Brian Glassic take a business trip to Kazakhstan to attend a product demonstration of a very different kind, an underground nuclear explosion that is able, or at least that is the pitch, to destroy the world's worst nuclear waste, the kind that Nick and Brian's company is paid to dispose of. It is the perfect setting to reflect upon the nature of advanced capital and neo-liberalism:

> Capital burns off the nuance in a culture. Foreign investment, global markets, corporate acquisitions, the flow of information through transnational media, the attenuating influence of money that's electronic and sex that's cyberspaced, untouched money and computer-safe sex, the convergence of consumer desire—not that people want the same things, necessarily, but that they want the same range of choices.
>
> (*U* 785)

When everything becomes electronic in this way, that is, digital, cyber, free-floating, then any desire can be met, for a price, of course, because "as desire tends to specialize, going silky and intimate, the force of converging markets produces an instantaneous capital that shoots across horizons at the speed of light" (*U* 786).

But if consumer products are everywhere in DeLillo, then so are the waste products they produce or are destined to become. If one is observant enough, one begins, like Nick Shay or his colleagues, "seeing garbage everywhere or reading it into a situation" (*U* 343). At higher levels of perception, one can even see "products as garbage even when they sat gleaming on store shelves, yet unbought" (*U* 121). In short, one can begin to see that every construction is haunted, doubled, double-banded, by its destruction, that every product is contrabanded by its waste. Waste is the other side, the underside, of consumer culture. In other words, "Waste is the secret history, the underhistory.... What we excrete comes back to consume us" (*U* 791). That is why we no doubt "feel a reverence for waste" (*U* 809). It is thus surely not by chance that so many of the ecological or individual disasters in DeLillo are wholly manmade—things like the airborne toxic event and the malady in Jack Gladney that it would have produced: "My body is growing a nebulous mass. They track these things like satellites. All this as a result of a byproduct of insecticide" (*WN* 283).

DeLillo's interest in waste, trash, and garbage is on fullest display in *White Noise* and *Underworld*, novels that are littered with trash from start to finish, whether it be the disposable products that pack our supermarkets and clog our trash compactors in *White Noise*, or all the crap that Jack will throw out over the course of several purges of home and office, or all the waste and detritus that fill our landfills and pollute our oceans in *Underworld*. But DeLillo's interest in trash goes way back before *White Noise*. Already back in *Great Jones Street*, someone muses that, one day, people "versed in the methods of counter-archaeology" (notice the "counter-" here) "will study us not by digging into the earth but by climbing vast dunes of industrial rubble and mutilated steel, seeking to reach the tops of our buildings" (*GJ* 209). Such study will be necessary, for there is, as the narrator of *Ratner's Star* puts it, "something about waste material that defies systematic naming" (*RS* 38), even though waste remains central to our systems of living. As Billy Twillig says as he thinks back to his boyhood in the Bronx, "much of local violence had garbage at its heart" (*RS* 251). Waste Disposal: the phrase alone is synonymous with syndicated crime if not systematic violence.

In *Underworld* DeLillo makes this long-standing obsession with garbage, trash, and waste into a central theme. The novel's main character, Nick Shay, works for a company called Waste Containment, a company that understood the significance and solemnity of waste and had devoted an entire philosophy to it:

> You stand at the head of a corridor and by the time you walk to the far end you have adopted the comprehensive philosophy of the firm, the

> *Weltanschauung*. I use this grave and layered word because somewhere in its depths there is a whisper of mystical contemplation that seems totally appropriate to the subject of waste.
>
> (*U* 282; see 278)

And the company had a finely honed mission statement to match that philosophy:

> We were waste handlers, waste traders, cosmologists of waste.... It was a religious conviction in our business that these deposits of rock salt would not leak radiation. Waste is a religious thing. We entomb contaminated waste with a sense of reverence and dread. It is necessary to respect what we discard.
>
> (*U* 88)

As he puts it later, "We were the Church Fathers of waste in all its transmutations" (*U* 102). Like the original Church Fathers, the upper echelons of Waste Containment even needed to know a little Latin: "Waste is an interesting word that you can trace through Old English and Old Norse back to the Latin, finding such derivatives as empty, void, vanish and devastate" (*U* 120). Nick actually traces his own interest in waste back to his early religious education:

> The Jesuits taught me to examine things for second meanings and deeper connections. Were they thinking about waste? We were waste managers, waste giants, we processed universal waste. Waste has a solemn aura now, an aspect of untouchability. White containers of plutonium waste with yellow caution tags.
>
> (*U* 88)

Nick was in his early forties, working as a corporate speechwriter and public relations aid when he got hired by the waste company. As he testifies, "I was ready for something new, for a faith to embrace" (*U* 282). That's when the waste business came calling, with its liturgies and its sacred sites—like the modern landfill:

> We stood above a hole in the earth, an engineered crater five hundred feet deep, maybe a mile across ... oddly and equally beautiful in a way, a prophylactic device, a gas-control system ... and I felt a weird elation, a loyalty to the company and the cause.
>
> (*U* 285)

This is, in short, "The scenery of the future. Eventually the only scenery left" (*U* 286).

The waste business thus has or is its own religion, with its gurus and prophets, the consultants and keynote speakers at waste conferences and conventions across the globe. While some condemn the waste, others—the more advanced—celebrate and worship it. As one garbage guru, trained as a "garbage archaeologist" (perhaps recycled from *Great Jones Street*), preaches to the assembled masses at a waste conference (*U* 281):

> Bring garbage into the open. Let people see it and respect it. Don't hide your waste facilities. Make an architecture of waste…. Get to know your garbage. And the hot stuff, the chemical waste, the nuclear waste, this becomes a remote landscape of nostalgia. Bus tours and postcards, I guarantee it…. Nostalgia for the banned materials of civilization, for the brute force of old industries and old conflicts.
>
> (*U* 286)

He could just be putting lipstick on a pig, as some would say, or he could actually be seeing a very different pig, and a brighter, more radiant future for all the really horrible stuff that most people simply want to ignore:

> The more dangerous the waste, the more heroic it will become. Irradiated ground. The way the Indians venerate this terrain now, we'll come to see it as sacred in the next century. Plutonium National Park. The last haunt of the white gods. Tourists wearing respirator masks and protective suits.
>
> (*U* 289)

He is, of course, speaking at the waste conference to the converted, the kind of people who are not unhappy about working in a building that "resembles a geometric turd" (*U* 163), the kind of people who visit the great landfills of the nation as if they were national parks—"the Fresh Kills landfill" on Staten Island, for example, "the King Kong of American garbage mounds" (*U* 163), the name of the landfill echoing an earlier, more wholesome reference to "Fresh Killed Chickens From The Farm" (*U* 57), as if "Fresh Kills" were at once the newest and the oldest name for waste, the most ancient and the most contemporary coming together in contraband fashion to tell future generations exactly who *we* were:

> Three thousand acres of mountained garbage…. It was science fiction and prehistory, garbage arriving twenty-four hours a day, hundreds of workers, vehicles with metal rollers compacting the trash, bucket augers digging vents for methane gas, the gulls diving and crying, a line of

snouted trucks sucking in loose litter. He imagined he was watching the construction of the Great Pyramid at Giza.

(*U* 184)

These are the kind of people—the kind of men (for it's mostly men)—who work at Waste Containment, the kind who, during a day off in LA, will visit not the Getty or the MOCA but the Watts Towers, a series of "openwork towers, three tall, four smaller ones," that someone named SR, Sabato Rodia, spent "thirty-three years building… out of steel rods and broken crockery and pebbles and seashells and soda bottles and wire mesh," a "jazz cathedral" made by "a master builder" out of waste (*U* 276–7; see 492), a great towering monument to trash in our times. It is this kind of dedication to the cause that explains why Nick, by the end of the novel, will have become "a sort of executive emeritus" at Waste Containment, sent around the world to visit colleges and research facilities to talk about waste (*U* 804).

In addition to all these reflections on trash and garbage, there is even poetic waxing about "raw sewage": "You treat it with loving care," says one of Nick's colleagues, who "went through the process in lushest detail, stroking certain words, drawing them out, oozy, swampy, semisolid, thick, slick, sludge" (*U* 301). Sewage is actually not just a species of the genus waste but the genus itself. For in the end, "all waste defers to shit," "all waste aspires to the condition of shit" (*U* 302). All this is build-up to the rumors regarding a ship that is endlessly sailing the world, unable to dock not because it is a "boatload of heroin," as once thought, but "a boatload of shit" (*U* 330; see 312), and perhaps also because there is a "a body buried there," "some mobster" maybe, "shot in the head execution-style" (*U* 331), which will carry its own associations for Nick Shay.

None of this is, of course, just some idiosyncratic preoccupation on the part of DeLillo or his characters. As the narrator testifies, this is "the age of house garbage, the age of construction debris and vandalized car bodies, the age of moldering mobster parts" (*U* 238). Ours is an age of "desperate crisis" as we try to deal with this "intractability of waste" (*U* 805). So ubiquitous, so unavoidable is it, that people have begun "trading garbage in the commodity pits in Chicago" (*U* 804).

Trash is thus everywhere in *Underworld*. After a week-long garbage strike in New York City, the streets are heaped with identical black plastic bags (*U* 376, 388, 446); Manx Martin helps a friend dump his restaurant garbage under the Whitestone Bridge (*U* 361–3); the FBI spies on mobsters by stealing their "household trash," careful to "substitute fake garbage, to allay suspicion" (*U* 558). Trash is everywhere in *Underworld* because it's everywhere in America. Hence all the reflections on just how rich the garbage of garbage-rich America really is: "They have garbage here you can furnish your house and feed your kids" (*U* 767). Albert Bronzini even begins what sounds like a thesis in Comparative Waste Studies, noting that the Ancient Mayans used to bury their dead not with valuable objects but "old broken things ... cracked vases ... chipped cups and tarnished bracelets. They used the dead as a convenient means of garbage disposal" (*U* 767).

But despite all this concern with trash and waste, it would be difficult to call DeLillo a traditional environmentalist. David Bell says in *Americana*, "I read two pages of script about the melting of the polar ice caps and then called my father" (*A* 95). DeLillo is against waste and for recycling, it seems, though he is skeptical about the rhetoric and religious fervor surrounding the latter. There is thus a critique of both America's penchant for wastefulness and destruction and its almost religious obsession with efficiency and recycling (*A* 118), which DeLillo treats with the same mock or maybe not so mock religiosity as waste itself. Jack Gladney in *White Noise*—the same one who was so fascinated by his finds in the family trash compactor (*WN* 259)—was already doing his best on this score, the best for himself and for the world at large: "I twirl the garbage bags and twist-tie them, swim laps in the college pool" (*WN* 15). But Nick Shay will take waste disposal at home to a whole new level, giving it almost as much fervent attention as he gives the macro-waste streams he treats at work. Nick recites his local recycling instructions like a prayer, like the rosary, with its five plastic, five glass, and five metal mysteries—the whole thing layered over, once again, with a bit of Latin:

> At home we separated our waste into glass and cans and paper products. Then we did clear glass versus colored glass. Then we did tin versus aluminum. We did plastic containers, without caps or lids, on Tuesdays only. Then we did yard waste.
>
> (*U* 89)

> On pickup days we placed each form of trash in its separate receptacle and put the receptacles, from the Latin verb that means receive again, out on the sidewalk in front of the house.... There is no language I might formulate that could overstate the diligence we brought to these tasks.
>
> (*U* 102–3)

Recycling is obviously not just the sign of being a good citizen but proof of being a good person. When asked to give an account of one's life in the afterlife, one could do worse than to begin: "We separate our household waste according to the guidelines" (*U* 803).

All these warnings about waste and our simultaneous fascination with it are mirrored throughout DeLillo by the warnings about and fascination with weapons. The connection is hardly fortuitous. As we read near the end of *Underworld*, "There is a curious connection between weapons and waste... maybe one is the mystical twin of the other" (*U* 791). That is in large part because the very purpose of weapons is to destroy and, as we say, lay waste to things. But it is also because enormous amounts of waste—and some of the most hazardous, the most vile—come out of the very production of these weapons. Hence the sort of utopic/dystopic vision near the end of *Underworld* of turning nuclear products against themselves, blowing up—and thereby neutralizing—the waste from old nuclear weapons and nuclear power plants with "low-yield nuclear devices" (*U* 794). It is the dream of turning waste upon waste in order to make it productive, the dream of turning waste against itself in a way that leaves no waste behind. This dream of getting rid once and for all of these materials with ungodly long half-lives is perfectly articulated by Viktor Maltsev, spokesperson for the company in Kazakhstan that is offering this unique service: "The fusion of two streams of history, weapons and waste. We destroy contaminated waste by means of nuclear explosions" (*U* 792). Seems like the perfect solution—though probably just a bit too perfect—for those "twelve hundred metric tons" of plutonium waste floating around in the world (*U* 795). Viktor concludes his pitch: "don't be surprised there will be tourists here someday" (*U* 792). Tourists, he says, because it will be important to help people in the future appreciate the spectacle of waste, to awaken them to its possibilities, to see it for what it is. The people at Waste Containment are, of course, already there, well ahead of the curve, their eyes already opened to what we will all see one day:

> "I'm doing real work, important work. Landfills are important. Trouble is, the job follows me. The subject follows me...."
>
> "You see it everywhere because it is everywhere."
>
> "But I didn't see it before."
>
> "You're enlightened now. Be grateful."
>
> (*U* 283)

4

Counterhistories

American History 2.0

How can we learn from the past unless we repeat it?

RS 64

There's something they aren't telling us. Something we don't know about. There's more to it. There's always more to it. This is what history consists of. It's the sum total of all the things they aren't telling us.

L 321

Longing on a large scale is what makes history.

U 11

There are many ways in which history, particularly American history, enters into DeLillo's novels, never as such, never not transformed, but still recognizable as what it was or was supposed to be. Memorialized there are many of the great events of twentieth- and early twenty-first-century American history, everything from Sputnik in 1957 (okay, not American, though it sure did light a fire under America (*U* 519)) and the Cuban Missile Crisis of October 1962, brought to us in *Underworld* through the comedic rants of one Lenny Bruce (*U* 505, 591), to the assassination of JFK in November 1963, the great Northeast Blackout of November 9, 1965 (*U* 633–7), the Moonie mass marriage in Yankee Stadium in 1976, the Challenger Space Shuttle disaster in 1986, and 9-11, to name but a few. These are the kind of events about which one says, "Where were you when … ?": "Where were you when Kennedy? Well, remember the time the lights went out. This place reminds me. The great Northeast blackout" (*U* 332).

Then, of course, there's the infamous baseball game in the Polo Grounds on October 3, 1951, the one that ends with Bobby Thomson's homerun blast—"They're calling it the Shot Heard 'Round the World" (*U* 669)—and the near simultaneous test by the Soviet Union of a nuclear weapon in the Kazakhstan desert. It was the kind of event that "makes people want to be in the streets, joined with others, telling others what has happened, those few who haven't heard—comparing faces and states of mind" (*U* 47). The contrast is developed in *Underworld* between this event and the mother of all twentieth-century American events, the assassination of JFK.

> When JFK was shot, people went inside. We watched TV in dark rooms and talked on the phone with friends and relatives. We were all separate and alone.... But when Thomson hit the homer, people rushed outside.
>
> (*U* 94)

But history also seeps into DeLillo's novels by way of proper names (Trotsky, for example, already in *Americana*, the name David Bell's office colleague Warburton uses to sign cryptic office memos (*A* 74)) and then again in *Libra*. Why Trotsky, we may wonder, and not Marx or Lenin? Well, maybe because "Trotsky had once lived, in exile, in a working-class area of the Bronx not far from the place Lee had lived with his mother" (*L* 34); "Trotsky in the Bronx, only blocks away" (*L* 101).

Libra is a novel not just about an historic event but about the forces that make history, the ways in which histories are written or constructed, and the desires of some to end their isolation by becoming part of history. Such is the case of Lee Harvey Oswald, who, even as a kid, wanted to read books with "subjects and ideas of historic scope, ideas that touched his life, his true life, the whirl of time inside him" (*L* 33). Whence his desire to experience history, to become "a man in history" or a world-historical figure (*L* 149; see 100), like Lenin or Trotsky:

> These were men who lived in isolation for long periods, lived close to death through long winters in exile or prison, feeling history in the room, waiting for the moment when it would surge through the walls, taking them with it. History was a force to these men, a presence in the room. They felt it and waited.
>
> (*L* 34)

As time goes on, Oswald begins to have "a sense of destiny," "locked in the miniature room, creating a design, a network of connections" (*L* 277), thinking that "the only end to isolation was to reach the point where he was no longer separated from the true struggles that went on around him." And "the name we give to this point is history" (*L* 248).

But of course history is not the sole possession of such men. Those planning the assassination, former CIA operatives, were also "men who believed history was in their care" (*L* 127). And when it's all over, when Kennedy is actually dead, it is Jack Ruby, at once spectator and actor, who understands as well as anyone just how big the thing would be: "This death was everywhere. Pictures of the grieving family.... This was an event that had the possibility of being bigger in history than Jesus" (*L* 428).

History is obviously not the sum total of facts but the ordering and the putting into narrative of those facts. As DeLillo reminds us, again in *Libra*, "facts are lonely things" (*L* 300). It is only out of "the endless fact-rubble of the investigations," then, "how many shots, how many gunmen, how many directions?" (*L* 300) that a history can be told, a history or a counternarrative, in short, a novel. As DeLillo writes in "In the Ruins of the Future," an essay published just a couple months after 9-11: "The Bush administration was feeling nostalgia for the cold war. This is over now. Many things are over. The narrative ends in the rubble and it is left to us to create the counternarrative" ("RF").

In another essay, "The Power of History," DeLillo speaks again of counternarratives, or of the way "language can be a form of counterhistory," the language of the novel, a language that attempts to deliver something that no history can, a language to "see inside the human works, down to dreams and routine rambling thoughts" ("PH"). In a word, "the novel is the dream release, the suspension of reality that history needs to escape its own brutal confinements" ("PH"). For fiction may not actually rescue history, but it certainly can recue, replay, and reframe it. In a word, it contrabands it, through a kind of doubling that confuses the original and its double. As someone asks in *Underworld*, "Is this when history turned to fiction?" (*U* 459) It's a tough question to answer, though it was perhaps already answered in *End Zone*, "History is the angle at which realities meet" (*EZ* 46). I am not exactly sure what that means, but it sounds right. Actually, it sounds like a theory of contraband.

Terrorism

We are willing to die, they are not. This is our strength, to love death, to feel the claim of armed martyrdom.

FM 178

Terror is the force that begins with a handful of people in a back room.

M 158

This room is the first minute of the new nation.

M 236

In this day and age, our day and age, literature can hardly avoid the topic of terrorism, and DeLillo's work will have confronted it from very early on. The opening of *Players* features a long, detailed description of an in-flight movie (yet another nod to our contemporary contraband life in the air) in which terrorists attack golfers (yet another sports reference) with automatic rifles (*P* 7–8). The rest of the novel then revolves around a terrorist shooting on the New York Stock Exchange and plans for future bomb attacks (*P* 65, 103, 183). And it ends with Lyle Wynant—the first of DeLillo's many, as we would now call them, "domestic terrorists" (*RD* 40; see 167–8)—in a hotel room in Toronto, waiting for the order to carry out an attack against the very stock exchange where he worked.

In *The Names* it becomes a question of attacking not some amorphous global system, epitomized by the New York Stock Exchange, but the country in which that exchange is located. It is here that the question of terrorists attacking America and Americans is broached head-on: "Terror.... In Europe they attack their own institutions, their police, journalists, industrialists, judges, academics, legislators. In the Middle East they attack Americans" (*N* 114). The reason for this, as risk analyst James Axton explains, is that "the others lack a certain mythical quality that terrorists find attractive.... America is the world's living myth. There's no sense of wrong when you kill an American or blame America for some local disaster" (*N* 114).

Between *The Names* and *Mao II* terror becomes even more prominent, even more pressing, both on the international stage and in DeLillo. It's the late 1980s and terror, the possibility of terror, is always in the back of people's minds. Brita, a well-known photographer of reclusive writers, says:

> Yes, I travel. Which means there is no moment on certain days when I'm not thinking terror. They have us in their power. In boarding areas I never sit near windows in case of flying glass.... I'm careful about reading matter. Nothing religious comes with me, no books with religious symbols on the jacket and no pictures of guns or sexy women.
>
> (*M* 40–1)

While DeLillo reflects on terrorism in almost every one of his works from *Players* forward, the two novels with the most sustained reflections on the matter are *Mao II* and *Falling Man*. Taken together, they can almost be read as a two-part debate about the nature and causes of terrorism, the first part from the 1980s—the rise of the Ayatollah Khomeini, terrorism organizations in Lebanon, and so on—and the second after 9–11.

Part one of the debate takes place between Bill Gray and George Haddad, with the latter arguing *for*, so to speak, the terrorists who have taken a hostage in Beirut: "We need a model that transcends all the bitter history. Something enormous and commanding. A figure of absolute being. This is crucial, Bill. In societies struggling to remake themselves, total politics, total authority, total being" (*M* 158). Terrorism is thus here understood, as one might have expected, as a conflict between competing narratives. The terrorist wants to be "noticed," to be sure, but what he wants above all else is to have his alternative narrative confirmed. And in order to do that violence seems necessary: "In societies reduced to blur and glut, terror is the only meaningful act.... Who do we take seriously? Only the lethal believer, the person who kills and dies for faith" (*M* 157).

It's a counternarrative that the terrorist is trying to impose—that's clear enough and, as a narrative, understandable enough. But the violence itself still seems incomprehensible. That the terrorist would commit him or herself to dying for a cause makes sense: "He will give his life for the cause. Perfectly in keeping.... The rightist kills his own leader. The leftist kills himself" (*P* 120). As someone says of the 1970s Baader-Meinhof terrorist group: "They committed suicide. Or the state killed them.... They were terrorists, weren't they? When they're not killing other people, they're killing themselves" ("BM" 106).

All that makes perfect sense. What initially doesn't make sense is the taking of innocent lives: "Only the terrorist stands outside. The culture hasn't figured out how to assimilate him. It's confusing when they kill the innocent. But this is precisely the language of being noticed, the only language the West understands" (*M* 157). Hence the power of outrageous acts such as kidnapping an innocent UN worker in Beirut. What we are looking at is a worldwide system of terror, inspired by ideology, perhaps, but aimed at terrorizing everyone, including and especially the innocent, that is, as always, the always relatively innocent: "Of course he's innocent. That's why they took him. It's such a simple idea. Terrorize the innocent" (*M* 129). It's simple and it's meaningful for the way it undermines all meaning: "When you inflict punishment on someone who is not guilty, when you fill rooms with innocent victims, you begin to empty the world of meaning.... This poet you've snatched. His detention drains the world of one more thimble of meaning" (*M* 200).

DeLillo seems to recognize something new about terrorism in *Mao II*, if not before. Having gone global, the point is to involve the media right from the start, since the mediatization is often the message of terror and the threat of terror can be just as terrorizing as the terror itself (see *M* 122, 124–5, 156). Though there are references to the Shining Path, the Sendero Luminoso, in Peru (*M* 175, 187), it is an unknown Maoist group in Beirut that is at the center of the final chapters of the novel. Brita, who earlier in the novel photographed Bill Gray, is now "on assignment for a German magazine... to photograph a local leader named Abu Rashid" (*M* 228). We could easily imagine that this is going to be the story of the West coming to impose its media and technology on the East or the Middle East. But when we get there we see that photographs are already more or less everywhere, already at the center of the conflict. In Brita's words, the place is "a millennial image mill" (*M* 229). "A pair of local militias" is seen "firing at portraits of each other's leader" (*M* 227). And when Brita finally locates Rashid's group, she finds "two hooded boys standing watch on the stairs with photographs of a gray-haired man pinned to their shirts" (*M* 231). The boys have pictures of Rashid on their t-shirts. When Brita asks why, Rashid responds: "It gives them a vision they will accept and obey. These children need an identity outside the narrow function of who they are and where they come from…. We teach them identity, sense of purpose. They are all children of Abu Rashid" (*M* 233). It's a technique Rashid seems to have learned from Mao himself, who, as we are reminded earlier, "used photographs to announce his return and demonstrate his vitality, to reinspire the revolution" (*M* 141). It is hard not to hear the song that runs in contraband in all our heads, the one recalled by Scott, who at one point leans toward Karen "to sing a bit of old Beatles, a line about carrying pictures of Chairman Mao" (*M* 223).

Interestingly, there is no explicitly religious dimension to terrorism in *Mao II*. Indeed it is stated that the terrorists themselves are *not* religious and are not acting out of any religious motivations. They are, on the contrary, a new brand of humanist, but one that opposes the image of the human forged in Europe. Abu Rashid explains:

> We teach that our children belong to something strong and self-reliant. They are not an invention of Europe. They are not making a race to go to God. We don't train them for paradise. No martyrs here. The image of Rashid is their identity.
>
> (*M* 233)

Europe is thus not to be imitated but opposed. Rashid's humanism is one in which men—men and women—are expected to surrender themselves not to God or religion or to some version of the afterlife but to a new political vision, one made in the likeness of the father that Abu Rashid has become for his followers.

> The boys who work near Abu Rashid have no face or speech. Their features are identical. They are his feature. They don't need their own features or voices. They are surrendering these things to something powerful and great.
>
> (*M* 234)

The vision here is thus not religious, though it requires a similar surrender—not to God but to man, to Mao's man. It is a vision that Mao believed could be realized through "thought reform," for Mao believed "it is possible to make history by changing the basic nature of a people" (*M* 236), and, to close the loop, Abu Rashid believes that this can best be achieved through terror: "He is saying terror is what we use to give our people their place in the world. What used to be achieved through work, we gain through terror. Terror makes the new future possible. All men one man" (*M* 235). But what about the UN hostage, Brita asks Rashid upon her arrival in Beirut?: "We sold him to the fundamentalists" (*M* 235).

Falling Man continues this conversation, this debate, about the nature of terrorism and about the fascination and power it exercises over us. The novel follows the final few months of a couple of the 9–11 terrorists, from the religious inspiration for their acts, their martyrdom—"They received instruction in the highest jihad, which is to make blood flow, their blood and that of others" (*FM* 173)—to the detailed planning of the attack: "Amir had stopped talking about Jews and Crusaders. It was all tactical now, plane schedules and fuel loads and getting men from one location to another, on time, in place" (*FM* 173). But the novel also includes something resembling, once again, a debate, a deadly serious debate about terrorism that is nonetheless not without DeLillo's humorous edge. The debate this time is between Martin Ridnour, who, like George Haddad, has a certain sympathy for those who are willing to die in order "to show how a great power can be vulnerable" (*FM* 46), and Nina, his partner. The arguments of Ridnour, who perhaps himself has a terrorist background in Germany (under the name of Ernst Hechinger), resemble on many scores those of Haddad. In fact, Ridnour himself sees a similarity between earlier terrorist organizations, the Baader Meinhof group, for example, and the authors of 9–11:

> He thinks these people, these jihadists, he thinks they have something in common with the radicals of the sixties and seventies. He thinks they're all part of the same classical pattern. They have their theorists. They have their visions of world brotherhood.
>
> (*FM* 147)

For Ridnour, the whole thing comes down, once again, to a conflict between two different visions of the world and two corresponding narratives: "They think the world is a disease. This world, this society, ours. A disease that's spreading" (*FM* 46). The conflict is not simply between the haves and the have-nots, for the latter do not want what the former have. It is between two different versions or value-systems of having: "One side has the capital, the labor, the technology, the armies, the agencies, the cities, the laws, the police and the prisons. The other side has a few men willing to die" (*FM* 46–7).

Two sides, two competing narratives: the whole thing can sound perfectly rational, comprehensible. And yet, for Ridnour, the true lives and motives of the 9-11 terrorists remain forever foreign and inscrutable: "Here, with these people, you can't even think it. You don't know what to do. Because they're a million miles outside your life. Which, besides, they're dead" (*FM* 64). The West thus faces here a power against which it is more or less helpless; and, even worse, it's a power the West contributes to despite itself (see *FM* 81).

The conflict is thus ideological, for the terrorists of 9-11 believe, just like Mao, that "the world changes first in the mind of the man who wants to change it" (*FM* 80; see *M* 236). There is also the same emphasis on discipline and rigor, on routine and regularity (*FM* 176), on rules and structures (*FM* 83), on codes and secrecy, on going unseen (*FM* 172). Believing that "death is stronger than life" (*FM* 172) is thus in nowise inconsistent with paying extreme attention to living, to breaking things down to the basics: "He prays and sleeps, prays and eats" (*FM* 176).

But there are, it seems, some important differences between these various terrorist groups. Martin is reminded by Nina that the religious commitment of the contemporary jihadists seems to make for a genuine difference in kind: "But we can't forget God. They invoke God constantly.... How convenient it is to find a system of belief that justifies these feelings and these killings" (*FM* 112; see 79–80). But that's not how Martin sees it, which is why he responds by speaking about "lost lands, failed states, foreign intervention, money, empire, oil, the narcissistic heart of the West" (*FM* 113). For Martin, the stakes are less religious than economic, political, geopolitical—a question of empire, as we saw earlier. As for Lianne, Nina's daughter, she wonders how any Westerner—even one with Martin's checkered past—can even try to defend them: "Maybe he was a terrorist but he was one of ours, she thought, and the thought chilled her, shamed her—one of ours, which meant godless, Western, white" (*FM* 195).

Rashid, recall, had said that "terror is what we use to give our people their place in the world" (*M* 235). Martin says something almost identical about the perpetrators of 9-11: "They want their place in the world, their own global union, not ours. It's an old dead war, you say. But it's everywhere and it's rational" (*FM* 116). It's rational and it's linked to both land and language: "Pick up a stone and hold it in your fist, this is Islam. God's name on every tongue throughout the countryside. There was no feeling like this ever in his life" (*FM* 172). But then the very next line seems to add something quite new to the equation: "He wore a bomb vest and knew he was a man now, finally, ready to close the distance to God" (*FM* 172).

Falling Man is a quintessentially double-banded DeLillo narrative that follows, on the one hand, the terrorists in the months, days, and minutes before the attacks on 9-11, and, on the other, Keith Neudecker in the minutes, hours, days, and then seconds just after the attacks—two narrative strands or bands that intersect in a single moment on a single day in September 2001 (*FM* 239). The narrative is all the more powerful for the way it goes back and forth between the two bands, where we at once see what Keith sees, as one of the two planes is "headed toward the Hudson corridor" (*FM* 237), and hear what Hammed Atta is thinking:

> Forget the world. Be unmindful of the thing called the world.... This is your long wish, to die with your brothers.... The pious ancestors had pulled their clothes tightly about them before battle. They were the ones who named the way. How could any death be better.
>
> (*FM* 238-9)

We are in his skin for a moment, or, better, in his head, given access to the contrabanded narrative that is running there. And when it hits, when the two bands intersect, it's like the bang at the beginning or the end of the world.

In his essay "In the Ruins of the Future," Don DeLillo—this time in his own name and not through some character—tries to develop the argument, the counternarrative, that George Haddad and Martin Ridnour had, in a sense, begun to sketch out. Those who commit acts of terror want to live, he writes, in the way they used to "before the waves of western influence. They surely see themselves as the elect of God whether or not they follow the central precepts of Islam. It is the presumptive right of those who choose violence and death to speak directly to God" ("RF").

At issue is God, then, and another temporality imposed by God, or imposed by the terrorists in the name of God: "the terrorists of September 11 want to bring back the past" ("RF" 34). They want to rob the world of its future by imposing upon it their version of the past: they are time bandits, trying to claim the future in order to close it down.

> Two forces in the world, past and future. With the end of communism, the ideas and principles of modern democracy were seen clearly to prevail, whatever the inequalities of the system itself. This is still the case. But now there is a global theocratic state, unboundaried and floating and so obsolete it must depend on suicidal fervor to gain its aims.
>
> ("RF" 40)

Two times and two forces, then, a contraband temporality, past and future, with the present being the place they intersect.

The attacks of 9-11, says DeLillo in "In the Ruins of the Future," have made everything more fragile, more threatened, vulnerable and ephemeral:

> The new Palm Pilot at a fingertip's reach, the stretch limousine parked outside the hotel, the midtown skyscraper under construction, carrying the name of a major investment bank—all haunted in a way by what has happened, less assured in their authority, in the prerogatives they offer.
>
> ("RF")

In *Zero K* the argument about terrorist violence gets one final article of impeachment: the primitive, archaic, atavistic nature of it all. It is as if the technology spoken of in the essay "In the Ruins of the Future"—the new Palm Pilot, etc.—went hand-in-hand with a new archaic violence of the hand: "Is there a longing for hand-to-hand, for crush his skull and smoke a cigarette. Car bombings at sacred sites. Rocket launchings by the hundreds" (*ZK* 243). There is the violence of hyper-sophisticated weapons systems and the violence of people who, already in *The Names*, kill with rocks and hammers and axes, people who kill with their "hands, in direct contact" (*N* 209). It's the archaic past resurfacing in a contemporary guise:

> Terror and war, everywhere now, sweeping the surface of our planet. And what does it all amount to? A grotesque kind of nostalgia. The primitive weapons, the man in the rickshaw wearing a bomb vest.... The small homemade explosive. And on the battlefield, assault rifles of earlier times, old Soviet weapons, old battered tanks.... Crush the innocent, burn the huts and poison the wells. Relive the history of the bloodline.... Websites that transmit atavistic horrors. Beheadings out of dreadful folklore.... Storm the village, kill the men, rape the women, abduct the children.
>
> (*ZK* 241–2)

We have seen how the novel is or can be a kind of counternarrative to the forces of history and historical events. That is, arguably, what DeLillo is attempting in *Falling Man*, a counternarrative that would make sense of what happened on 9-11, or that would try to interrogate the limits of sense. But it would seem that terrorism is not just one theme or topic among others for the contemporary novelist. There is, it appears, an even more intimate connection between them. As Bill Gray argues in *Mao II*: "There's a curious knot that binds novelists and terrorists" (*M* 41). In the beginning of the novel, Brita is traveling the world to find writers who, like Bill, live in secret locations like terrorists. She even says to Scott who is taking her to see Bill for the first time, "I feel as if I'm being taken to see some terrorist chief at his secret retreat in the mountains" (*M* 27). Later in the novel, Brita has shifted her attention from reclusive writers to terrorists in hiding—in Beirut, for example (*M* 229).

The identification of the novelist with the terrorist thus becomes one of the central themes of *Mao II*. It is George Haddad, again, who argues for the writer's identification with, or at least understanding of, the terrorist: "And isn't it the novelist, Bill, above all people, above all writers, who understands this rage, who knows in his soul what the terrorist thinks and feels? Through history it's the novelist who has felt affinity for the violent man who lives in the dark" (*M* 130; see 156–7). "It's the novelist who understands the secret life, the rage that underlies all obscurity and neglect. You're half murderers, most of you" (*M* 158).

On the one hand, the writer—the novelist—wields a force to be feared, a counterforce, precisely, to the powers that be: "Every government, every group that holds power or aspires to power should feel so threatened by writers that they hunt them down, everywhere" (*M* 97). That's on the one hand. On the other hand, the writer is today becoming totally irrelevant:

> Years ago I used to think it was possible for a novelist to alter the inner life of her culture. Now bomb-makers and gunmen have taken that territory. They make raids on human consciousness. What writers used to do before we were all incorporated.
>
> (*M* 41)

When the nightly news replaces the novel, and then the Palm Pilot the nightly news, when there is no longer any "great secular transcendence," then maybe the only way to reshape the world is through terror (*M* 72). Haddad argues: "Beckett is the last writer to shape the way we think and see. After him, the major work involves midair explosions and crumbled buildings. This is the new tragic narrative" (*M* 157).

There is the writing that threatens, maybe even terrorizes, but then there is the writing that imagines what it is like to be terrorized, writing from the side of the victim, as it were. In *Mao II* again Bill Gray does not just try to get that UN worker released from captivity in Beirut, going so far as to suggest trading himself for the captive (*M* 97–9, 132); he also begins to write about him, and then actually *as* him, imagining himself to be a captive, a hostage held in a basement room, yet another underworld, the site, it seems, of every counternarrative:

> There was something at stake in these sentences he wrote about the basement room. They held a pause, an anxious space he began to

recognize. There's a danger in a sentence when it comes out right, a sense that these words almost did not make it to the page.

(*M* 167; see 110, 202–4)

Because that's the other thing about a counternarrative: it can always not take place, or can be immediately erased, or can arrive stillborn into the world. Or else, in the best or worst of cases, it can simply become part of history, and so just another stop on the tour. In *Zero K*, for example, we are reminded of some of that good old-fashioned early twentieth-century anarchist terrorism for which there are now historical tours, near Broad Street in New York, for instance, where "a tour leader spoke to his umbrella'd group about the scars on the wall caused by an anarchist's bomb a hundred years ago" (*ZK* 179). Was that terrorism the same as the one experienced in that same city a century later, two iterations of the same age-old revolt, or are we talking about terrorisms of very different stripes? Will there be a century from now similar "umbrella'd groups" touring the site where the World Trade Center towers once stood, similar groups dreaming of a similar "ambuscade"? (see *S* 69).

9/11, The Twin Towers

"I think of it as one, not two," she said. "Even though there are clearly two towers. It's a single entity, isn't it."

U 372

"The second plane, by the time the second plane appears," he said, "we're all a little older and wiser."

FM 135

Today, it is impossible to speak of terrorism in the United States without evoking September 11, 9–11, or the Twin Towers. But it so happens that the Towers, which opened in 1973, are often, eerily, and from very early on, in the background of DeLillo's novels. Indeed it seems in retrospect that DeLillo's New York has revolved from the very beginning not around the Empire State Building or the Chrysler Building or any other individual building but around the two World Trade Towers, the North one and the South, the one defined in relation to the other, and both of them today still defined, in the memorials of them at today's World Trade Center, through the negative images or footprints of themselves.

If every construction is doubled, haunted, by its destruction, if destruction is the inevitable contraband of every construction, then the World Trade

Towers are absolutely emblematic of this structural law. Indeed the possibility or even the fantasy of skyscrapers falling—skyscrapers in general and the World Trade Center buildings in particular—is there almost from the beginning of DeLillo's work. Someone says in *End Zone*, the year before the World Trade Center opened, "I liked to think of huge buildings toppling" (*EZ* 21; see *AZ* 367). In *Players*, Pam, one of the main protagonists, works for the Grief Management Company headquartered, where else, in the World Trade Center. "It was her original view that the World Trade Center was an unlikely headquarters for an outfit such as this. But she changed her mind as time passed. Where else would you stack all this grief?" (*P* 18) To Pam, moreover, "the towers didn't seem permanent. They remained concepts, no less transient for all their bulk than some routine distortion of light" (*P* 19; see 14–15, 24, 48, 81). Jack Laws (not far from Lawton, and Lawton, Bill Lawton, not far from Bin Laden (see *FM* 37, 72-3)), the partner of Pam's co-worker, Ethan, says one night as they are watching the New York skyline: "That plane looks like it's going to hit.... I was sure it would hit" (*P* 84). This is the same Jack Laws, by the way, who will commit suicide by self-immolation later in the novel.

In *Mao II* the two towers return with an even greater emphasis on their doubleness, their duplicity, their twinness, the way they repeat or seem to repeat themselves, in short, their double-bandedness. It is as if the towers themselves were conspirators: "My big complaint is only partly size. The size is deadly. But having two of them is like a comment, it's like a dialogue, only I don't know what they're saying" (*M* 40). They are there, talking to one another, "looming"—a quintessential DeLillo word because it evokes always two things, in contraband, the thing looming and the thing over which the first thing looms: "the Trade towers stood cut against the night, intensely massed and near. This is the 'loomed' in all its prolonged and impending force" (*M* 87). They are twins, "fraternal" twins, it seems, but of different genders: "One has an antenna." "The male" (*M* 87; see *N* 185). Finally, in *Mao II*—itself the title of a painting, or a series of paintings, by Andy Warhol—there's a painting called Skyscraper III, a painting that seems to haunt in retrospect all the towers that have ever been built at One World Trade Center Place:

> In Tokyo she saw a painting reproduced in an art journal and it was called *Skyscraper III*, a paneled canvas showing the World Trade Center at precisely the angle she saw it from her window and in the same dark spirit. These were her towers, standing windowless, two black latex slabs that consumed the available space.
>
> (*M* 165)

Then there's *Underworld*, of course, from the seemingly premonitory cover image of a bird (and there are so many birds in DeLillo) that looks like a plane about to crash into one of the towers to references to the "the unfinished grid of the World Trade Center" (*U* 385), the towers under construction, "already towering, twin-towering" (*U* 372), the two towers "siamesed" when seen from a certain angle, "joined at the waist by a transit crane" (*U* 487). Two towers joined at the waist but also, it seems, joined in waste—proleptically, prophetically. As Brian Glassic surveys the Fresh Kills landfill on Staten Island, "three thousand acres of mountained garbage," "the towers of the World Trade Center were visible in the distance and he sensed a poetic balance between that idea and this one" (*U* 184). It is as if he had a sense that it might not be long before the rubble from those towers ended up in that same landfill.

If there is a single word to describe the forces of destruction that haunt every construction, and perhaps the World Trade Center in particular, it would have to be *transience*, a word that is of more than just passing interest for DeLillo. Pam in *Players* is already intrigued by a humanoid version of it when she walks "beneath a flophouse marquee":

> TRANSIENTS. Something about that word confused her.... The functional value had slipped out of its bark somehow and vanished. Pammy stopped walking, turned her body completely and looked once more at the sign. Seconds passed before she grasped its meaning.
> (*P* 207)

Just a year later, in *Running Dog*: "This quality of transience appealed to Selvy. It had the advantage of reducing one's accountability, somehow" (*RD* 24; see *GJ* 263). And then many years later, in *Point Omega*: "Things in war are transient. See what's there and then be prepared to watch it disappear" (*PO* 29).

The events of 9-11 would be the culmination of these fears or fantasies of transience and impermanence, and *Falling Man*—a title that is itself duplicitous, double, like the towers themselves, since it names at once the man or men, the people, who infamously jumped off the burning towers, one of them perhaps Rumsey, Keith's co-worker, and the performance artist who repeats or imitates this fall in the weeks following 9-11—would be ground zero for thinking the transience of the towers. If the time and space of the towers were already central to *Players*, the event or events of 9-11 have a way of confusing or collapsing both time and space in *Falling Man*. In the opening pages of the novel, we hear how Keith, having emerged from one of the towers, "walked away from it and into it at the same time," the people around him with "faces in collapse" (*FM* 4).

After 9–11, everything changes, including time, the way we count and mark time. There is the time before the planes and then there is the time after: "fifteen days after the planes" (*FM* 69), "everything now is measured by after" (*FM* 137–8), "thirty-six days after the planes" (*FM* 170). Years later, when Lianne brings her son to an anti-war protest, things are still being measured in terms of "after": "Three years past, since that day in September" (*FM* 182). Only in the final pages, years later still, is Lianne "ready to be alone, in reliable calm, she and the kid, the way they were before the planes appeared that day, silver crossing blue" (*FM* 236).

The construction and destruction of the World Trade Towers were thus there in DeLillo from the beginning, at once fantasies and provocations. Martin Ridnour says in *Falling Man*:

> That's why you built the towers, isn't it? Weren't the towers built as fantasies of wealth and power that would one day become fantasies of destruction? You build a thing like that so you can see it come down. The provocation is obvious.
>
> (*FM* 116)

The collapse of the towers haunts them when they are standing and, once they are gone, their spectral presence haunts the spaces they once occupied, like the bottles and shapes in the two Giorgio Morandi still lives in Nina's apartment, that is, the two *natura morta* that Nina once thought she would like to die looking at:

> Two of the taller items were dark and somber, with smoky marks and smudges, and one of them was partly concealed by a long-necked bottle. The bottle was a bottle, white. The two dark objects, too obscure to name, were the things that Martin was referring to.
>
> "What do you see?" he said.
>
> She saw what he saw. She saw the towers.
>
> (*FM* 49)

The second band or contraband, the spectral death of living towers or the still life of a *natura morta*, is thus never just a dialectical response to what has come before it. The second is not that which simply comes in response to the first, to what is already there, but that which actually helps produce the first as first, the counterband that produces the band that would then be recognized retrospectively as having come first. Our recognition of what happened on 9–11, for instance, comes not from our direct experience of it, whatever that might mean, but from the mediatization of the event and the repetition of its images. First the two planes—a description from *Falling Man* that is inspired, clearly, by the now iconic TV images: "God's name on the tongues of killers and victims both, first one plane and then the other, the one that was nearly cartoon human, with flashing eyes and teeth, the second plane, the south tower" (*FM* 134).

Two bands or two tracks, then, two different planes—because, in DeLillo, there had to be, necessarily, fatally, two, a second plane to help us recognize what had happened with the first, and then the people in the two towers, because there had to be two towers, allowing those who would survive, some of them, like Keith Neudecker and Florence Givens, to watch themselves sometime in the future, in the towers, being hit, at once alive and would-be-dead.

> They would all be dead, passengers and crew, and thousands in the towers dead, and she felt it in her body, a deep pause, and thought there he is, unbelievably, in one of those towers, and now his hand on hers, in pale light, as though to console her for his dying.
>
> (*FM* 134–5)

On September 11, the planes come in succession, close in time but not simultaneous, separated by some seventeen minutes, "first one plane and then the other" (*FM* 134). The towers are thus hit at different times and they fall at different times. As Babette and Jack know and fear in *White Noise*, one of them will inevitably go before the other, one will collapse before the other; the south one, hit second, will thus collapse twenty-nine minutes before the north one, which will stand alone for nearly half an hour: "He drove east a ways and looked again and there was only one tower. One tower made no sense" (*FM* 21).

Repetition, then, because "by the time the second plane appears, we're all a little older and wiser" (*FM* 135). We are no longer the same by the time of the second plane, not to mention the time of the second fall ("In time he heard the sound of the second fall" (*FM* 5)). Two times, then, along with two towers and two planes, the second in each case giving meaning to the first, making it what it was, what it will have been.

First the North Tower, which was hit first, and then the South Tower, which fell first, Keystroke 1, Keystroke 2, Mao (I), Mao II, and then maybe even "DeLillo," with that one L followed by two, a city skyline maybe, with soaring towers held in place by low-rise vowels in an alphabet city.

Creation and Ruin

We feel a private thrill, admit it, at the sight of beauty in flames.

A 118

Come on, hurry up, plane crash footage.

WN 64

"Why is ecology so boring to read about?" she said. "For the same reason that destruction is such fun."

GJ 71

I don't think this is the kind of disaster that leads to sexual abandon. One or two fellows might come skulking out eventually but there won't be an orgiastic horde, not tonight anyway.

WN 150

White Noise is, as we have already seen, a novel about consumer culture in America, about shiny bright products and the dark waste they produce. As such, it is also a novel about the way consumer culture leads to violence and destruction and the way violence and destruction are produced and consumed in American culture—like a spectacle. Recall those Friday nights in the Gladney household, the whole family gathered around the TV eating Chinese take-out, comfortably ensconced in their upper-middle class smalltownness, watching foreign disaster footage (*WN* 64–6). They can watch and eat take-out because they know that "these things happen to poor people who live in exposed areas," that "society is set up in such a way that it's the poor and the uneducated who suffer the main impact of natural and man-made disasters" (*WN* 114). The temptation for those on the right side of the tracks or the safe side of the disaster is thus to sit back and enjoy the show.

Already in *End Zone* we find people enjoying natural disasters—extreme weather, for example—on TV: "we watched a program composed of film clips of hurricanes, tornadoes and avalanches. It was one of the most fascinating things I had ever seen" (*EZ* 97). And the really terrible or amusing thing, depending on how you look at it, or who you are looking at, is that we seem to need these things:

> Because we're suffering from brain fade. We need an occasional catastrophe to break up the incessant bombardment of information…. Words, pictures, numbers, facts, graphics, statistics, specks, waves,

particles, motes. Only a catastrophe gets our attention. We want them, we need them, we depend on them. As long as they happen somewhere else.

(*WN* 66)

As DeLillo himself suggests in "The Power of History," "we depend on disaster to consolidate our vision." All this explains why, for example, the infamous "airborne toxic event" in *White Noise* evokes not just panic but, in someone like Jack's son Heinrich, jubilation and self-discovery:

> I'd never heard him go on about something with such spirited enjoyment. He was practically giddy. He must have known we could all die. Was this some kind of end-of-the-world elation? Did he seek distraction from his own small miseries in some violent and overwhelming event? His voice betrayed a craving for terrible things.
>
> (*WN* 123)

Murray Siskind has, of course, his own theory about spectacular violence. It boils down to this: it is meant to be celebrated and enjoyed. He tells his students:

> It's a celebration. A reaffirmation of traditional values and beliefs. I connect car crashes to holidays like Thanksgiving and the Fourth. We don't mourn the dead or rejoice in miracles. These are days of secular optimism, of self-celebration.
>
> (*WN* 218)

As Murray says to Jack, "Look past the violence. There is a wonderful brimming spirit of innocence and fun" (*WN* 219). It's advice that Jack seems to follow when he sees a car crash during the airborne toxic event: "The scene of injured people, medics, smoking steel, all washed in a strong and eerie light, took on the eloquence of a formal composition" (*WN* 122).

This celebration of destruction is perhaps not unrelated to the pleasure of ruins. When, in *Running Dog*, train passengers ride through Harlem—this is the Harlem of the 1970s—they "grow silent as the train passes through.... It isn't shock or gloom so much as sheer fascination that brings on the hush. The pleasure of ruins" (*RD* 42; 175). It is a fascination that, in *Mao II*, links New York City to Beirut, two cities in ruins. While we see people in Beirut coming "out of stifling shelters in their underwear to sweep away the rubble and buy bread" (*M* 111), people in New York look at their crumbling streets and buildings and observe, "It's just like Beirut." And then there is, of course, in the same New York of about a decade later, the "ash ruins" of ground zero in the aftermath of 9-11: "The only light was vestigial now, the light of what comes after, carried in the residue of smashed matter, in the ash ruins of what was various and human, hovering in the air above" (*FM* 246).

It is perhaps why one can imagine a form of tourism that would indulge not the fantasies of some ideal past that never really existed but the ruin that is at the heart of all these things. As one of the nuns thinks in *Underworld*: "You travel somewhere not for museums and sunsets but for ruins, bombed-out terrain, for the moss-grown memory of torture and war" (*U* 248; "AE" 87). For catastrophes, whether "natural" or man-made, are terrible, lamentable things, though also, and at the same time, totally awesome, "spectacular, part of the grandness of a sweeping event" (*WN* 127).

There is therefore death on an individual level, the death of the individual, each time unique, each time a drama, the event by which a unique individual is undone (more on that later), and then there is the shared death of disaster or catastrophe, the death that threatens entire peoples or populations. That's the kind of death that looms on the horizon with the airborne toxic event: "the cloud resembled a national promotion for death, a multimillion-dollar campaign backed by radio spots, heavy print and billboard, TV saturation" (*WN* 158).

DeLillo has thus been talking about disasters for decades. But something seems to have shifted of late in the frequency or the intensity of these events and in his talk about them:

> Don't you see and feel these things more acutely than you used to? The perils and warnings? Something gathering, no matter how safe you may feel in your wearable technology. All the voice commands and hyper-connections that allow you to become disembodied.
>
> (*ZK* 127)

It is not clear where this voice is coming from, or what exactly it is talking about, but the least that can be said is that it is ominous. While DeLillo's list of plagues, disasters, and catastrophes was already pretty complete before *Zero K*, each new novel being the occasion to update the list, the inventory in *Zero K* seems to leave little out:

> He spoke in detail about food systems, weather systems, the loss of forests, the spread of drought, the massive die-offs of birds and ocean life, the levels of carbon dioxide, the lack of drinking water, the waves of virus that envelop broad geographies.... Then there was biological warfare with its variant forms of mass extinction. Toxins, agents, replicating entities. And the refugees everywhere, victims of war in great numbers, living in makeshift shelters, unable to return to their crushed cities and towns, dying at sea when their rescue vessels capsize.
>
> (*ZK* 126–7)

It's like the end of the world in contraband, all the wars of the past century telescoped together, with intimations of a Third World War on the horizon, the Third or maybe even the Fourth, the one that Einstein infamously said would be fought with "sticks and stones."

War and Peace

War brings out the best in technology.

EZ 85

If anybody kills on a grand scale, it'll be the Pentagon. On a small scale, watch out for your local police.

EZ 159–60

The war is dragging into its third week…. People are not enjoying this war to the same extent that people have always enjoyed and nourished themselves on war, as a heightening, a periodic intensity.

"HM" 29–30

PEACE IS COMING—BE PREPARED.

U 318

Just as there is a lot more in DeLillo's work about destruction and violence than creation and harmony, even if the two always go together, so there is a lot more about war than peace. A simple look at his protagonists' areas of interest or specialization tells the story: disciplines and specialties of choice include such things as Grief Management (*P* 18), Risk Assessment (*N* 11), War Assessment (*EZ* 82), Advanced Disaster Management (*WN* 205), Waste Containment (*U* 278), Hitler Studies (*WN* 4), and so on. So when it's not some catastrophe or natural disaster looming or in the making, it's some war that is in the background, whether the Second World War, the Korean War, the Cold War, the Vietnam War, the Gulf Wars, etc. There are a lot of wars, to be sure, but it is not as if DeLillo is making any of them up. The thesis regarding wars seems linked, at least in part, to what we saw earlier regarding technology and our insatiable desire to see it put to good use, even if that entails laying waste to things and killing people: "War is the ultimate realization of modern technology. For centuries men have tested themselves in war…. War was the great challenge and the great evaluator. It told you how much you were worth" (*EZ* 83).

The Vietnam War looms in the background of DeLillo's early novels, the draft, for example, in *End Zone* (*EZ* 21) and *The Names*. As James Axton says to his eleven-year-old son, with words that anyone who lived through the Vietnam era should be able to identify with: "It was our favorite war, your mother's and mine. We were both against it but she insisted on being more against it than I was. It got to be a contest, a running battle. We used to have terrific arguments" (*N* 184; see 181, *AZ* 206). It was everything it was cracked up to be, as Matt Shay in *Underworld* came to see firsthand: "He'd served in Vietnam, after all, where everything he'd ever disbelieved or failed to imagine turned out, in the end, to be true" (*U* 418).

There is a theory running throughout several later DeLillo novels that the Cold War, with all its threats of nuclear annihilation, at least made the world understandable and therefore, a little less uncertain. With the end of the Cold War and the proliferation of nuclear arms beyond the two superpowers, things have become scarier because they are less and less unpredictable.

> Power meant something thirty, forty years ago. It was stable, it was focused, it was a tangible thing. It was greatness, danger, terror, all those things. And it held us together, the Soviets and us.... Violence is undone, violence is easier now, it's uprooted, out of control, it has no measure anymore, it has no level of values.
>
> (*U* 76; 170)

While the Cold War "winding down" would thus seem to be a good thing, a promising thing, it is possible that "when the tension and rivalry come to an end, that's when your worst nightmares begin" (*U* 170). For "the atomic fact" still remains ("MD" 123), the end of the Cold War notwithstanding, and new technologies have come along to amplify the fear:

> Laser technology contains a core of foreboding and myth.... we approach the weapon with our minds full of ancient warnings and fears. (There ought to be a term for this ironic condition: primitive fear of the weapons we are advanced enough to design and produce.)
>
> ("HM" 35)

Modern war and "mythic images" thus go together in DeLillo (*EZ* 223). The more sophisticated the weapons, the more primitive the fears. The more science advances, the more it resembles some ancient religion:

> There is a kind of theology of fear that comes out of this.... Now god is the force of nature itself, the fusion of tritium and deuterium. Now he's the weapon. So maybe this time we went too far in creating a being of omnipotent power. All this hardware.
>
> (*EZ* 80)

These last lines come from a conversation in *End Zone* between Gary Harkness, an undergraduate at Logos College, and Major Staley, the campus ROTC recruiter. It occurs in the latter's motel room (for the motel is, in DeLillo, the house in contraband, a counterplace for our contraband lives) during one of their several "war simulation" get-togethers (*EZ* 79, 219). It's odd and no doubt "inappropriate," a scenario that would raise a red flag on any compliance test, but Gary Harkness doesn't complain and Staley does have something to teach. He is an expert on the US nuclear arsenal (*EZ* 156), with fun facts about insects surviving nuclear war (*EZ* 206), and so on, though he is not to be confused, he says reassuringly to Gary, with "some kind of monstrous creature who enjoys talking about the spectacle of megadeath" (*EZ* 85). As he says before one gaming session, "We might not even get to the point of using nuclear weapons" (*EZ* 221).

But, in the end, Gary is just as smitten as Staley by the talk of nuclear war and other kinds of catastrophe: "I liked reading about the deaths of tens of millions of people. I liked dwelling on the destruction of great cities" (*EZ* 20). And he is not the only student at Logos College to be "plagued by joyous visions of apocalypse" (*EZ* 223). The only girl he is really attracted to regularly wears an orange dress with "a mushroom cloud appliquéd on the front" (*EZ* 41), and Taft Robinson, the school's star football player, has developed a more than passing interest in "atrocities," "with a special emphasis on kids" (*EZ* 240).

Harkness and Staley are a good match for each other and for these war simulation games. As Harkness says: "I continued to look forward to each new puddle of destruction. Six megatons for Cairo. MIRVs for the Benelux countries" (*EZ* 43).

> We're talking a one-megaton device. All right, you're standing nine miles from ground zero. If it's a clear day, you get second-degree burns. Guaranteed. One hundred megs, you may as well forget it. If you were seventy-five miles out, you'd still get second degree. Depending on the variables, your house might even ignite.
>
> (*EZ* 80)

As one might imagine, and as we have seen in countless other contexts in DeLillo, the fun is to be found as much in the language of disaster and destruction as in the imagining, "words and phrases like thermal hurricane, overkill, circular error probability, post-attack environment, stark deterrence, dose-rate contours, kill-ration, spasm. Pleasure in these words" (*EZ* 21).

What Gary and Staley indulge in is, in theory, just a game, but it is this kind of game theory that makes one wonder whether the war itself would not be gamed out in just this way. And it is not the only game with such morbid overtones. Earlier in *End Zone* there is the game "Bang, you're dead" (*EZ* 31–2), which provides no small amusement on the Logos College campus. It's already a reprise, of sorts, of the very dark "Godsave" game in *Americana*, invented by a guy killed in Vietnam:

> It was really a peculiar form of conversation, almost a religious chant. It even had a name. It was called Godsave.... Godsave the 94 woman and children I vaporized this morning, he'd say.... Godsave the blind monk I incinerated with nape.... It was like a religious ceremony but full of ironies you don't find in most religions.
>
> (*A* 280–1)

It is like the game "I spy with my little eye" but with more sinister implications, and it bears some comparison with the "pray for x" game in *Mao II*: "All the hostages, pray for them stashed in their closets and toilets. All the babies, pray for them lying in rag hammocks. All the refugees, pray for their dead and wait for the shelling to subside" (*M* 239). It's sick and it's funny; it's funny-sick, and it says something profound about us as a culture or a species.

In *Point Omega* we meet yet another theorist of war, Richard Elster, expert strategist of the war in Iraq, the so-called Second Gulf War, or more simply and accurately, the US invasion of Iraq. According to Elster, war has become completely detached, removed from the lives it affects and the places it destroys: "They think they're sending an army into a place on a map" (*PO* 28). War has become more and more abstract, but that does not prevent it from being marketed and sold through promotion efforts worthy of Madison Avenue, the one we saw to be so hard at work elsewhere in DeLillo: "We tried to create new realities overnight, careful sets of words that resemble advertising slogans in memorability and repeatability" (*PO* 28–9). Things like, because it is hard not to remember, Desert Storm or Infinite Justice or Iraqi Freedom.

Elster carries these speculations even further. Questioning the reasons for the war in Iraq, its excesses, its crimes, and its use of torture, he writes an article about the word, the extraordinary word, "rendition," as in "extraordinary rendition" (*PO* 33). But Elster also seems to suggest that behind it all is a violence for the sake of violence, a violence whose aim is not some idea or material thing but the end of consciousness itself, a sort of death drive or desire on the part of consciousness to return to inorganic matter.

> Something's coming. But isn't this what we want? Isn't this the burden of consciousness? We're all played out. Matter wants to lose its

self-consciousness. We're the mind and heart that matter has become. Time to close it all down. This is what drives us now.

(*PO* 50)

There is thus war, the simulation of war, and then there is the confusion or conflation, the counterbanding, of these various levels of violence in language. *The Names* revolves around a ritualistic kind of violence, a seemingly necessary and preordained violence, a violence that appears related to language itself (*N* 115, 293). There is the violence of games and game theory, a violence that, at least in theory, is under control, even if part of the game can always be to intimidate the enemy by feigning an irrational, uncontrolled, and completely mad violence. Raphael Vilar's "philosophy of destruction" in *Players* (*P* 182) involves just such a "calculated madness" (*P* 108), the art of appearing so irrational that no form of violence is off the table. In *Running Dog* there's a character with a similar theory, someone who has learned to "terrorize people—cops more than once, men with guns—simply by displaying rage that bordered on the irrational" (*RD* 206). The point of such calculated madness is, of course, to make it uncertain whether it really is calculated, whether we are not in fact dealing, as seems to be the case with a faction of the Happy Valley Commune in *Great Jones Street*, with a "mindless violence... the only truly philosophical violence," one that avoids "any and all implications, political and otherwise" (*GJ* 191). There would thus be "revolutionary violence," along with "the secret longing it evokes in the most docile soul" (*P* 8), the kind of violence that "needs a burden, a purpose" (*C* 196), and then there would be a mindless, goalless, pointless violence, beyond all reasons and implications, a violence that is perpetrated neither for material gain nor for some idea or ideology but simply for itself, violence for violence's sake. That's the kind of violence speculated about already in *Great Jones Street*:

> Man the primate has been violent for only forty thousand years. What started it was abstract thought. When man started thinking abstractly he advanced from killing for food to killing for words and ideas. Maybe with mindless violence we're going into a new cycle. No more abstract thought and no more concrete thought. Violence for nothing.
>
> (*GJ* 192)

Then there is the question, so basic and yet so easy to ignore, of what it means, exactly, to kill someone, whether in war or elsewhere. The question is posed in the following passage in relation to killing someone through a telescopic lens. Imagine how many times more magnified the question becomes when it's a question of dropping bombs from tens of thousands of feet or by drone from thousands of miles away:

> The force of a death should be enormous but how can you know what kind of man you've killed or who was the braver and stronger if you have to peer through layers of glass that deliver the image but obscure the meaning of the act? War has a conscience or it's ordinary murder.
>
> (*L* 298)

Finally, after all this violence and all these wars, past and present, from the Second World War to the Russian invasion of Ukraine in *Zero K*, all these wars at once real and virtual, there are the looming threats of a Third World War, already audible in the forebodings of a radio preacher in *Americana* who warns that "Failure to comply with this order will result in a worldwide orgy of bloodshed that will make World War II seem like a Quaker picnic in New Harmony, Indiana" (*A* 369). The possibility of some Third World War will have thus been there from the beginning in DeLillo, accompanied always by a sort of ironic smile, because it's always good to check in from time to time to see "whether the World War III idea is any more viable than it was a week ago in the light of recent developments on the international scene" (*A* 65), and because how else are we to face something so shattering? In *Underworld*, just outside the military installation where Matt Shay is designing sophisticated weapons systems to fight and/or prevent the next world war, protesters carry "a sign stretched between wooden uprights, *World War III Starts Here*" (*U* 404). It's just a sign, a sign to be read, a sign of the future, DeLillo seems to suggest, because when the thing actually starts, an all-consuming world war, it will take someone far outside it all to see it happening and read the signs. So it is that in the short story "Human Moments in World War III" the war is experienced or narrated not by someone in the middle of it all, someone on the ground, as it were, but by an astronaut looking down on an earth at war from his orbiting space capsule: "The war has changed the way he sees the earth" ("HM" 25). This is narrative contraband pushed to its atmospheric limits, as far from the earth as one can get and still see it, far enough not to be touched by the violence and yet close enough still to be moved by it. There it is below, the whole big blue ball of wax, going up in smoke, or at least smoldering and on the verge.

As for the other side of war, the contrabanded side of war, there is, occasionally, if we are lucky, peace, or at least the prospect of peace, peace in the form of peace protests and protestors. It's the kind of thing for which DeLillo is obviously sympathetic, though almost never without, again, a touch of irony or skepticism. There is, for example, in *Falling Man* the anti-war protest that Lianne takes Justin to in August 2004 (the 29th, to be precise, Charlie Parker's birthday), "a march against the war, the president, the policies" (*FM* 181), and, in *Underworld*, the October 1967 protest against the Vietnam War and Dow Chemical at the University of Wisconsin in Madison, where protesters took over the university radio station and confronted police armed with tear-gas, protesters so certain of their cause that they "ran toward the gas because they thought the moral force of their argument would neutralize the effect of the chemicals" (*U* 602). There is also the 1966 anti-Vietnam War protest at the famous "Black & White Ball" (*U* 560) at the Plaza in New York, a protest that begins predictably enough, with the invitees being "cursed in rhyming couplets" (*U* 567), though it then erupts into a sort of protest-performance art piece that prefigures the anti-globalization protests of *Cosmopolis*.

> Everything happened at once. Figures in raven faces and skull masks. Figures in white winding-sheets. Monks, nuns, executioners.... They formed a death rank on the dance floor, halting the music and sending the guests to the fringes.... Then they opened their mouths, saying nothing, and directed hollow stares at the guests.
>
> (*U* 575-6)

It's a protest all right, to cite *Cosmopolis*, but it's also something else, something more: "the spectacle, the protest, whatever it was—the mockery of their sleek and precious evening" (*U* 577): it was the other side, the dark side, of the black-and-white ball.

There are protests and protesters and then there are people who simply come to see if not the futility of it all at least the indefensible role they are playing in it. In *Underworld* this role of social conscience is played by Charles Wainwright, affectionately known as Chuckie, whose father, the ad man, bought the famous baseball from the Polo Grounds off Manx Martin. Here is Chuckie having serious second thoughts about all the lives he and the bombs he had been dropping had taken in Vietnam:

> The mean and cutting fun had gone out of it for Chuckie. He didn't want to kill any more VC. And he was developing a curious concern for the local landscape. Tired of killing the forest, the trees of the forest, the

birds that inhabit the trees, the insects that live their whole karmic lives nestled in the wing feathers of the birds.

(*U* 614)

Having lost that killer instinct that those around him still had, Chuckie would wake up in the middle of night "thinking there's got to be a more productive way to spend your time... than dropping bombs on people who never said a cross word to you" (*U* 615). Because once the shooting starts or the bombs start dropping, some of DeLillo's characters come to realize, there is no logical end to the destruction, the category of "enemy" being so open-ended and so flexible that it will be tempting to take everyone out just to be sure.

The bombs fluttered down on the NVA and the ARVN alike, because if the troops on both sides pretty much resemble each other and if their acronyms contain pretty much the same letters, you have to bomb both sides to get satisfactory results. The bombs also fell on the Vietcong, the Viet Minh, the French, the Laotians, the Cambodians, the Pathet Lao, the Khmer Rouge, the Montagnards, the Hmong, the Maoists, the Taoists, the Buddhists, the monks, the nuns, the rice farmers, the pig farmers, the student protesters and the war resisters and flower people, the Chicago 7, the Chicago 8, the Catonsville 9—they were all, pretty much, the enemy.

(*U* 612)

In the end, DeLillo does give peace a chance, and, in *Underworld*, he even gives it, rather than war, the last word. We are at this point in the novel inside the internet, another sort of underworld, another contraband place, capable of doubling and drawing into it everything on the outside, transforming and remaking it in its own image. We are online, and our narrator seems to be searching, searching for his own past and for traces of the last century in America, a century that had seen two world wars and the use of two nuclear bombs, all of that visible right there on the internet. He continues searching and eventually he becomes focused on a word, "a single seraphic word," which the narrator—and seemingly DeLillo himself—wants to explore and perhaps bring into the world, to bring to life what is written there online:

You can examine the word with a click... you can summon the word in Sanskrit, Greek, Latin and Arabic, in a thousand languages and dialectics living and dead, and locate literary citations, and follow the word through the tunneled underworld of its ancestral roots... and you try to imagine the word on the screen becoming a thing in the world... a word extending itself ever outward, the tone of agreement or treaty, the tone of repose... the sunlit ardor of an object deep in drenching noon, the argument of binding touch, but it's only a sequence of pulses on a dullish screen and all it can do is make you pensive—a word that spreads a longing through the raw sprawl of the city and out across the dreaming bourns and orchards to the solitary hills.

Peace.
(*U* 826–7)

5

Countermeasures

Self and Others

Eventually he provided a résumé—background, education, past employment, so forth. All of it was verifiable, none of it true.

RD 156

You're pretending to be exactly who you are. That's the curious thing.

U 103

Don't tell me I'm crazy. I fucking know I'm crazy. Tell me I'm a little brave, a little determined. I want to hear someone say I follow things to the end.

N 157

"I'd like to lose interest in myself," I told Murray. "Is there any chance of that happening?" "None. Better men have tried."

WN 152

Be yourself. Only don't go too far.

RS 18

There are in DeLillo about as many ways to keep one's identity secret as there are ways to have an identity in the first place. There are spies and undercover agents pretty much everywhere (see RD 8), people living under assumed names or identities, people hidden behind their image—"The fella's all image…. He's a bunch of little electronic dots, that's all he is" (RD 31)— or their "dummy corporations" (RD 50; see 143). And then there are all the people acting "on behalf of a person or group that doesn't want his, her or its identity known to the world at large" (RD 16). These are all ways of disappearing or of helping others to disappear in DeLillo's novels, and they are all liberally represented.

But what about the people who are not hiding or concealing their identities for some purpose? Can they be known? Who are these people? These characters? Well, David Bell, the narrator of *Americana*, is pretty clear right from the start about his prospects of knowing those closest to him: "Pike was a living schizogram, as were Sullivan, and Bobby Brand, whom I have yet to introduce, and my father and departed mother, and perhaps myself" (*A* 51). The problem of identity goes far beyond trying to find the true identity lurking behind the mask, the virtual dots, or the dummy corporations. Because once you strip off the mask, peel away all the layers or decode the dots, there may be no one there at home—at least not anyone we can know: "What's inside the form and structure?" Seems like "this mind and soul, hers and everyone's, keep dreaming toward something unreachable" (*FM* 232).

And so even bodies can seem strange—and not only to others but also to ourselves: "Whose body have I been wearing all these years?" (*RS* 426) This can happen through disease, Guy Banister in *Libra*, for example, suffering from early Parkinson's, experiencing dizzy spells and a trembling hand, "way out there, as if it belonged to someone else" (*L* 139). Or it can just be the way one is. Elster's daughter Jessie in *Point Omega* is something of an extreme case in point: "she had to touch her arm or face to know who she was…. She wasn't a child who needed imaginary friends. She was imaginary to herself" (*PO* 71). It is perhaps not surprising that she will disappear or evaporate into thin air, or else become dust or stone—unfindable, in any case.

Even one's face can appear foreign as soon as its veneer of familiarity wears off: "Your face is your life. But your face is also submerged in your life. That's why you don't see it. Only other people see it. And the camera of course" (*FM* 115). The face is thus a mask and the mask one puts on the face can be more revealing than the face itself. J. Edgar Hoover proves this fundamental truth when putting on his costume for the famous Black & White Ball in New York City: he "looked at the mask as if it had a life, an identity of its own…. It was a sleek black leather mask with handlebar extensions and a scatter of shiny sequins around the eyes…. The mask transformed him" (*U* 561–2).

If everyone is ultimately unknowable in this way, unfathomable even to him or herself, then it becomes difficult to pin down the precise cause of anyone's actions, the self behind any genuinely good decision or catastrophic blunder. So Matt thinks of his brother Nick:

> When Nick dies a team of metaphysicians will examine the black box, the personal flight recorder that's designed to tell them how his mind worked and why he did what he did and what he thought about it all, but there's no guarantee they'll find the slightest clue.
>
> (*U* 447)

The one thing we can know about ourselves, it seems, is that we are unknowable—to others and to ourselves. As James Axton says of Owen

Brademas: "I would never completely understand Owen, know his reasons, know the inner shapes and themes. This only made the likeness"—that is, Axton's likeness to Brademas—"more plausible" (*N* 294). As Lee Harvey Oswald says of David Ferrie, who is certainly a paragon of strangeness but not an absolutely unique case, "This man is strange even to himself" (*L* 45). It is perhaps only this strangeness, in the end, that we can know about ourselves, a strangeness that may not be unrelated to that inkling we have of our own deaths: "Every lost moment is the life. It's unknowable except to us, each of us inexpressibly, this man, that woman…. It's what we call self, the true life, he said, the essential being. It's self in the soft wallow of what it knows, and what it knows is that it will not live forever" (*PO* 63). Keith Neudecker seems to sense something of this at the beginning of *Falling Man*, a sense of who he is from the absence he has just discovered inside him on the morning of 9-11: "Things inside were distant and still, where he was supposed to be" (*FM* 3).

Sometimes, however, this strange or estranged identity can be awakened in us not by some catastrophe but by wonder, by a visitation, in short, by the strangeness of another, which can begin by something so strange and so small as a hair, as when Lauren "picks a hair out of her mouth" in *The Body Artist* (*BA* 10), "a hair in my mouth," as she says, "from someone else's head" (*BA* 11). It's an interruption but perhaps also an intervention. The arrival of Mr. Tuttle in Lauren's house, a stray boy who comes as unexpected as that stray hair, reads like a response to her friend Murielle's advice just a bit earlier in the novel about how to get over her husband Rey's death: "you have to direct yourself out of this thing, not into it. Don't fold up" (*BA* 39). It is Mr. Tuttle, it seems, who will keep Lauren from folding in upon herself. She tells him, "I came here to be by myself…. I will give you a chance to tell me who you are. But I don't want someone in my house" (*BA* 46). But before long she will be naming him after a high school science teacher ("She thought it would make him easier to see"), feeding him and giving him sponge baths from head to toe, private parts included (*BA* 48). All that, it seems, in order to come back to herself.

Of course, if Mr. Tuttle helps Lauren not to lose herself in herself, he does so only by posing new and perhaps even more extreme questions of identity. "Like someone you could easily miss. Like someone you technically see but don't quite register in the usual interpretative way. / Like a man anonymous to himself" (*BA* 95). But no matter how extreme a case he may be, Mr. Tuttle is hardly alone in being alone and foreign to himself. All the questions about identity that he poses will thus eventually get worked out or at least reposed in Lauren's art itself. As a critic reviewing her performance piece puts it, her art is "about you and me. What begins in solitary otherness becomes familiar and even personal. It is about who we are when we are not rehearsing who we are" (*BA* 109–10). In the words of "The Starveling," it is about what we are when we have "no other self... no fake self, no veneer," when we are "barefaced, bare-souled," "stripped of the faces that come naturally to others" ("S" 205–6). But what are we, exactly, when we are not rehearsing, when we are stripped of the faces we normally wear? What happens when the "voice running through [our] head" changes narrative or stops talking altogether (*U* 701)? What happens when one becomes like the hostage in Beirut in *Mao II*, someone for whom the days were not connected, for whom "there was no one to remind him who he was" (*M* 111)? In other words, what happens when one is forced to live a life without another's words, a life without contraband?

Already in *Americana* David Bell's mother suggests that East and West seem to have a different relationship to others—and thus to individuality. "The more magical a race is, the less significant the individual is. Magic overwhelms everything. We in the West value human life almost desperately because we have no magic" (*A* 184). This is just the beginning of DeLillo's decades-long interrogation and exploration of the themes of identity, solitude, loneliness, and isolation. Here is just one of DeLillo's many images of loneliness, a compact, isolated image, an image in isolation that doubles the isolation itself: "Keith in the shower this morning, standing numbly in the flow, a dim figure far away inside plexiglass" (*FM* 23)—an image, a lonely image, that nonetheless communicates with others, Artis in *Zero K*, for example, remembering having discovered herself, or her loneliness, one day years ago in the shower (see *ZK* 17–18).

The shower, then, as a precursor of the Convergence, which poses all kinds of questions about identity and solitude, about what it means to be an individual and to be alone: "We are here to learn the power of solitude. We are here to reconsider everything about life's end.... Think of being alone and frozen in the crypt, the capsule.... Solitude in extremis.... But are you anyone without others?" (*ZK* 67). Jeffrey sees his father, or at least the body that was his father's, in the Convergence and gets a little confused:

> It was hard to connect the life and times of my father to this remote semblance. Had I ever thought of the human body and what a spectacle it is, the elemental force of it, my father's body, stripped of everything that might mark it as an individual life. It was a thing fallen into anonymity, all the normal responses dimming now. I did not turn away. I felt obliged to look.
>
> (*ZK* 251)

If Jeffrey is to find any way out of this confusion, it will happen not there, in the Convergence, but back in New York City, in the sounds of another boy who just may remind him of himself.

In DeLillo, it seems that everyone is lonely, everyone a loner of sorts, even when they are sharing a life with others. As someone—though it could be pretty much anyone—says in *Amazons*:

> I'm lonely all the time. I'm lonely when I'm by myself and I'm lonely in a crowd. TV makes me lonely, radio makes me lonely, airports make me loneliest of all. Maybe the answer is a family. But I'm afraid my kids won't respect me.
>
> (*AZ* 73)

We read of Lee Harvey Oswald and his Russian wife Marina in *Libra*: "They'd get an apartment with a balcony, their own furniture for a change, modern pieces, sleek and clean. These are standard ways to stop being lonely" (*L* 371). But as we slowly close in on November 22, 1963, Lee needs other, more dramatic ways to escape the isolation. "Summer was building toward a vision, a history. He felt he was being swept up, swept along, done with being a pitiful individual, done with isolation" (*L* 322; see 456). It is this fear of isolation, "the scariness of being alone" (*L* 342), that will link Oswald to Ruby (*L* 343), the one who is killed in that Dallas police station basement joined to the one who kills through a shared loneliness.

Nick Shay too admits to having been a loner all his life—and, speaking here at age forty-three, he wishes to change this, or sort of: "I've always been a country of one. There's a certain distance in my makeup, a measured separation like my old man's, I guess, that I've worked at times to reduce, or thought of working, or said the hell with it" (*U* 275). He goes on to explain this distance or separation in a way that links him to his old man—or at least to his image of him: "there's an Italian word, or a Latin word, that explains everything... *lontananza*. Distance or remoteness, sure. But as I use the word, as I interpret it, hard-edged and fine-grained, it's the perfected distance of the gangster" (*U* 275). Being with his wife Marian helps, to be sure, but it doesn't end the isolation. The night of the Great Northeast Blackout, for example, Nick, who is living out west but visiting New York, returns to his darkened hotel room and thinks of calling Marian but ends up not doing it:

> I didn't call Marian. I felt a loneliness, for lack of a better word, but that's the word in fact, a thing I tried never to admit to and knew how to step outside of, but sometimes even this was not means enough, and I didn't call her because I would not give in, watching the night come down.
>
> (*U* 637)

It is not surprising, then, that it would be George the Waiter's loneliness that really gets to Nick, that gets under his skin, even more than that fascinating needle he sees George sticking in his arm. "Pushing forty," "a bachelor for life" living with his eighty-year-old grandmother, George spends his spare time in a basement room "playing solitaire" and shooting up (*U* 778, 721–2), and "maybe this is what interested Nick," "the fact that George was the loneliest man he'd ever known" (*U* 724; see 747, 808). It is not surprising that George would strike such a chord of loneliness in Nick and cause him to do something that neither of them, or both of them, had always been waiting for.

Of course, the individual cannot really feel isolated without all the others around to feel isolated from. On your best days, then, you may want to ask yourself, "Who are these people, minute to minute and year after year?" (*ZK* 54) And on your very best, and most sympathetic, "What did it mean, the first time a thinking creature looked deeply into another's eyes?... the gaze that demonstrates we are lonely in our souls?" (*BA* 85).

These are serious questions, but if knowing oneself is so difficult, one can only imagine how hard it is to know another. In most of DeLillo's novels, this seems not only hard but downright impossible. This is already and maybe even especially clear when one considers people from a distance, detached from their lives and the illusions of sense and order that those lives tend to impress upon us: "I listened to the air blast as they passed beneath me, car after car, drivers making instantaneous decisions, news and weather on their radios, unknown worlds in their minds... *Who are they? Where are they going?*" ("HS" 180). But it can also happen when one watches someone up close. A stranger on the street, for example: "I watched her, knowing that I could not invent a single detail of the life that pulsed behind those eyes" (*ZK* 175). Or even one's own spouse or child, who, at a certain level, is just as unknowable, inscrutable, absolutely secret as that stranger on the street. This fundamental truth can be grasped at any time, but perhaps especially when the other is asleep. It is, in its stunning simplicity, a perfect contraband moment: watching someone sleep. For "there's something tender about sleep. It's so totally unprotected" (*V* 38). There is something so vulnerable but also so secret about a person asleep, even more than closed off and unknowable:

> This is what you feel, looking at the hushed and vulnerable body, almost anyone's, or you lie next to your husband after you've made love and breathe the heat of his merciless dreams and wonder who he is, tenderly ponder the truth you'll never know, because this is the secret that sleep protects in its neural depths, in its stages, layers and fold.
>
> (*BA* 54; see 71–2)

It is no coincidence that Jack Gladney likes watching people sleep, and particularly children (his own, fortunately). It's something spiritual, even devotional:

> Watching children sleep makes me feel devout, part of a spiritual system. It is the closest I can come to God. If there is a secular equivalent of standing in a great spired cathedral with marble pillars and streams of mystical light slanting through two-tier Gothic windows, it would be watching children in their little bedrooms fast asleep. Girls especially.
> (*WN* 147; see 183)

Watching others sleep can thus be a religious experience. But it can also be rather creepy, a violation or the possibility of violation. In *Valparaiso*, camera crews want to film Michael asleep, just to see what he looks like when he is totally unprotected. In *Underworld* Nick watches the innocent, sleeping figure of Brian, who has not been so innocent with Nick's wife, thinking of when and how hard to slap his sleeping head:

> I sit and watch him sleep and I eat my food.... How right for this old-fashioned face, narrow and boyish, that I could probably crush with five earnest blows. I imagine this with some satisfaction. Dealing a serious blow.
> (*U* 795)

It is not easy, maybe it is even impossible, to gain access—real access—to the life of another. Nick Shay tries with his mother: "He tried to hear the rustle of her life, the fly buzzing in the room of the woman who lives alone" (*U* 201). But if Sister Grace is right, he could not have gotten very far, for she "believed the proof of God's creativity eddied from the fact that you could not surmise the life, even remotely, of his humblest shut-in" (*U* 245–6). As Klara Sax (not far from the Greek *sarx*, meaning "flesh") once says, no one could know "the mystery of living in her skin" (*U* 498).

The Individual and the Crowd

Russ Hodges: "When you deal with crowds, nothing's predictable."
U 15

And this is what you fear, that history is passing into the hands of the crowd.
M 162

Think in collective terms was the cry. The individual must disappear.

L 186

"So what you're saying."
"Take him off the calendar."
"Clip him."
"Turn him into a crowd."

L 432

If individuals are always strange and unknowable in DeLillo, inscrutable to others and even to themselves, they today face the further risk or indignity of getting absorbed or lost in the "crowd." While there were obviously masses of people in the past, mobs and throngs, hordes and multitudes, DeLillo seems to suggest that these were perhaps not exactly "crowds." Crowds, it seems, are a more recent thing, the invention, perhaps, of certain technologies and mediatizations—photography, film, and television—a crowd coming into existence *for* these technologies, it seems, rather being simply reproduced and rebroadcast by them. And, of course, with the explosive growth in human population in the twentieth century, with 7.7 billion people living in the world today, and 512 cities with over a million people, 33 of these with over 10 million, and the ubiquitousness of the media in all those cities, crowds have become a new unit of measure for human beings. DeLillo puts it presciently if not prophetically in his novel of 1991 *Mao II* when he says, "the future belongs to crowds" (*M* 16).

But DeLillo will have been a thinker of crowds from the very beginning, crowds at once home and abroad, domestic and foreign, domesticated and unleashed. There are crowds on the streets of New York City already on the opening pages of *Americana*, and then crowds in almost every work thereafter, crowds in conjunction with the themes of repetition, loneliness, the masses, mass production, and so on. While DeLillo's aesthetic is always best expressed by the motto "least is best" (*GJ* 5), crowds are what must be thought today, the mass Moonie wedding in Yankee Stadium at the beginning of *Mao II* being the first premise in the argument for crowds, or the argument for understanding the future through crowds. Of course not everyone is so enthusiastic, the father of Karen, for example, one of the brides. The fact that marriage had made not only his daughter and her appointed husband but all sixty-five hundred couples—the more the marrier, seems to have been idea—into "one body now, an undifferentiated mass" (*M* 3), "really scares him, a mass of people turned into a sculptured object…. They are a nation, he supposes, founded on the principle of easy belief. A unit fueled by credulousness" (*M* 7). Karen's father sees nothing redeeming in the fact that "they all feel the same, young people from fifty countries, immunized against the language of self" (*M* 8).

Crowds are everywhere in DeLillo because they are our future, all of our futures. Just in *Mao II*, after the mass marriage, there are "bodies rolling in a sea swell" in the televised scenes of a soccer crowd (*M* 32), crowds of Maoists in China, a "great mass of blue-and-white cotton" (*M* 163; see "HS" 168), crowds in Tehran after the death of Ayatollah Khomeini, "delirious crowds swirling beneath enormous photographs of holy men" (*M* 174), an agglomeration of humanity so large that "the camera could not absorb the full breadth of the crowd," a crowd that "had no edge or limit and kept on spreading" (*M* 188), the image accompanied by people "calling out a name under the chalk sky, millions, chanting" (*M* 181).

They could be chanting in English, Arabic, or Hindi, Farsi or German—a crowd that has gathered for a funeral, or a ballgame, or a Nazi rally, all orchestrated for the big screen, as Jack Gladney would have known: "Crowd scenes predominated. Close-up jostled shots of thousands of people outside a stadium after a Goebbels speech, people surging, massing, bursting through the traffic" (*WN* 25), "crowds ... hypnotized by [Hitler's] voice, the party anthems, the torchlight parades" (*WN* 73). The question of crowds is thus inseparable from that of the media, the question being whether the media is there to capture the crowd or whether the crowd comes into being only because of the media.

It's a different kind of crowd, but a crowd nonetheless, that gathers at the Polo Grounds, as opposed to Yankee Stadium, that famous day in October 1951. It begins with a kind of anticipation, with people waiting to become the crowd they know they can be, waiting "to be carried on the sound of rally chant and rhythmic handclap, the set forms and repetitions. This is the power they keep in reserve for the right time" (*U* 19). And then it begins happening: "This is how the crowd enters the game. The repeated three-beat has the force of some abject faith, a desperate kind of will toward magic and accident" (*U* 36). Finally, the thing becomes a force of its own, desire on a scale that goes beyond an aggregation of individuals. "They're coming into open roar, making a noise that keeps enlarging itself in breadth and range. This is the crowd made over, the crowd renewed" (*U* 37). It is at this point that the "cheering or rooting" becomes "a territorial roar" (*U* 37; see 92, 100, 132, 366, 428, 443–4, 820; *AZ* 150), which you can even hear down below when you are getting a hotdog or a beer and something happens in the stadium above, "a chambered voice rolling through the hollows in the underbody of the stadium" (*U* 24).

Underworld in fact begins by following the fourteen-year-old Cotter Martin, playing hooky, sneaking in to the Polo Grounds, and hoping—rather than fearing, this time—to get lost in the crowd:

> This is just a kid with a local yearning but he is part of an assembling crowd, anonymous thousands off the buses and trains, people in narrow columns tramping over the swing bridge above the river, and even if

they are not a migration or a revolution, some vast shaking of the soul, they bring with them the body heat of a great city and their own small reveries and desperations, the unseen something that haunts the day— men in fedoras and sailors on shore leave, the stray tumble of their thoughts, going to a game.

(*U* 11)

You follow him for a bit, like the stadium security people who are trying to catch him after he has jumped the turnstile, but soon "you lose him in the crowd" (*U* 14; see 430). Being "lost in the crowd"—that seems to be both the fear and the attraction, the danger and the promise of living in the twentieth or twenty-first century. Hundreds of pages later in the novel, back in New York City, it will be another crowd that will assemble to witness yet another miracle—not a game-ending homerun but, as we will see later, the appearance on a billboard of a recently murdered girl's face.

Crowds gather to celebrate an event—a marriage, a miracle ballgame or the miraculous resurrection of a young girl on a billboard, or else, and sometimes unbeknownst to them, a pageant of death, like the one in Dealey Plaza on November 22, 1963:

> Street by street the crowd began to understand why it was here.... A contagion had brought them here, some mystery of common impulse, hundreds of thousands come from so many histories and systems of being, come from some experience of the night before, a convergence of dreams, to stand together shouting as the Lincoln passed. They were here to be an event, a consciousness.
>
> (*L* 393–4; see 391)

Language, loss of self, a collective unconscious or a sort of collective speaking in tongues—one can understand why DeLillo would be interested in crowds, irrespective of their location, their race, or their religion. In the end there is a certain religion to the crowd itself:

> The crowd was gifted at being a crowd. This was their truth. They were at home, she thought, in the wave of bodies, the compressed mass. Being a crowd, this was a religion in itself, apart from the occasion they were there to celebrate.
>
> (*FM* 185)

There is something paradoxical about crowds: while they often come together "in the name of death," in "tributes to the dead," with "processions, songs, speeches, dialogues with the dead, recitations of the names of the dead" (*WN* 73), the idea of the crowd is to keep death at bay, to absorb the individual and raise the collective into some immortal form: "To become a crowd is to keep out death. To break off from the crowd is to risk death as an individual, to face dying alone. Crowds came for this reason above all others. They were there to be a crowd" (*WN* 73). It is as if the crowd were to the individual what the underworld is to the world above, what the unconscious—teeming with images and desires—is to consciousness, what dreams and nightmares are to waking life.

Both Bill Gray in *Mao II* and Owen Brademas in *The Names* are at once frightened and fascinated by the possibility of losing themselves in a crowd, the possibility of blending in and losing themselves "in something larger" than themselves: "You're totally alone in the foreground but you're also part of the swarm, the shifting jelly of heads looming over your little face" (*M* 89). Bill will thus travel to Beirut under the pretext of trying to help get a UN worker released from captivity, though we understand that he ultimately goes there in order to find himself by losing himself in a crowd. For Owen Brademas, there's the same ambivalence: "Masses of people scare me. Religion. People driven by the same powerful emotion. All that reverence, awe and dread. I'm a boy from the prairie" (*N* 24). He too, then, is deathly afraid of such crowds, afraid of what will happen when crowds gather to witness a solar eclipse in India, one of those monstrous miracles with which DeLillo's novels often end: "It would happen in five days, being total in the south... Owen looked out the window, wanting not to dwell on this cosmic event, the trampled bodies it would produce, the voices massed in chant" (*N* 279). Like Bill Gray, Owen Brademas is at once drawn to and repelled by "the nightmarish force of people in groups, the power of religion," for "masses of people suggested worship and delirium, obliteration of control, children trampled" (*N* 276). It is frightening and, as a result, totally fascinating:

> a whirlwind of human awe and submission. To be carried along, no gaps in the ranks, to move at a pace determined by the crowd itself, breathless, in and of them. This is what draws me to such things. Surrender. To burn away one's self in the sandstone hills. To become part of the chanting wave of men, the white cities, the tents that cover the plain, the vortex in the courtyard of the Grand Mosque.
>
> (*N* 296)

To surrender oneself in or to a crowd is perhaps "a grace," "to lose oneself in the mortal crowd, surrendering, giving oneself over to mass awe, to disappearance in others" (*N* 285). Brademas is seriously tempted by such a thought. And yet he also recognizes the difficulty any Westerner, and maybe particularly himself, would have losing himself in this way:

> To infiltrate Mecca. Imagine it, to enter the city with one and a half million pilgrims, cross the border within the border, make the *hadj*. What enormous fears would a man like me have to overcome, what lifelong inclinations toward solitude, toward the sanctity of a personal space in which to live and be.
>
> (*N* 296)

From *End Zone* to *Zero K*, DeLillo is keenly aware of the power—of the promise and the peril—of crowds:

> A million pilgrims face Mecca. Think of the power behind that fact. All turning now. And bending. And praying. History is the angle at which realities meet.
>
> (*EZ* 46)

> The woman at the table was speaking about great human spectacles, the white-clad faithful in Mecca, the hadj, mass devotion, millions, year after year, and Hindus gathered on the banks of the Ganges, millions, tens of millions, a festival of immortality.
>
> (*ZK* 63)

DeLillo's fascination with crowds can be seen not only in what his characters say about them but also in what he himself has written, in his own name, outside or beyond all fiction. DeLillo ends his essay "In the Ruins of the Future," published not long after 9–11:

> But the dead are their own nation and race, one identity, young or old, devout or unbelieving—a union of souls. During the hadj, the annual pilgrimage to Mecca, the faithful must eliminate every sign of status, income and nationality, the men wearing identical strips of seamless white cloth, the women with covered heads, all recalling in prayer their fellowship with the dead.
>
> Allahu akbar. God is great.
>
> ("RF")

DeLillo's point seems to be that the future is crowds not only here on earth but even beyond. No one-on-one intake interviews with St. Peter, no personal attention from a benevolent, paternal God who treats everyone as his favorite child, but an afterlife of surging, crowded souls, moving and buzzing in contraband, the airwaves rife with countless voices merged in a sort of cosmic cacophony, not the harmony of the spheres but the deafening sound of a crowd.

Prophylactics and Purifications

We are down to eating and sleeping, if that. Rudiments, she thought. Whatever the minimum. That's what we're down to.

P 201

It's the little things that give you the edge.

RD 176

This is a time for discipline, mental toughness. We're practically at the edge.

WN 132

If crowds in particular, and others in general, are a threat to the individual, to the self, then countermeasures must be taken to guard against them, to keep the other in general out or at a distance. Whence the need to clean, scrub, and scour, to get rid of germs and contaminants, to protect oneself from others and seal oneself off from the outside. Sometimes it's just a question of sealing out a bad memory. Take the steak knife used by a certain wife in *Zero K* to stab her husband in the shoulder. It is perhaps no great surprise that the husband in question would consider it forever unusable for regular eating purposes:

> I made it a point to throw away the steak knife because I didn't think it would be a suitable utensil for us to use again even if we'd all gathered together and devised scrubbing methods that would render the thing blood-free and germ-free and memory-free. Even if we'd all agreed on the most fastidious methods.
>
> (*ZK* 100–1)

Cleanliness is, to be sure, next to godliness, but the god-fearing in DeLillo always tend to take it just a little too far, that is, to the point of obsession. Take Sister Edgar, "a cold-war nun who'd once lined the walls of her room with Reynolds Wrap as a safeguard against nuclear fallout" (*U* 245; "AE" 83; see "IA" 60). She wakes up every morning, looks out the window, and thinks: "That's creation out there, little green apples and infectious disease" (*U* 237; "AE" 73). Everything thus has to be scoured with disinfectants, though even that is not enough because Sister Edgar "hadn't cleaned the original disinfectant in something stronger than disinfectant. She hadn't done this because the regression was infinite. And the regression was infinite because it is called infinite regression" (*U* 251; see "AE" 90). And it is called an infinite regression because it quickly regresses into an infinitely proliferating series of questions:

> At the sink she scrubbed her hands repeatedly with coarse brown soap. How can the hands be clean if the soap is not? This question was insistent in her life. But if you clean the soap with bleach, what do you clean the bleach bottle with? If you use scouring powder on the bleach bottle, how do you clean the box of Ajax? Germs have personalities. Different objects harbor threats of various insidious types. And the questions turn inward forever.
>
> (*U* 237–8; see "AE" 74)

Everything that enters the home or the body must thus be cleaned and scrubbed, and then cleaned and scrubbed again with various forms of household cleaners and disinfectants, which also fill the cupboards of DeLillo novels: Ajax, Camay soap, Ivory liquid—even mob boss Carmine Latta in *Libra* has "a man who washed his pocket money in Ivory liquid to keep it germ-free" (*L* 175). And when Sister Edgar herself goes out she must be even more protected, "shielded from organic menace," which is why she wears a pair of "latex gloves," as "protection against the spurt of blood or pus and the viral entities hidden within, submicroscopic parasites in their soviet socialist protein coats" (*U* 241, "AE" 79; see *U* 187). "Soviet Socialist" because Sister Edgar "knew in her heart" that Ismael—one of the reasons for the gloves—had "AIDS... Human Immunodeficiency Virus. Acquired Immune Deficiency Syndrome. Komitet Gosudarstvennoi Bezopasnosti" (recall that related trio at *WN* 303), and that "the KGB was responsible for the disease itself, a product of germ warfare" (*U* 243–4). The depth of Sister Edgar's fear of these little pieces of the other, these sheddings and secretions, will make her reaction to the apparition of Esmeralda at the end of the novel all the more remarkable, all the more miraculous, as "she yanks off her gloves and shakes hands, pumps hands with the great-bodied women who roll their eyes to heaven" (*U* 822).

As for other Edgar, J. Hoover, a master at tracking and compiling information on all kinds of foreign agents, it was "the unseeable life-forms" that dismayed him most (*U* 18). He probably would have been unable to decide whether the Soviet Union or germs posed the greatest threat to American security. Actually, he, like Sister Edgar, would have probably thought it to be a false alternative. That is why he has "an air-filtration system in his house to vaporize specks of dust," at the same time as "he finds a fascination in cankers, lesions and rotting bodies so long as his connection to the source is strictly pictorial" (*U* 50). "At home Edgar sat on a toilet that was raised on a platform, to isolate him from floorbound forms of life" (*U* 560). So great was Edgar's fear of contamination that it would follow him all the way to the tomb, "a lead-lined coffin" designed "to protect his body from worms, germs, moles, voles and vandals," as well as "safe from nuclear war, from the Ravage and Decay of radiation fallout" (*U* 577–8). Unlike his ecclesiastical counterpart, J. Edgar will not get over his phobia by the end of *Underworld*. Only one Edgar will be the beneficiary of a miracle of that magnitude.

In addition to cleaners and disinfectants designed to wash off or neutralize foreign agents once they have attached themselves to us, there are all those protective devices designed for keeping foreign things out in the first place. Things like condoms. In *Underworld* there is a long scene between Nick and Brian Glassic in a store in Phoenix called "Condomology"—and "that's what it was all right, condoms, the whole place was condoms" (*U* 109). It's a sort of reprise of the supermarket scenes from *White Noise*, only this time it is focused on a single product in various shapes, flavors, and materials, condoms for every occasion (*U* 108–14). Just before entertaining Nick with "a little Churchill—*We shall wear them on the beaches*," etc. (*U* 111), Brian, who is having an affair with Nick's wife, tells Nick all about his prophylactic past.

> My brother carried a rubber in his wallet all through adolescence. He showed it to me once, I think I was twelve. Flipped open his wallet and showed me this little wizened thing like a deflated penis and I don't think I ever recovered.... Sex alone was tough enough to encounter. This was technology they wanted to wrap around my dick. This was mass-produced latex they used to paint battleships.
>
> (*U* 110)

Brian and Nick then do some comparative shopping at Condomology, contrasting the new type that's "odor-free" and unconstricting with "the old cheap latex that binds the sex member and reduces the sensation and smells bad" (*U* 114), the kind that smells like "shower curtains" or "car upholstery" or "big blocky garment bags where you store the clothes you never wear" (*U* 113). Brian ends up buying the latter for his teenage son; as he rationalizes it, "I want him to pay a price for being sensible" (*U* 114). It is during this same scene that Brian and Nick have this little exchange, which is reproduced here just to remind us of all those good things we saw earlier about brands and brand loyalty and product placement:

> A young woman stood near the door, a Ramses logo tattooed on her earlobe. "My kid's got one of those," Brian said. "Only it says Pepsi. Should I be grateful?" "Which kid?" "Which kid. What's the difference?"
>
> (*U* 111)

There are condoms, therefore, and there are gloves, and both can provide protection. But Eric's mother, apprised of her pubescent son's newly developed habit, knows the dangers of confusing the two, of putting the wrong glove on the other hand, so to speak:

> One of her kitchen gloves was missing—she had many pairs—and she wanted to believe Eric had borrowed it for one of his chemistry assignments. But she was afraid to ask. And she didn't think she looked forward to getting it back.... And the gloves protected her from scalding water and the touch of food scraps. Erica loved her gloves.
>
> (*U* 519; see 581)

But fastidiousness and various forms of compulsive behavior are really just the flipside of the need that almost all of DeLillo's characters will have at some point to discipline themselves, to purge excess, to pare things down, to isolate or seclude themselves in order to prepare for some kind of ritual encounter. Indeed there is in almost every DeLillo novel a moment when things need to get reduced to the minimum, a moment when rigor and discipline are required. As Chester Greylag Dent says from far down beneath the sea in his nuclear submarine in *Ratner's Star*, "True greatness always involves a period of complete withdrawal" (*RS* 347). Or as reclusive rock star Bucky Wunderlick says of his self-imposed exile in an apartment in New York's NoHo district: "Great Jones Street was a time of prayerful fatigue. I became a half-saint, practiced in visions, informed by a sense of bodily economy, but deficient in true pain. I was preoccupied with conserving myself for some unknown ordeal to come" (*GJ* 19; see 60).

For all their differences, Bell, Selvy, and Bucky all seek a kind of spiritual transformation through rigor and discipline. It is not unlike the kind of self-discipline and self-sacrifice in *End Zone*, sometimes wholly steeped in irony, sometimes just lightly frosted. Coach Creed says, for example, "I've seen a good football player who didn't know the value of self-sacrifice.... I've never seen a good football player who wanted to learn a foreign language" (*EZ* 199). And then he makes a connection to the Sioux Indians, just as in *Americana*:

> Our inner life is falling apart. We're losing control of things. We need more self-sacrifice, more discipline.... The Sioux purified themselves by fasting and solitude. Four days without food in a sweat lodge. Before you went out to lament for your nation, you had to purify yourself. Fasting and solitude.
>
> (*EZ* 200)

"Famous for creating order out of chaos" (*EZ* 10), Coach Creed's commandments came in the form of one-liners, highly condensed pep talks that could fit on a stone tablet: "Don't ever get too proud to pray," "Do not drag-ass," and so on (*EZ* 11). On the wall of the coach's office there are neither football pictures nor pinups but "a page torn from a book, a black-and-white plate of a girl praying in a medieval cell" (*EZ* 198). Turns out to be St. Teresa of Avila (*EZ* 202; see *RS* 51), a Spanish mystic, since football and mystical visions seem to require the same discipline and self-abnegation, the same commitment to pain. As Gary Harkness says to star running back Robinson Taft about the Coach Creed rhetoric that drew Taft to Logos College: "He sold you on pain and sacrifice.... No sporting press to record your magic. No cameras. He got you on pain" (*EZ* 237). It comes as little surprise, then, that at the end of the novel Gary would refrain from food and water for several days, turning himself into some kind of ascetic (*EZ* 241–2). We don't know what will ultimately happen to him, just as we don't know what will happen to David Bell or Bucky Wunderlick after their final withdrawals into solitude and isolation. Only one thing is certain: if they are to become anything, a certain discipline, rigor, and sacrifice will be required. For it is not just football, a particularly brutal sport, or rock stardom, a notoriously destructive lifestyle, that requires these things but even a discipline as different as, say, mathematics. As the head of the Logicon Project says to Billy Twillig in *Ratner's Star*: "You're a mathematician. You work till you drop.... Sacrifice" (*RS* 305). It's probably a line that inspired DeLillo himself as he was trying to complete *Ratner's Star*.

Glenn Selvy in *Running Dog* is perhaps not just a case in point but a model or a paradigm. At the beginning of the novel, Selvy is rigorous, self-disciplined, meticulous. He leads a transient life, which has "the advantage of reducing one's accountability, somehow" (*RD* 24), an inconspicuous life, "a calculated existence," "life narrowed down to unfinished rooms" (*RD* 54; see 63). He even trained himself "to look different. There's exercises you can do. Muscular contractions" (*RD* 159). And this discipline extends all the way down to good hygiene, proper care for one's equipment, and other seemingly unrelated rules for better living:

> Shaving. Proper maintenance of old combat gear. Seats on the aisle in planes and trains. Sex with married women only. These were personal quirks mostly, aspects of his psychic guide to survival.
>
> (*RD* 81)

When we see Selvy deviate from these rules—"Sex with an unmarried woman. Two and half days without a shave. Minor lapses." (*RD* 83)—we know something's up. When he does it again—"It was interesting that he'd done it again. Sex with an unmarried woman." (*RD* 135)—we know that something major, something life-changing or life-taking, is in the offing. His return to Marathon Mines, the camp where he once trained, signals that the showdown is near, that "this is the end of the line" (*RD* 182).

Not so much an imitation as a doubling, a double-banding that is never completely serious and never wholly ironic, a doubling that smuggles in the serious under the cover of mockery and humor and converts traditional terms, gestures, and tropes into pastiche, Selvy is always at once himself and another. He says to Nadine Rademacher that he is really an Indian and that his name is "Running Dog" (*RD* 160). All that remains, therefore, is a ritual death and burial, the one he had been training for without knowing it: "All this time he'd been preparing to die. / It was a course in dying. In how to die violently. In how to be killed by your own side, in secret, no hard feelings…. It was a ritual preparation" (*RD* 183). Hence Selvy prepares, travels to the right place, finds the right weapon, strips himself bare, and waits for his assassins, all, it seems, as part of the ritual, an exercise in the "art of dying," a Western showdown with Eastern overtones (*RD* 186; see 192). As Selvy says to his friend Levi who has followed him to the abandoned training camp, "Dying is an art in the East" (*RD* 233). Hence Selvy dies a ritual death out in the desert at Marathon Mines, and Levi leaves him, according to the ritual, "in a sitting posture," more propitious, it appears, for "leaving the earth-plane" (*RD* 245).

It's all about rigor and the ritual that accompanies it. The narrator says about the Moonie mass marriage at the beginning of *Mao II*, "Forty days of separation before they're alone in a room, allowed to touch and love. Or longer. Or years if Master sees the need. Take cold showers. It is this rigor that draws the strong" (*M* 10). Rigor is a kind of countermeasure or counterweight to the disorder and wayward desires of everyday life. It is what gives meaning to our lives and our deaths, a way to take the sting out of death, or to remove the chaos, or to turn that chaos to some advantage:

> We start our lives in chaos, in babble. As we surge up into the world, we try to devise a shape, a plan. There is dignity in this. Your whole life is a plot, a scheme, a diagram.... To plot is to affirm life, to seek shape and control.
>
> (*WN* 291–2)

There's Selvy, there's Levi, and then there's Lee in *Libra*, reading his brother's Marine Corps manual, more or less learning it by heart, and what attracts him is nothing other than that idea of rigor:

> There was no end of things to quote from the manual. The book had been written just for him. He read deeply in the rules, impressed by the strictness and precision, by the stream of awesome details, weird, niggling, perfect.
>
> (*L* 42)

Oswald is interested in the discipline, or at least the idea of discipline, that goes into being a marine, or else a spy (*L* 111), or a revolutionary. For it is, paradoxically, self-discipline, self-denial, and self-abnegation that enhance the powers of the self in all these domains. It's a lesson that FBI Director J. Edgar Hoover also learned early on:

> Edgar's own power had always been double-skinned. He had the power of his office of course. And also the power that his self-repression gave him.... Edgar had earned his monocratic power through the days and nights of his self-denial, the rejection of unacceptable impulses.
>
> (*U* 573)

We see a similar rigor and discipline, though turned toward other ends, in *The Body Artist* in Lauren Hartke's "breathing exercises," her "bodywork" (*BA* 37), in "the prayerful spans of systematic breathing, life lived irreducibly as sheer respiration" (*BA* 57). For Lauren, stripping down, shaving, depigmenting herself, bleaching her close-cropped hair, removing residues and greases and dead skin, scouring her body from head to toe—all that is ritual preparation to becoming something or someone else. "This was her work, to disappear from all her former venues of aspect and bearing and to become a blankness, a body slate erased of every past resemblance" (*BA* 84; see 97).

Everyone at some point hopes to gain just a little edge, and it is rigor and discipline that can provide that edge. Why does Bill Gray go to Beirut? Because "he wanted to imagine what it was like to know extremes of isolation" (*M* 154; see 183), an isolation that is "unsparing, stony, true, the root thing he'd been rehearsing all these years" (*M* 197–8). Why does Matt Shay agree to go into the desert to do weapons research? Because of "the self-knowledge he might find in a sterner life, in the fixing of willful limits" (*U* 413). And all this explains why Matt's older brother Nick, after killing George the Waiter, appreciates so much the rigor and discipline offered by a correctional facility for juveniles. "The minute I entered correction I was a convert to the system.... I believed in the stern logic of correction" (*U* 502; see 261).

There are big-time transformations, concentrated efforts, self-abnegations or self-denials on the scale of saints or psychotics, monumental attempts to will oneself "into tighter being" (*U* 604), and then there are micro-moments of rigor and discipline, small resolutions that one hopes will lead to bigger commitments. James Axton says in *The Names*: "I resolved to stop drinking, although I'd had only a couple glasses of wine in the last week or so. It was a setting of limits I thought I needed. A firmness and clarity, a sense that I could define the shape of things" (*N* 192).

It is all about creating meaning and structure, whether we are talking about saints, terrorists, or capitalists. For Eric Packer too is rigorous, "ruthlessly efficient. Talented, yes. In business, in personal acquisitions. Organizing [his] life in general" (*C* 31). He has his own "meditation cell" (*C* 5) and imagines Kendra Hays, his bodyguard and lover, "washing his viscera in palm wine in a ceremony of embalming" (*C* 208). Again, all this is never without a certain ironic distance, and yet that distance always has a way of folding back upon the inside and very quickly hitting home.

Rituals of self-fashioning or self-perfecting, of outfitting or purging oneself, are thus everywhere in DeLillo. Take, for example, the famous moving-in scene at College-on-the-Hill in *White Noise*, where the narrative goes through in great detail all the items the incoming students are bringing onto campus and into their dorm rooms, everything from "boxes of blankets, boots and shoes, stationary and books" to "the cartons of phonograph records and cassettes; the hairdryers and styling irons; the tennis rackets, soccer balls, hockey and lacrosse sticks,... the controlled substances, the birth control pills and devices; the junk food still in shopping bags—onion-and-garlic chips, nacho thins, peanut creme patties," etc. etc. (*WN* 3). Well, that scene has its counterpart in Jack's many attempts to purge himself or his belongings before his confrontation with Mink. Here is just one of those purges:

> I started throwing things away. Things in the top and bottom of my closet, things in boxes in the basement and attic. I threw away correspondence,

old paperbacks, magazines I'd been saving to read, pencils that needed sharpening. I threw away tennis shoes, sweat socks, gloves with ragged fingers, old belts and neckties. I came upon stacks of student reports, broken rods for the seats of director's chairs. I threw these away. I threw away every aerosol can that didn't have a top.

(*WN* 222)

And here's another one, not quite as amusing but more indicative of where purges eventually go:

I threw away shelf paper, faded stationery, manuscripts of articles I'd written, galley proofs of the same articles, the journals in which the articles were printed…. There was an immensity of things, an overburdening weight, a connection, a mortality…. I just wanted to get the stuff out of the house.

(*WN* 262; see 294)

This is more than just spring cleaning: it's a genuine purge. And yet such exceptional purges or purifications are perhaps never wholly distinct from the kinds of things DeLillo characters do at home on a more or less daily basis in the privacy of their own bathrooms.

The Shit, the Shower, the Shave, and the Haircut

I no longer take my classic morning crap after breakfast. Everything's slower and dumber.

ZK 223

Every man wants to grow a beard before he dies. It's one way of saying fuck you to everybody.

A 246

It was the very beard I would have grown in 1969 if Janet Savory, my second wife, Heinrich's mother, hadn't argued against it.

WN 65

Murray had a little Amish beard that came straight down off his lower lip like a baggage tag.

AZ 42

He didn't know what he wanted. Then he knew. He wanted to get a haircut.

C 7

There is, then, in almost every DeLillo work, some kind of ritual purge or sacrifice, some preparation for a transcending event. This can involve, as we have seen, various kinds of exercises or disciplines, plans and preparations, on a large scale. But it often begins with smaller things, within a more circumscribed field, that is, with the body, which initially does not need to be trained or sculpted or shaped but just cleaned and groomed. Hence the rigor and ritual we have been looking at are often attached to everyday gestures of expelling, washing, and cutting in order to face the day. And so it all often begins with a shit, a shower, a shave, and, when you are preparing for something a little bigger, a haircut.

For none of this is as simple or banal as it seems. In addition to the secret of the other, the secret that the other is, beyond or at the limits of language, and the secret of ourselves, the secret of who we are down deep, there is the contraband we carry around inside us, most of it unknown even to us, the secrets—the secretions and the excretions—of our own unknown but daily lives. Our body itself is thus not some shell or machine for a soul or a self to be lodged within but a whole "hidden system" of "tallowy secretions, glandular events of the body cosmos, small festers and eruptions, impacted fats, oils, salt and sweat, and how nearly scholarly the pleasures of extraction" (*BA* 84). In short, every body has its underworld, which at once makes that body work and threatens always to irrupt from within to destroy it. As such, it often informs us of things we would rather not know, answering the question posed in *Underworld*: "Why do bad smells seem to tell us something about ourselves?" (*U* 104). Attention to the body and its functions is thus essential, DeLillo seems to be suggesting, if we are to understand anything about who we are. And attention does not mean reverence, let alone worship, since "worship of the body always ends in fascism" (*RS* 361).

DeLillo seems to take great pleasure in extracting or describing in detail some of these secretions and excretions, everything from excrement, the most revered or reviled of bodily wastes, to vomit, saliva, sperm—even "navel sludge" (*RS* 262). The drunken scatological orgy somewhere in Texas near the end of *Americana* (*A* 372) is just one in a now very long series of scenes or descriptions in DeLillo featuring secretions, excretions, or discharges of various kinds.

In *Amazons* there is the whole problem of how to handle the "wastage" of the ailing hockey player during his five-months of sleep therapy inside a Kramer cube—more on that later (*AZ* 225). In *End Zone*, the appearance of a bit of excrement in the desert leads to a long excursus on the matter of shit (*EZ* 88–9), the association of waste, the desert, and a certain faith or religiosity being thereby established well before *Underworld*. In *Mao II* we see the author Bill Gray obsessing about his next novel but then seemingly just as concerned to shake "the last drop of pee off his dick" (*M* 212), super-attentive to every last drop of bodily fluid coming out of him, as if it were a sign of his "true life," his vast and infinitely interesting inner life: "the ooze of speckled matter, the blood sneeze, the daily pale secretion, the bits of human tissue sticking to the page" (*M* 28). Bill was a well-known writer, to be sure, but before or in addition to that "he was a sitting industry of farts and belches. This is what he did for a living, sit and hawk, mucus and flatus" (*M* 136). And as Bill knows, "The biographer who didn't examine these things... couldn't begin to know the catchments, the odd-corner deeps of Bill's true life" (*M* 136). ("Hawking," notice, because some bodily practices are more poetic than others. Hawking takes focus and usually comes with age, while, say, puking is something any youthful enthusiast can do. That is why, as we read in *Players*, "Hawking is to puking as haiku is to roller derby" (*P* 162), an analogy that Aristotle would have needed another *Poetics* to explain.)

It might be thought that only DeLillo's older characters take such a deep personal interest in these excretions or bodily functions, but even fourteen-year-old Billy Twillig is taken by "the jams and scabs of his own living body" (*RS* 363). His interest did, admittedly, have its limits; for example, "Excrement worried him a bit. Shitpiss. He did not have reveries about excrement" (*RS* 37). As for saliva, "there were few things more pleasantly disgusting, he believed, than watching his own spit hit the dust, half quivering with fragments of earth, a tiny spoonful of drool" (*RS* 363). It has some pretty interesting properties, spit does, the way it "bunches and wobbles when it hits the dirt, going sandy brown" (*U* 25)—or the way it freezes, as one might recall from the very beginning of *Americana*, when put on top of an ice cube tray, an ice cube tray in someone else's refrigerator during a party, no less (*A* 10, 195). In *Point Omega* Jim Finley looks at Elster looking at his handkerchief and thinks: "I didn't know what he saw in that handful of mucus but he kept looking" (*PO* 97). And the looking continues right up through *Zero K*: "He paused here to remove a handkerchief from his trouser pocket and blow his nose, unconditionally, with follow-up swipes and blots, and this made me feel better. Real life, body functions" (*ZK* 129).

There's everyday mucus and phlegm and spit but then there's the morning crap, a sacred ritual for everyone from Jack Ruby to Lauren Hartke, despite all their differences: "He took the newspapers he'd bought that morning and went into the toilet.... It was the best part of his day.... His mind settled down when he was crapping. There was a restfulness and calm" (*L* 351). "There's nothing like a raging crap, she thought, to make mind and body one" (*BA* 35). It's hardly surprising that this latter would take such an interest in the sheddings of her own body, "skin in flakes and scales and little rolling boluses that she liked to hold between her fingers and imagine, unmorbidly, as the cell death of something inside her" (*BA* 84).

These are the everyday secretions, the kind that reassure us and tell us who we are, or the kind that begin to worry us and the doctors treating us. Dr. Bazelon (or the person playing him) asks in *The Day Room*: "Are your bowels regular? Are you crapping? Describe your stool for me… Tell me about the color of your stool" (*DR* 35). Even with what would seem to be the most natural, most life-giving, of bodily fluids, there is the possibility of intrusion, substitution, or fabrication. In *The Day Room* again, Grass says of "his own" blood: "Some of it is mine, some of it is mass-produced in the Republic of Korea. It's polyester blood. Pick your own color" (*DR* 10). And that is perhaps the future of blood—a future in which blood actually has futures, options and short-selling: "I've invested heavily in blood futures. I have a direct line to the trading floor for polyester blood" (*DR* 13). Jack Gladney takes a similarly keen interest in blood, especially when he realizes upon entering the hospital that it is Mink's blood, not his own, that he is looking at: "The rain had stopped. I was shocked at the amount of blood we were leaving behind. His, mainly" (*WN* 314).

As for semen, it needs to be put in a category and a paragraph of its own, though a character in *Ratner's Star* is uncertain about what that category should be: "Softly had never set eyes on his own semen. He regarded this fluid not primarily as a transporting medium but as some defensive secretion of the body, a reaction (perhaps) to danger or excessive stress" (*RS* 367).

Secretions tell us a lot about ourselves and the world around us. In *Ratner's Star*, the Jesuit/scientist/scatologist Armand Verbene, S.J., claims they can tell us everything:

> The ants and their semifluid secretions teach us that pattern, pattern, pattern is the foundational element by which the creatures of the physical world reveal a perfect working model of the divine ideal…. These ants simply crawl and secrete. These are the pattern ants. They enter, they exit, they secrete. These are the ants of red ant metaphysics.
>
> (*RS* 157–8, 160)

There is endless amounts of talk in DeLillo's novels about all these everyday secretions and excretions, from the toilet trivia contest in the faculty dining room at College-on-the-Hill (*WN* 68) to the whole question of what happens to Eric Packer's waste as he tools around New York City in a limo with its own toilet: "I noticed the toilet. It's one of the first things I noticed. What happens to your waste?" (*C* 190). And whenever anyone is traveling, whether on a road trip in the United States or through southern Greece, you can bet that the narrator will not be able to resist embroidering a bit on all on the shitholes and pissholes encountered during the journey:

> Bowls with no seats. Pissing in sinks. The culture of public toilets. All those great diners, movie houses, gas stations. The whole ethos of the road. I've pissed in sinks all through the American West.... I pissed in a sink in Utah when it was twenty-two below. That's the coldest I've ever pissed in a sink in.
>
> (*WN* 68)

> It was the terminal shithouse of the Peloponnese.... It had a history, a reek of squatting armies, centuries of war, plunder, siege, blood feuds. I stood five feet from the bowl to urinate, tip-toed. How strange that people used this place, still. It was like an offering to Death, to stand there directing my stream toward the porcelain hole.
>
> (*N* 183–4)

It is no surprise that all these thoughts of dirt, germs, and secretions inevitably lead to thoughts of death, to the question of whether there is anything beyond these bodily elements. Lianne in *Falling Man* thinks back to something she once heard: "Human existence had to have a deeper source than our own dank fluids. Dank or rank. There had to be a force behind it, a principal being who was and is and ever shall be" (*FM* 231; see *RS* 29). Something more than shit, in short, though shit may be the royal road to this deeper source.

Underworld is, in many ways, one big object lesson in human waste, everything from men pissing *en masse* at the baseball game in the Polo Grounds (*U* 21), or pissing individually, like Manx Martin, using "the fa-cil-i-tees... taking a king leak" (*U* 143), to Jackie Gleason vomiting up beer and bits of hotdogs during that same baseball game (*U* 44), to rumors of a cargo ship filled with excrement sailing the oceans, unable to dock because of the stench (*U* 302; see 278), to Nick Shay's work at Waste Management. And then there's the story of Marvin Lundy's first trip through Eastern Europe with his new bride Eleanor, where the smell of Marvin's bowel movements becomes more and more rank the further east they go:

> He began to dread the moment after breakfast every day when it came time for him to haul himself to the toilet. / What is the word, ignoble? / Marvin thought of his bowel movements as BMs, a phrase he'd heard an army doctor mutter once.
>
> (*U* 309–10)

The smell, "his smell," "was a secret he had to keep from his wife" (*U* 310), but "the deeper into communist country, the more foul his BMs" (*U* 311). However natural and personal, the smell became "infused with ... geopolitics" (*U* 312), and with worries over whether his new wife would be able to accept his nasty secret:

> He realized this was probably a normal part of every early marriage, smelling the other's smell, getting it over and done with so you can move ahead with your lives, have children, buy a little house, remember everybody's birthday, take a drive on the Blue Ridge Parkway, get sick and die.
>
> (U 310)

But Marvin Lundy is not wrong to be afraid of his secretions—even just the smells—invading another's space. Such infiltration or such a crossing of borders between self and other is often disconcerting, even when it's something far less offensive than another's excrement, something so seemingly harmless as a hair. Recall how Lauren in *The Body Artist* "picked a hair out of her mouth" (*BA* 10): "A hair in my mouth," she says, "from someone else's head" (*BA* 11; see *RS* 280). It's an experience we've all had, and Lauren will have it more than once: "She felt something wispy at the edge of her mouth, half in half out, that could only be a hair" (*BA* 69). It's just a little thing, a minor irritation, but its intrusion seems to suggest the "intimate passage of the hair from person to person and somehow mouth to mouth across years and cities and diseases and unclean foods and many baneful body fluids" (*BA* 12). It can come from any number of sources, a neglectful food provider or a former lover, who has perhaps transmitted more than just a hair (see *RS* 280), or, as in *The Body Artist*, from a strange person hiding somewhere in your house, the kind who, once you find him and realize he is harmless, you will want to give a sponge bath to, right down to the private parts (see *BA* 48).

After the shit, the shower, and the sponge bath, the next serious task on the morning's to-do list is, for many a DeLillo character, the shave. For to shave or not to shave is not just a simple question of hygiene or grooming but, as with whether to get a haircut or not, as we will soon see, a serious question of how to live, a question, in the end, of life and death. In *Libra* one of the former CIA agents planning the assassination "slept on a cot in grubby clothes but made it a point to shave every day," because "shaving had an impact on his morale and he needed all the help he could get" (*L* 128). When Bill Gray in *Mao II* stops shaving—and begins to ignore at the same time the pain in his abdomen—we know that the end is near, that he too is on some kind of suicide mission, involved in some unnamed ritual of death or self-sacrifice (*M* 200): "He liked the sense of soldierly preparation, the diligence and rigor that helped him pretend he knew what he was doing" (*M* 122). In *Point Omega* one can track the health of the two main protagonists, Elster and Jim Finley, by following their respective hygienes; while the former is utterly undone by the disappearance of his daughter, the latter tries to maintain a certain rigor and order in his life: "He stopped shaving, I made it a point to shave every day, do nothing different" (*PO* 85). "He began to resemble a recluse who might live in a shack on an abandoned mining site, unwashed old man, shaky, stubbled" (*PO* 87).

After 9–11, those who were affected but not wholly devastated by the events attempted to recreate for themselves a rigor and a discipline. Lianne, for example, "was content in the small guarded scheme she'd lately constructed, arranging the days, working the details, staying down, keeping out" (*FM* 182). As for her estranged husband, Keith, he "stopped shaving for a time, whatever that means" (*FM* 67). But of course we know that means. For terrorists such as Mohammed Atta, preparing in Hamburg for 9–11, not shaving meant that they were beginning to prepare for serious things: "They were all growing beards…. The beard would look better if he trimmed it. But there were rules now and he was determined to follow them. His life had structure. Things were clearly defined" (*FM* 79, 83).

When you see someone in a DeLillo novel stop shaving, or shaving everything, or doing something out of the ordinary with the hair on their body, then you know something momentous is on the horizon. Take Ross in *Zero K*, for example, who first grows a beard, contrary to his habits, and then shaves it off: "My father had grown a beard. This surprised me…. Was this the beard a man grows who is eager to enter a new dimension of belief?" (*ZK* 7) "There was something I hadn't realized until now. Ross had shaved his beard" (*ZK* 101; see *LL* 9). So the beard's the first step. Later, it's the full body-shave, head-to-toe, preparation for entering one's capsule in the Convergence: "The barber put Ross in the chair and worked quickly…. Hair shed everywhere, head showing small ruts and lesions" (*ZK* 232–3).

A haircut or a shave—or the opposite—is thus always a ritual or rite of passage, the mark of transition to another life, to a counter-life of some kind. When Klara Sax asks Nick Shay, having not seen him for nearly forty years, "You're leading a regular life," and Nick answers, "Shave every day" (*U* 71), we know that neither the question nor the answer is as banal or straightforward as it seems.

Finally, then, after the shit, the shower, and the shave, there is—typically less routine and therefore even more significant—the haircut. As someone says in the short story "Human Moments in World War III," "What an interesting thing a haircut is, when you think of it" ("HM" 41). The haircut is one of those seemingly minor themes or leitmotifs in a DeLillo novel (sort of like shoes, only at the other end of the body) that comes to play a central role almost every time. A haircut can be, first of all, a sign of power and authority, a mark of distinction carefully maintained, say, by "great big barbered network executives" with "aftershave in their voices," executives who "on the speakerphone… sound like God coming through the roof of a thirteenth-century cathedral" (*V* 65; see 104). For having "expensively cut hair" (*WN* 58) is sometimes all it takes to give one a certain authority, an American in Athens, for example, maybe CIA, maybe not, but something has to explain "the perfect part in his hair" (*N* 261). And when you are in advertising, like Charlie Wainwright, you want to give the impression that you know what you want and that you won't get pushed around, and you can get all of that out of a haircut: "He got fascist haircuts done by Spadavecchia of Milan—his *school* actually, since Gianni was frequently overbooked" (*U* 530). Murray Siskind, who knows a thing or two about how to create authority, will credit Babette with having "important hair" (*WN* 19), the big disheveled look that shouldn't be touched. Of course, sometimes, no matter how much time and money one puts into it, the haircut just doesn't seem to fit the head (see *WN* 58), or doesn't seem to create the impression one wants: "Who cuts your hair? Did they arrest the mass murderer who cuts your hair?" (*U* 485; see *WN* 58).

Haircuts can thus serve many purposes or mean many things. A son can sometimes get a haircut just to piss off his father. Such was the case of Jeffrey Lockhart as a kid: "I shaved a strip of hair along the middle of my head, front to back—I was his personal antichrist" (*ZK* 14). But most of the time a haircut is an indication of some kind of commitment, the exterior sign of some change in mission or motivation. Ann Maitland says to James Axton, jokingly though it could have been in earnest:

> I think you ought to grow a beard or shave your head. We need a physical demonstration of your commitment to these deep ideas. I'm not sure you're altogether serious. Give us something to believe in. A shaved head would do wonders for this group.
>
> (*N* 5)

When you see a DeLillo protagonist grooming himself, often ritualistically, in some way, you know that the battle, the confrontation, the moment of reckoning, is not very far off. In short, the cut is always the hair-trigger for an event.

Hair is thus always interesting in DeLillo, from Selvy's ritual shaving to the hairs of Bill Gray stuck in his typewriter (*M* 201) (or, in *White Noise*, in the computer "circuits" (*WN* 151)) all the way down to the sight of "female hair down there" (*RS* 320; see 243–4 and 276), the hair that stops fourteen-year-old math genius Billy Twilling dead in his tracks. So interesting is hair that, in "Human Moments in World War III," DeLillo imagines one astronaut giving another a haircut as they orbit the earth ("HM" 41; see also "S" 191, 201).

And then there's nature's way of giving haircuts—Heinrich's naturally receding hairline, for which Jack, the father, feels somewhat guilty, whether for the genes he has passed on or the environment he has raised his son in, albeit "unwittingly, in the vicinity of a chemical dump site, in the path of air currents that carry industrial wastes capable of producing scalp degeneration" (*WN* 22; see 45, 181). And then there is Rumsey, a victim of baldness before becoming a victim on 9–11: "Baldness in Rumsey, as it progressed, was a gentle melancholy, the pensive regret of a failed boy" (*FM* 123). While so many things separated Oswald from Ruby, they had going bald in common— in perfect contrast, of course, to JFK's full head of well-groomed hair. It's why Ruby never went anywhere without wearing a hat, to conceal his "balding head," and why "he took scalp treatments that he felt were doing some good although he doubted it" (*L* 267). As for Lee, his mother thinks there's something suspicious, maybe even conspiratorial, about his premature balding: "Because his hair was coming out, which he says himself, from a full head of hair to badly thinning in front that you could practically see his scalp…. Judge, this is a family where the men have always displayed full heads of hair and he is still a boy" (*L* 243).

Hair is thus there from the beginning, hair, haircuts, and barber shops, from *Americana* (*A* 279) and *Amazons* (*AZ* 137, 325–6, 330) to *Great Jones Street* (*G* 260) and *Cosmopolis*. David Bell says in *Americana*: "I went into the bathroom, took off my shirt and began shaving my chest with an electric razor. It was a ritual cleansing of the body, a prelude to the sacred journey" (*A* 124). This will be followed by a number of shaves and showers, and, after Bell's movie has been completed, a ritual cutting of nails and a few stray hairs: "I showered and shaved. With my curved scissor I clipped some hair from my nostrils. I looked not bad, things considered, the film-segment done and torn out of me" (*A* 334; see 335, 377). Though very different from Bell, Glenn Selvy appears cut from the same cloth when it comes to hair. That is why Selvy's friend Levi plans to prepare Selvy's dead body, according to ancient ritual, by beginning with his hair: "First Levi would sit and chant, directing the escape, the separation of the deceased from his body, as taught by the masters of the snowy range…. You started by plucking a few strands of hair from the top of the dead man's head" (*RD* 245–6). The only problem, of course, is that Selvy had been scalped by his assassins so that when Levi finally arrives there is no hair to pluck (*RD* 240). But the intention was there, and this little passage from *White Noise* can be read as completing the ritual, even though it's the hair of the living and not the dead that is cut: "This is how it ended for him, with his attendants cutting off their hair and disfiguring their own faces in barbarian tribute" (*WN* 100).

There is hair in *Underworld* from beginning to end, with references just in the opening pages to "brilliantined men" (*U* 12) and men who "need a haircut" (*U* 13) and that "bowl-cut" look (*U* 15) and Einstein—"What Einstein?" "Albert, with the hair" (*U* 26). Much later, we meet the "polymerized hairpiece" of Marvin Lundy (*U* 315) and, later still, Rosemary Shay's "Mother Hubbard hairdo" (*U* 698). And then there are all the barbers, real barbers, George the Barber, for example, who cut hair for a living, but then also Albert Bronzini, who keeps a little barber's kit in a Garcia y Vega cigar box, "fine cigars since 1882," and uses it on occasion to give his good friend Eddie Robles an amateur haircut (*U* 223).

> He had no idea how to cut hair. He'd done Eddie's hair a number of times but hadn't worked out a method.... The idea was to get the hair off the guy's head and onto the floor.
>
> (*U* 225)

In *Libra* there are people who seem not to care much about their hair (*L* 25), people who pay great attention to it—like the guy who grows it down his neck, "a rat's tail ... painstakingly braided" (*L* 292), and the Soviets, who, after recovering U-2 pilot Gary Powers, took care to give "the prisoner a peasant haircut" (*L* 193), and people, or really just one person, David Ferrie, because he truly is one of a kind, who "suffered from a rare and horrific condition that had no cure," "alopecia universalis" (*L* 316), to give it a name, which caused his body to be "one hundred percent bald. It looked like something pulled from the earth, a tuberous stem or fungus esteemed by gourmets" (*L* 29). Instead of watching himself in a mirror at the barber shop as the hair came off, he would "wince ... in front of mirrors when he pasted on his homemade eyebrows and mohair toupee" (*L* 29), a "faded red ... object that resembled some windblown piece of street debris" (*L* 66), "tufts of fur glued to his head, like handfuls of animal hair just pasted on" (*L* 313).

Getting a haircut or a shave—these can be big religious rituals or else little familiar acts of devotion, discipline, or memory, the kind of thing a son might do with a father, or remember having done with him or seen him do. Nick Shay, for example, has memories of his father shaving, "a towel draped over his shoulder, wearing his undershirt, his singlet, and the blade made a noise I liked to listen to" (*U* 106). But the archetypal example of this is to be found in *Cosmopolis*, where, at the very beginning of the novel, mega-rich Eric Packer looks at his reflection in the glass skyscraper whose luxurious penthouse he owns and suddenly realizes what he really wants, this man who has or could have pretty much anything he wants: "The tower gave him strength and depth. He knew what he wanted, a haircut" (C 9). Thus begins Packer's all-day odyssey across Manhattan to a barbershop in Hell's Kitchen where he used to go with his father as a kid. It might be the memories or the mirrors or both, but haircuts have a way of bringing us back, of causing us to reflect. Because if you want to know *who* will do something in DeLillo, you would probably do well, as always, to follow the money. But if you want to know *when* they will do it, just follow the hair.

6

Counterforces

Life and Death

What should I say? That the term itself—my life—is a desperate overstatement…. Some people are able to use that term and make it sound like a throbbing corporate enterprise.

V 44

"Do you say yes to life?" "I guess so. Sure, why not."

RS 56

I want to die after a long traditional illness. What about you?

PO 106

"I'm dying, David." "Don't generalize, Wendy."

A 25

"Do you believe love is stronger than death?" "Not in a million years." "Good," he said. "Nothing is stronger than death."

WN 284

In *White Noise* the always incisive Murray Siskind has an interesting theory about life. The idea, as he explains it to Jack, is that "there are two kinds of people in the world. Killers and diers. Most of us are diers" (*WN* 290). But to make it more interesting, there is only a certain amount of psychic energy in the world and it has all been doled among the killers and diers. It is thus a zero-sum game in which killers can get more psychic energy only by recuperating for themselves the life force—the "life-credit"—of those they kill. "If he dies, you cannot. To kill him is to gain life-credit. The more people you kill, the more credit you store up. It explains any number of massacres, wars, executions" (*WN* 290). The idea is that by killing others one not only resists death at the hands of others but extends one's own life through the life force of those others. Murray goes on: "The killer, in theory, attempts to defeat his own death by killing others. He buys time, he buys life" (*WN* 291).

That's Murray's theory of life in the abstract. Here's that theory turned into advice for Jack, who is thinking of killing the person with whom his wife is having an affair: "Be the killer for a change. Let someone else be the dier. Let him replace you, theoretically, in that role…. The more people you kill, the more power you gain over your own death" (*WN* 291). When Jack actually goes through with the attempt, it is precisely Murray's theory that he recalls: "I tried to see myself from Mink's viewpoint. Looming, dominant, gaining life-power, storing up life-credit" (*WN* 312).

The theory is perfectly Suskindian in its scope and ambition. And it seems to be shared by others in DeLillo's corpus. Owen Brademas says in *The Names*, for example: "I came away from the old city feeling I'd been engaged in a contest of some singular and gratifying kind. Whatever he'd lost in life-strength, this is what I'd won" (*N* 309). A similar dynamic seems to be behind the cult murders in the same novel (see *N* 175), or, in *Cosmopolis*, the assassination of the Russian media mogul with whom Packer is friends: "He died so you can live" (*C* 82). In *The Day Room*, Grass, reminiscent of Packer, expresses a similar view: "I live in a great steel tower that reflects the blazing sun. People catch fire just walking by. The more bodies that pile up around you, the greater your equity, the stronger your power, the longer you live" (*DR* 12).

The point here seems to be that, without having to go so far as planning to take another's life, living a life of one's own requires a certain taking control, developing a plot line of one's own, and that is often to the detriment of others.

> We start our lives in chaos, in babble. As we surge up into the world, we try to devise a shape, a plan. There is dignity in this. Your whole life is a plot, a scheme, a diagram…. To plot is to affirm life, to seek shape and control.
>
> (*WN* 291–2)

But then there is something else, something a little less clear, something called in *Point Omega*, and in a couple of other different places, "the true life."

> The true life is not reducible to words spoken or written, not by anyone, ever. The true life takes place when we're alone, thinking, feeling, lost in memory, dreamingly self-aware, the submicroscopic moments.
>
> (*PO* 17; see 34)

Whatever this life is, it is not, it would seem, a life beyond life or a life after life. It is perhaps more like a hyperlife, a life at the outer edge of words, a life in a relation of contraband with what inhabits life from the beginning, that is, with death. Perhaps we would need to return to St. Augustine for that one. Or else to Murray Siskind, whose theories about death are every bit as enthusiastic as those we just saw him express about life. He says—again to Jack: "There are numerous ways to get around death. You tried to employ two of them at once. You stood out on the one hand and tried to hide on the other" (*WN* 288). Two ways to avoid death: first, to stand out and do great things, that is, to be a killer rather than a dier, and, second, to run and take cover. When we are thus unable to do the former, "We repress, we disguise, we bury, we exclude." We try to run away from the looming threat hanging over us, and "some people do it better than others" (*WN* 288).

But repression is not, of course, the same thing as forgetting, so that, in the end, death is just about all we think about (*WN* 38, 282). Even fourteen-year-old Billy Twillig cannot help being consumed by the thought (*RS* 327; see *RS* 37). Beneath all the banter and the humor, all the denial and repression, all the disguises and exclusions, death is and remains the ultimate preoccupation of life in DeLillo's works, the ultimate contraband, the other side of life that is not really a side at all. The entire plot of *White Noise* revolves simultaneously—in perfect contraband fashion—around both the pursuit of death, Jack's attempt to kill Mink, aka Mr. Gray, and his attempt to avoid or to forget about death. But the two strands are even more tightly braided than that. Jack threatens Mink with death because of this latter's promises to help others, and his wife Babette in particular, not to mention himself, get over their fear of death. For the drug Dylar had been "designed to solve an ancient problem. Fear of death. It encourages the brain to produce fear-of-death inhibitors" (*WN* 227–8). Pop a pill, which itself "silently self-destructs" (*WN* 211)—there it is again, the dream of perfect self-annihilation—and chemicals are released to "interact with neurotransmitters in the brain that are related to the fear of death" (*WN* 200). It's "technology with a human face," designed to quell the human fear of death (*WN* 211). Beneath all the humor and the posing, the prose is deadly serious. Because when the ironic coating dissolves, what we are left with is a fear so ancient and deep that no one can ignore it, not even Jack, even though he ultimately rejects the idea of Dylar because, he says, "I was not a believer in easy solutions, something to swallow that would rid my soul of an ancient fear" (*WN* 211).

Beneath all the healthiness in the world there is thus an incurable illness, one that not even Dylar can cure—the knowledge that we are going to die. It's a knowledge that can be expressed in a simple rule of thumb, elegantly laid out in *Zero K*: "If someone or something has no beginning, then I can believe that he, she or it has no end. But if you're born or hatched or sprouted, then your days are already numbered" (*ZK* 131). Here's the same idea, the same knowledge, in *Amazons*: "My days are numbered. I'm like a space object with a decaying orbit" (*AZ* 12). This knowledge would not be so problematic if it were not always accompanied by fear, by an often debilitating fear, as if the fear of death were in the end as big a problem as death itself. We read in *White Noise* again: "It's almost as though our fear is what brings it on. If we could learn not to be afraid, we could live forever." "We talk ourselves into it. Is that what you mean?" (*WN* 282). Or again in *The Day Room*: "Disease is not the illness. Disease is just a symptom of the illness." "What is the illness?" "Knowing that you're going to die" (*DR* 19). It is an illness that, in *The Names*, seems to distinguish the human animal from all others: "We know we will die. This is our saving grace in a sense. No animal knows this but us" (*N* 175). For anyone like Jack Gladney, anyone who has been born, hatched, or sprouted, the verdict is in, even if we don't quite know when the sentence will be carried out: "I'm tentatively scheduled to die. It won't happen tomorrow or the next day. But it is in the works" (*WN* 202). And even if we did, we wouldn't believe it or we would try to work our way around it. When Murray asks Jack, "Would you prefer to know the exact date and time of your death?" Jack answers:

> Absolutely not. It's bad enough to fear the unknown. Faced with the unknown, we can pretend it isn't there. Exact dates would drive many to suicide, if only to beat the system.
>
> (*WN* 285)

So we know and we try not to know; we know that every minute could be our last—to sum up such a very dire situation in very trite words—and yet we forget from one minute to the next until the truth is all of a sudden staring us in the face. Because it can happen from one day to the next, to almost everyone's surprise:

> "I just saw him yesterday in the market. How could he be dead?"
> "How long does it take?"
> "I'm only saying."
>
> (*U* 706)

Of course there are certain places, privileged place, where death happens pretty routinely—starting with war and natural disasters, as we already saw—but there are also places of privilege for thinking about death, "on airplanes, in hospitals," places where this knowledge is more palpable than usual, where "we sense the presence of death …. The hush of death" (*DR* 7), as Wyatt says in *The Day Room*, places where the hum or, rather, the "white noise" of death can be detected beneath all the commotion, a staticy crackle beneath the living din. It is no coincidence that *The Silence* begins aboard a plane returning to New York from Paris, where the "twin drones of mind and aircraft" do their best to keep thoughts of death at bay until the loud knocking begins in the airplane's underbelly and the French cabin crew no longer translates the panicked words of the captain from the flight deck (*S* 3–4).

So there is a lot of talk about death in DeLillo, but there is no one way of defining or understanding it. In *Zero K* the questions come fast and furious: "Can we call them dead?" "Death is a cultural artifact, not a strict determination of what is humanly inevitable" (*ZK* 71). "What does it mean to die?" / "Where are the dead?" / "When do you stop being who you are?" (*ZK* 70). These are not just academic questions but questions that anyone who has ever had to watch a friend or parent or loved one die has had to ask:

> I didn't know whether to regard the physical form they were working on as "the body." ... The other thing I didn't know was what constituted the end. When does the person become the body? There were levels of surrender, I thought.... It occurred to me that there was more than one official definition, none characterized by unanimous assent. They made it up as the occasion required. Doctors, lawyers, theologians, philosophers, professors of ethics, judges and juries.
>
> (*ZK* 139–40)

Whatever it is and however one defines it, death remains the underside or the contraband of life. It is always there, though "at an incandescent distance" (*V* 52), far in the future, or already back in childhood, in one's distant past, in the underground. Alex in *Love-Lies-Bleeding* recalls being with his father on the subway and seeing his first corpse: "All life drained out of him ... Gray like an animal. He belonged to a different order of nature" (*LL* 8). Gray like a dead animal, gray like a subway rat, or Gray like Mr. Gray, the Dylar-peddler of *White Noise*.

There is life, there is the event of death, which is incompatible with life, a complete break with life, and then there is the time, which can be brief or extended, of *dying*, the time in which life and death are intimately linked (see *U* 713). There are those who, like Win Everett in *Libra*, have a feeling for "the long fall," a "general sense" that they are dying (*L* 79), and then there are others, most others, who seem to be surprised, caught off guard by their dying (see *L* 186, 188). This element of surprise is part of the fascination of the Texas Highway Killer video, a sort of memento mori for the contemporary world:

> Seeing someone at the moment he dies, dying unexpectedly. This is reason alone to stay fixed to the screen. It is instructional, watching a

man shot dead as he drives along on a sunny day. It demonstrates an elemental truth, that every breath you take has two possible endings.

(*U* 159–60)

It is this time of dying that is explored in *Love-Lies-Bleeding* and *Zero K*. Alex, as Lia says, is "in a place that is blessed by death," in "last life," living an "exalted time" that "no one has the right to deprive him of" (*LL* 30), no longer alive, exactly, and yet not quite yet dead: "No longer and not yet. This is where he is" (*LL* 48).

It is this in-between state, this contraband state, that gives a certain authority to those who have been condemned to death by law or medicine or some other fate. Murray Siskind, Elvis expert, knows this too. He says to Jack after Jack suspects he has been fatally poisoned in the airborne toxic event: "Your status as a doomed man lends your words a certain prestige and authority. I like that…. You're growing in prestige even as we speak. You're creating a hazy light about your own body" (*WN* 284; see "HS" 165). But then who is not doomed in this way and who would be able to affirm that the man doomed to die soon, tomorrow, say, is not the most subject to denial or repression, to dreams of a reprieve or an afterlife? In fact, "Doesn't the fact of imminent death encourage the deepest self-delusion?" (*ZK* 85). And can't it breed in those who must bear witness to this imminent death not respect or awe but the most forthright if not heartless sorts of comparison? Here is Murray, who is once again one of our best guides to these dark depths of the human soul, responding to the news of Jack's illness:

> "Better you than me."
> I nodded gravely. "Why does this have to be said?"
> "Because friends have to be brutally honest with each other."
>
> (*WN* 293)

If death is the contraband of life, its opposite or its other side, it is also that which gives "a precious texture to life, a sense of definition" (*WN* 228). In *Cosmopolis* it seems to be the threat of death that, for Eric Packer at least, actually brings along with it the possibility of finally living:

> He didn't know how long it was since he'd felt so good…. it was the threat of death at the brink of night that spoke to him most surely about some principle of fate he'd always known would come clear in time. / Now he could begin the business of living.
>
> (*C* 106–7)

From *White Noise* to *Zero K*, the mortal protagonists seem to be in agreement: "The defining element of life is that it ends" (*ZK* 70). Someone who talks to those waiting to enter the Convergence seems to be on exactly the same page: "I want to die and be finished forever. Don't you want to die? ... What's the point of living if we don't die at the end of it?" (*ZK* 40). Our death, our knowledge of death, would thus seem to be, so the argument goes, that which makes life so precious. To which someone like Jack Gladney might respond, "What good is a preciousness based on fear and anxiety? It's an anxious quivering thing" (*WN* 284). He might thus have been tempted, like Ross in *Zero K*, to give the Convergence a whirl, to take a chance on an eventual resurrection or second life within this life—if only just to see, a hundred or two hundred years from now, how well Hitler Studies are faring in the United States, and, while he's at it, whether there still is a United States. It is the ultimate fantasy, the Convergence is, and the ultimate contrabanding of life and death.

Mourning

She claims my death would leave a bigger hole in her life than her death would leave in mine. This is the level of our discourse. The relative size of holes, abysses and gaps.

WN 101

I know you're in mourning or whatever the hip equivalent of mourning is.

GJ 124

I'd never felt more human than I did when my mother lay in bed, dying.... This was a wave of sadness and loss that made me understand that I was a man expanded by grief.

ZK 248

"We die once, big-time." (*FM* 177): that would seem to be a truism of the first order, all fantasies of the Convergence aside. But for those who remain after this one, big-time event—for "the family," as they say, or for the other member in a couple—there is mourning, which is not a one-time thing but an enduring, protracted, seemingly endless process. While there is often a resistance to the traditional gestures of mourning in DeLillo, there is mourning nonetheless, and such mourning has come to occupy a more and more central place in DeLillo's works. Lia speaks this way of Alex at a memorial service in NYC in *Love-Lies-Bleeding*:

There are no stories. You're here for the wrong reason. If you're here to honor his memory, it's not his memory, it's your memory, and it's false. There are no stories. There are other things, hard to express, so deep and true that I can't share them, and don't want to. In the end it's not what kind of man he was but simply that he's gone. The stark fact. The thing that turns us into children, alone under the sky.

(*LL* 83)

And then there is this gesture of memory, of survival: "I'll go back home and climb into the burning hills, where he worked, and scatter his ashes there. He goes nowhere now, into nothing. What powerful work he had it in mind to make. Untitled, unfinished. But not nothing" (*LL* 83; see *ZK* 73). It can all appear rather abstract, or detached, but Lia also understands "how two people can live together and when one of them dies, the other has to stop living. The other can't live a single day or a single week. A day may be passable, livable. A week, too long and dark. One dies, the other has to die" (*LL* 82). This devastation at the death of another had already been entertained as a possibility in *The Body Artist*, entertained but eventually overcome:

> Why not sink into it? Let death bring you down. Give death its sway. / Why shouldn't the death of a person you love bring you into lurid ruin? You don't know how to love the ones you love until they disappear abruptly…. Why shouldn't his death bring you into some total scandal of garment-rending grief? Why should you accommodate his death? Or surrender to it in thin-lipped tasteful bereavement? … Sink lower, she thought. Let it bring you down. Go where it takes you.
>
> (*BA* 116)

Lauren's body work *in extremis* seems to be an attempt to work through or work out this death, Rey's death, her husband's death, though also her mother's:

> She worked herself up along the doorpost, slowly, breathing completely, her back to the fluted wood, squat-rising, drawing out the act over an extended length of time. Her mother died when she was nine. It wasn't her fault. It had nothing to do with her.
>
> (*BA* 124)

The Body Artist is a work of mourning, as is *Zero K*, and maybe even *Point Omega*—all later works—but one could also throw in *Americana* as well since the death of David Bell's mother hangs over the entire novel. And didn't Pammy in *Players* work for a company housed in the World Trade Towers called Grief Management, "writing a direct-mail piece on the subjects of sorrow and death" (*P* 62)? Maybe all of DeLillo's works are also, somehow, about mourning. Maybe all of them could be summarized this way: "One more sadness at the middle of things" (*N* 177).

There are, then, in DeLillo simple moments of mourning, tender moments, if you will: "She missed Albert's mother" (*U* 746). And then there are moments of loss that somehow make one feel fuller and truer. Nick Shay is, perhaps surprisingly, the best witness here:

> When my mother died I felt expanded, slowly, durably, over time. I felt suffused with her truth.... She is part of me now, total and consoling. And it is not a sadness to acknowledge that she had to die before I could know her fully. It is only a statement of the power of what comes after.
>
> (*U* 804)

But then there is what might be called advance mourning, anticipatory mourning, the kind that accompanies the question we looked at earlier in *White Noise*, "Who will die first?" (*WN* 15, 30)—a question that remains open right up until the moment when it is answered. Before then, there is just speculation and longing and confusion and something like a prayer for more time:

> The truth is I don't want to die first. Given a choice between loneliness and death, it would take me a fraction of a second to decide. But I don't want to be alone either.... Let us both live forever, in sickness and health, feebleminded, doddering, toothless, liver-spotted, dim-sighted, hallucinating. Who decides these things? What is out there? Who are you?
>
> (*WN* 102–3)

There are reflections on various ways of treating the dead, from burial (like Selvy—in a sitting position), to cremation, to being shot into space. "Bury or cremate?" "They put them in a wall nowdays. It's a popular thing," says Albert Bronzini (*U* 233). But nowadays, "They have a new thing, maybe you heard," says Albert's friend Eddie. "Called space burials.... They send your ashes into space.... You go up with about seven hundred other ashes in the same shot.... Ten thousand dollars a pound" (*U* 225–6).

And then there is the Convergence (which could have been called the Contraband). It is the future, it seems, of death and dying, but a future that is, in many ways, already upon us. Anyone who has recently been to a cremation ceremony will recognize some of the tropes and something of the topos of the Convergence, the words, the language, the images, the solemnity.

As we saw earlier in our discussion of crowds, DeLillo also probes the idea of state funerals and mass mourning, everything from the funeral procession of Brutha Fez in *Cosmopolis* to the huge crowds mourning the death of the Ayatollah Khomeini in 1989 in Iran, a "frenzied mourning" in which the living try through chants and clothes-rending "to bring the dead man back among them" (*M* 188–9). It is "the story of a body that the living will not yield to the earth" (*M* 190).

But there is one last "kind" of mourning in DeLillo that deserves mention here—the *impossible* kind, a mourning that is impossible because the dead leave no world in which to mourn, because they take the world down with them and make it impossible for the ones left behind to continue to live on. As we read in *Cosmopolis* of Eric Packer, "When he died he would not end. The world would end" (*C* 6). Spoken of Packer from Packer's point of view, it is an expression of Packer's consummate egoism and boundless narcissism. But when spoken about another it seems to say something other and even more true about the catastrophe or the scandal of another's death.

Hence *Zero K*. Initially, Ross Lockhart imagines a mourning that would not go that far, that would still leave him a place in the world to mourn: "Suffer the loss, live and suffer and hope it gets easier—not easier but so deeply embedded, the loss, the absence, that I can carry it" (*ZK* 143). Ross tells his son that he decided not to join Artis in the Convergence because that "would have been the kind of surrender in which [he] gains control instead of relinquishing it" (*ZK* 143), his way, in short, of still trying to own the end of the world. After all, "Is a man of epic wealth allowed to be broken by grief?" (*ZK* 138). But when Ross later decides to join Artis in the Convergence, it is, it seems, no longer with this ambition to own this end of the world, since he has, in effect, already undergone it: Artis took the world with her when she died, and Ross feels he has no other choice but to try to join her in the next one.

The Afterlife

There was a picture on the wall of Jack Kennedy holding hands with Pope John XXIII in heaven. Heaven was a partly cloudy place.

WN 316

I guess that sort of thing is mostly auto-suggestion though. I can talk myself into almost anything. When I die I'll talk myself into another womb and start all over. That's what they do in Tibet—people who couldn't even get into Princeton entering fresh wombs like crazy.

A 312

Jack: *"And nothing survives? Death is the end?"*
Nun: *"Do you want to know what I believe or what I pretend to believe?"*
WN 319

There is thus death and mourning, collective and individual, and then there are stories—promises—of overcoming death and bringing mourning to an end. This is, for some, the death told of by religion, tales of "the dead who will come out of the earth to lash and cudgel the living, to punish the sins of the living—death, yes, triumphant" (*U* 249; see "AE" 88; see also *WN* 137, *N* 303). It's a somewhat consoling tale, so long as you are among the cudgelers, but there are other versions where the dead are promised an even better fate: "Read up on reincarnation, transmigration, hyperspace, the resurrection of the dead and so on…. Seriously, you can find a great deal of long-range solace in the idea of an afterlife" (*WN* 286). It is of course pretty clear from the language here that DeLillo himself doesn't really *believe* in any of that, that there is in the end no triumph over death. As Lia says in *Love-Lies-Bleeding*, there is not even "peace when someone dies. There's nothing" (*LL* 28). There are secret lives and underworlds but no other world, no afterlife. That kind of religious vision seems debunked by religious figures themselves, from Sister Herman in *White Noise* to Sister Edgar in *Underworld*. This little exchange from *Ratner's Star* seems to express DeLillo's ultimate views on the matter: "What do you suppose happens to a person after death?" "He remains in that state" (*RS* 241–2).

But the fact that there is no transcendental counterband, as it were, no life after or beyond or transcendent to this life, does not mean that there are no miracles and that there is not faith. We will see a bit later that almost every DeLillo novel ends with a kind of miracle, a secular miracle, if you will, a moment of grace or wonder that is not incompatible with faith but does not suggest anything like an actual, living afterlife.

There are, in the end, other ways of living on after death—even if it means there is no one there, exactly, to do the actual, human living. All the forms of mediatization that fill the works of DeLillo (cinema, video, literature, the internet, and so on) are all ways of "living on" or "surviving," ways of having one's image or one's name continue on after death. One can be alive and kicking one day and then, all of a sudden, the only thing that remains—and it does remain for a time—is one's name or image, a neural or digital afterlife that seems to be about the best any of us can hope for. The Tiresias-like Vija Kinski says to Eric Packer in *Cosmopolis*:

There you sit, of large visions and prideful acts. Why die when you can live on disk? A disk, not a tomb. An idea beyond the body…. Will it happen someday? Sooner than we think because everything happens sooner than we think. Later today perhaps. Maybe today is the day when everything happens, for better or worse, ka-boom, like that.

(*C* 105–6)

Kinski could have said, "*ho gar kairos engus*," that is, "for the time is near," the time is coming not for a death that will obliterate all memory of what life once was but a death that will download all that memory onto a computer or onto a site where that memory can live elsewhere—or maybe, today, everywhere. For Packer, one could do a whole lot worse, because "what did he want that was not posthumous?" (*C* 209).

The Convergence of *Zero K* would seem to be the realization of this dream of a cyber life after death, a cyber life that even promises a continuation or another shot at *this* life. It is, in many ways, the ultimate counterband life, for it brings together, it makes converge, life and death, this time and another, the present and the future. It is a way to own the end of the world, a way to overcome it, giving oneself over to technology in anticipation of a day when one's memories, one's life, are miraculously downloaded back into a living body and restored. It is something "located at the far margins of plausibility"—so out there, as Ross says, that "no one could make this up" (*ZK* 115)—but it corresponds to some of our deepest longings. The idea is that "the time will come when there are ways to counteract the circumstances that led to the end," ways to make it so that "mind and body are restored, returned to life" (*ZK* 8), a "second life" (*ZK* 20). It is not "a new idea," just one "that is now approaching full realization" (*ZK* 8). "Life after death." "Eventually, yes" (*ZK* 9).

It's a twenty-first-century idea with very ancient roots, "a promise more assured than the ineffable hereafters of the world's organized religions" (*ZK* 74), but not so different from the "life everlasting" that has always belonged "to those of breathtaking wealth... Kings, queens, emperors, pharaohs" (*ZK* 76). For Ross, the modern billionaire, there would be neither monument nor pyramid: "the pod would be his final shrine of entitlement" (*ZK* 117).

But once the freezing is done, how is one to think of the "life" lived by these people, or these once-people, "dead, or maybe dead, or whatever they were, the cryogenic dead, upright in their capsules" (*ZK* 74), "shaved and naked, standing and waiting" (*ZK* 203–4), "dormant in a capsule," waiting for their "cyber-resurrection" (*ZK* 245)? What is to be made of that "phantom life within the braincase," that "floating thought" (*ZK* 238), those "lives in abeyance" (*ZK* 141)? For those who remain living in their wake, things are a bit clearer. For example, what remains for Jeffrey, looking at Artis, is a memory of her story and the echo of a word:

I wasn't ready to leave. I remained, eyes closed, thinking, remembering. Artis and her story of counting drops of water on a shower curtain. Here, the things to count, internally, will be endless. *Forevermore.* Her word. The savor of that word. I opened my eyes and looked a while longer, the son, the stepson, the privileged witness.

Artis belonged here, Ross did not.

(*ZK* 258)

There is a convergence, therefore, and then there is not. The Convergence is the counterbanding of death and life, of one life and another, still unimaginable life. It is also the convergence of life and art. The statues in the Convergence resemble at once buried antiquities and the bodies about to be frozen. Jeffrey says, "Could I avoid interpreting the figures as an ancestral version of the upright men and women in their cryonic capsules, actual humans on the verge of immortality?" (*ZK* 133) Humans as statues, then, and statues of or as humans (see *ZK* 231–2; see *U* 793). If the Convergence is the counterbanding of life and death, past and future, then the "veer" is the very place of contact between the two bands, the tenuous site where life and death touch or veer into one another.

Curiously enough, *Zero K* was not the first time DeLillo thought about cryogenics. It's an idea that was already in *Americana*, though with a little less reverence: "Once we figure out how to thaw the sons of bitches, we'll have mass resurrections from coast to coast" (*A* 301). DeLillo seems to have been digging around in this direction for some time. Alex Macklin's final earth work is oddly Convergence-like, as is the very setting for much of *Ratner's Star*, a vast underground cycloid complex, "a figure of magical properties," a shape that could be applied "to a building, a city, a giant tombstone if need be" (*RS* 78). Moreover, Billy's introduction into the structure is not unlike Jeffrey's—"The two men led him through a series of subcorridors that ended at the mouth of a masonite labyrinth" (*RS* 16)—and his room, called a "canister," reads in retrospect like a forerunner of the rooms in *Zero K*. And then, right at the center of the novel, in the depths of the "Great Hole" of "Field Experiment Number One," there is "a vast underground chamber largely in a natural state" that contains "remnants of ancient architecture" (*RS* 211), the place of the ceremony for Shazar Lazarus Ratner, the Jewish scientist from Brooklyn who will give precious advice to Billy Twillig from inside his "ultrasterile biomedical membrane environment" (*RS* 211), a membrane or tank that Billy, having been an "incubator baby," knows a little something about (*RS* 222). It's as if this setting from a novel from 1976—with all these people in tanks, tubes, pods, canisters, and so on—had itself been resurrected in 2016 for *Zero K*.

But then there is the "Kramer cube" of *Amazons*, that is, Kramer with a K in *Amazons* with a z. This is no doubt the most striking precursor or early model of the Convergence in *Zero K*. "A self-contained unit" that "hummed with the power of life and death" (*AZ* 223), this is the box in which an ailing hockey player (Shaver's the name) will be placed for five months of "sleep therapy" (*AZ* 121). Like the Convergence, it's a medical contraption, but it feels like one is entering "the four-thousand-year-old tomb of some prophet or king" (*AZ* 224). As the non-ailing one outside the cube, Cleo Birdwell, is able to say about the ailing Shaver inside: "He looked better than I did. Immortal, somehow" (*AZ* 237). Cleo imagines that "he would never wake up, and never get old, and never die. They would keep him in a little cubbyhole at the Smithsonian" (*AZ* 237).

And just as in *Zero K*, as soon as there is one person in the box or in the Convergence there is the dream of two, the dream of accompanying someone into eternity or another life—Ross with Artis in *Zero K*, Cleo with Shaver in *Amazons*.

> I pictured us in twin Kramers, millions of years after the Great Population Explosion…. We are discovered by aborigines when Australia and North America collide. They climb aboard, so to speak, and head east with their boomerangs to my apartment, where Shaver and I are asleep in matching striped pajamas.
> (*AZ* 326)

Even the glow or the radiance that those who enter the Convergence take on is already there on the faces of those sleeping their way—or so Cleo hopes—to good health and restoration in the Kramer cube: "Shaver *did glow*. There was a sweet, gentle, innocent, restful look about him. I could only hope it wasn't the Glow of Death, or Madness, or Slow Starvation" (*AZ* 349). The dream of outwitting or outrunning or somehow living on in spite of disease and death has thus been part of DeLillo's work from *Americana* and *Amazons* to *Zero K*.

There are thus full-blown visions of an afterlife, denials of such an afterlife, scientific attempts to achieve a sort of afterlife, and then simpler things, like spirits, from the "kite-souls" of *Americana* (*A* 245; see 170) to the "spirit woman" of *Falling Man* (*FM* 234) and the "spirit birds" with which *Point Omega* concludes: "Sometimes a wind comes before the rain and sends birds sailing past the window, spirit birds that ride the night, stranger than dreams" (*PO* 117). Spirit birds, then, transient things of wonder, a flutter, a blur, and then they are gone.

The Apocalypse

He handed me a pamphlet called "Twenty Common Mistakes About the End of the World."

WN 137

The time is coming.

FM 82

Wars, famines, earthquakes, volcanic eruptions. It's all beginning to jell.

WN 136

In the works of Don DeLillo, references to the apocalypse, the end times, or the end of the world are, for some reason, almost certain to get a good laugh. Perhaps it is because the end of the world offers such great opportunities for contraband. Take, for example, just this description in *Mao II* of Karen, newly married Moonie, "holding a cluster of starry jasmine and thinking of the bloodstorm to come" (*M* 7). It's that contrast between the way she looks and what she is thinking that is so powerful and, thus, so entertaining. Same thing in *Zero K* when the Monk tells Ross that "the place where he would reside, in a preserved state, was very deep in the earth—deeper still than this cloistered hall. Possibly even safe from world's end. The Monk spoke enthusiastically about world's end" (*ZK* 95). Ross Lockhart got it right in his very first words in *Zero K*: "*Everybody wants to own the end of the world*" (*ZK* 3).

The apocalypse is, obviously, the ultimate contraband story, the story of an end of one world and the beginning of another—whether in heaven, hell, or some hell on earth. The most graphic depiction of that story is, of course, the one that falls into the hands of J. Edgar Hoover in the opening pages of *Underworld* in the form of the painting by Pieter Bruegel titled "The Triumph of Death":

> It is a color reproduction of a painting crowded with medieval figures who are dying or dead—a landscape of visionary havoc and ruin.... Across the red-brown earth, skeleton armies on the march.... Death himself astride a slat-ribbed hack, he is peaked for blood, his scythe held ready as he presses people in haunted swarms toward the entrance of some helltrap ... he asks himself why a magazine called Life would want to reproduce a painting of such lurid and dreadful dimensions. But he can't take his eyes off the page.
>
> (*U* 41)

This is the first appearance of a theme that will run from one end of the novel to the other, from a street preacher quoting scripture—"No one knows the day or the hour. I believe this is Matthew twenty-four" (*U* 140)—to Lenny Bruce screaming about the end of the world as part of his comedy routine during the Cuban Missile Crisis: "*We're all gonna die!*" (*U* 508). No one knows when it's coming, but the whole thing about the apocalypse—or the rapture—is that people often think they do: "Look at this. The Rapture is approaching. October twenty-eight. They give the exact date" (*U* 127).

While there are other—many other—apocalyptic tales in DeLillo's work, and already in *Americana* (see *A* 330-1), *Underworld* gives a shape if not a face to the apocalypse. It is "the Unthinkable," and since the mid-1940s that Unthinkable has taken the shape of a mushroom cloud, which began to cast its shadow over the entire world during that Cuban missile crisis, as it became clear "how little it would take to make the thing happen—the first night on earth when the Unthinkable crept up over the horizon line and waited in an animal squat" (*U* 508). It is hard not to be reminded of what DeLillo said earlier about technology, our technology, the kind that is "crucial to civilization" and get threatening to it, "crouched and undecidable," ready to "go either way" (*C* 95). *Underworld* is there to remind us, if reminding is still needed, that this Unthinkable is still there, squatting and crouched, undecidable, and perfectly able to pounce.

The Omega Point, the Death Drive

"I'm afraid to die," she said. "I think about it all the time. It won't go away."
"There must be something else, an underlying problem."
"What could be more underlying than death?"

WN 197

Why are terminal events so pleasing, I wonder?

GJ 223

How fragile we are. Isn't it true? Everyone everywhere on this earth.

ZK 126

The Triumph of Death.

U 9

Suicide as much as murder, self-destruction as much as destruction, manmade disasters and ruin as much as nature's own ways of wreaking havoc—that is the inclination, the inevitable drive, of many of DeLillo's characters, from Glenn Selvy to Bill Gray to Eric Packer, with David Bell, Gary Harkness, Nick Shay and a few others somehow managing to survive, at least for a time, their own self-destructive tendencies. That is the way of all characters and it is the way of all plots, the way of all lives and all life, as if every affirmation of life were contrabanded by its own death and destruction, as if the path of every mortal being—including all these alpha males—ended at the omega point. From individual suicide to planetary death, everything seems to move in the same direction.

Excluding all the suspicious suicides that Nicholas Branch tries to treat as a series of coincidences, all the strange deaths and ruled suicides of those intimately or remotely involved in the Kennedy assassination or the investigation of it, like that of George de Mohrenschildt, "in March 1977, in Palm Beach, [dead] of a blast through the mouth with a 20-gauge shotgun" (*L* 58), suicide is everywhere in DeLillo. There are probably just as many self-inflicted gunshot wounds or gun deaths as there are shootings or killings of others. In *Americana* there is the tale of a young girl who is ordered by her father to kill her dog with a .22 and who ends up killing herself instead (*A* 363); in *Point Omega* there's Elster's daughter, who has probably committed suicide in the desert (*PO* 82, 89); in *End Zone* there's an assistant football coach who "shot himself in the head with an ivory-handled Colt .45"—and you can see how important it is, here as always, to get the name of the gun right (*EZ* 70; see *GJ* 243–4); and in *Falling Man* there's Lianne's father who wanted to avoid "the long course of senile dementia" and so "made a couple of phone calls from his cabin in northern New Hampshire and then used an old sporting rifle to kill himself" (*FM* 40; 130). "Died by his own hand. / For nineteen years, since he fired the shot that killed him, she'd said these words to herself periodically, in memoriam" (*FM* 218; see 169). "Died by his own hand," she says, because there is one strong argument that can always be used to justify suicide, the same one that is used to explain entering the Convergence: "We are born without choosing to be. Should we have to die in the same manner?" (*ZK* 252).

So it turns out to be a pretty popular thing in DeLillo, dying by one's own hand. In *The Body Artist* Rey Robles does it, dying by "a self-inflicted gunshot wound" (*BA* 27). In retrospect, we might have seen it coming. The last words Lauren spoke to Rey as he was going out the door were about picking up some Ajax, the name not just of a cleaning product, available in both powder form and as a liquid in "a bottle with a pistol-grip attachment" (*BA* 32), but also of a Greek warrior who committed suicide:

> Ajax, son of Telamon, I think, if my Trojan War is still intact, and maybe we need a newspaper because the old one's pretty stale, and great brave warrior, and spear-thrower of mighty distances, and toilet cleanser too.
>
> (*BA* 86–7)

Later in the novel, Lauren uses a bottle of the same Ajax, in mock imitation, it seems, of Rey's suicide:

> She cleaned the bathroom, using the spray-gun bottle of disinfectant. Then she held the nozzle of the spray gun to her head, seeing herself as doing what anyone might do.... It was the pine-scented bottle, the pistol-grip bottle of tile-and-grout cleaner, killer of mildew, and she held the nozzle, the muzzle to her head, finger pressed to the plastic trigger, with her tongue hanging out for effect.
>
> This is what people do, she thought, alone in their lives.
>
> (*BA* 114)

This is what people do, some people at least, like Jeffrey Lockhart, in *Zero K*: "I looked in the mirror over the bureau and simulated a suicide by gunshot to the head. I did it three more times, working on different faces" (*ZK* 227).

Dying by one's own hand is indeed something people do in their lives. In DeLillo, it's just about as frequent as getting shot in the hand. Jack Gladney, for example: "'We're shot,' I said, lifting my wrist in the air" (*WN* 315; see 313 and *LL* 38), or Packer, who shoots himself in a hand that then feels or looks like the hand of another: "It seemed separate from the rest of him, pervertedly alive in its own little subplot" (*C* 197). And you know who else shot himself in the hand? Lee Harvey Oswald, of all people, when he was stationed with the Marines in Japan. "I believe I shot myself" (*L* 91), he tells the hospital personnel. His service file thus reads, though no one quite believes it: "Patient dropped his '45 caliber automatic, pistol discharged when it struck the floor" (*L* 92). But what does it mean for a writer who writes or types by hand to write of characters who are constantly getting shot in the hand by their own design?

Dying by one's own hand: it's a way to describe suicide in general, for there are other ways to commit suicide—Oswald tries a razor at one point (*L* 151–3)—though the preferred means remains the gun. That's because the thing about guns is that they are made to go off, almost effortlessly, of their own accord, automatically, with just a little pressure applied by a finger that is so well suited to the task that it's called the trigger finger. It takes just a little squeeze, or sometimes just the uttering a name, like "Nancy Babich," to make the thing go bang (*C* 146).

But we mustn't forget self-immolation, which is maybe even more dramatic and no doubt requires greater commitment than shooting oneself in the head. Early on in *Cosmopolis*, Eric Packer sees a Tibetan monk setting himself aflame, and he admires this act, and wants "to imagine the man's pain, his choice, the abysmal will he'd had to summon" (*C* 98). When Kinski protests that "It's not original," Packer responds, more earnestly than we've seen him in the novel, "He did a serious thing. He took his life. Isn't this what you have to do to show them that you're serious?" (*C* 100). It is indeed a serious thing, self-immolation, and it is not original to *Cosmopolis*. In fact, it's something of a recurring theme in DeLillo's work. Jack in *Players* commits suicide in this way. "His arms were in front of him, hands crossed at about the same place his ankles were crossed. This had seemed ceremonial, the result of research on his part" (*P* 198). In *Libra*, the wife of a CIA operative is taken by a newspaper article about "a Buddhist monk who sets himself on fire. Because these are the things that tell us how we live" (*L* 261). Finally, in *Zero K* there is a film running in the Convergence of just such an immolation: "After a moment they began, in sequence, left to right, seemingly unplanned, to take up the bottles and pour the liquid on chest, arms and legs …. They were formless, soundless, screaming" (*ZK* 61–2); "monks, yes, in Tibet, in China, in India, setting themselves aflame … men dying for a cause" (*ZK* 85). It's a serious thing, self-immolation, as is, to be sure, death by starvation—the kind we see in *The Names*: "She will try to kill herself…. Starvation. Drawn-out, silent, losing the functions one by one. What is better in a place like India than starvation? … For such people, dying is a methodology" (*N* 292).

In addition to these explicit suicides, these deaths that would be, as they say, "ruled a suicide," there are all kinds of people in DeLillo's novels who are, to use another expression, on a sort of "suicide mission." Selvy's retreat into the desert near the end of *Running Dog* and his death at the hands of a Vietnamese hit-man is as much a ritual suicide as an assassination (see *RD* 107). The same goes for Bill Gray, who seems to be following a death wish in his trip from New York City to Athens, Cypress, and Beirut. By ignoring his health, masking without treating his pain, he seems to be following a decidedly suicidal trajectory. Rather than spending his old age back in NYC, living there with "someone to push him ever sunward" (*M* 201), he pushes himself over the edge elsewhere. Even Jack Ruby can be said to have committed suicide. He calls a friend not long before he does what he did and says: "If you ever pick up the phone and hear a voice that says I'm killing myself and you think it's my voice, Jack Ruby, then I'm telling you right now

I'm not bluffing" (*L* 349). And then there are the terrorists of 9-11, who commit suicide, in effect, for some "vision of heaven and hell, revenge and devastation" (*FM* 178; see 174, *P* 146).

Cosmopolis too is the tale of Eric Packer's self-destruction. His trip across the city in his automobile, his stretch limousine, becomes, in the end, an almost literal *autokheir*, death by one's own hand (*kheir*), or through one's own *auto*, a will to self-destruction that Packer pursues with a singular zeal. As Vija Kinski notes, "Even when you self-destruct, you want to fail more, lose more, die more than others, stink more than others. In the old tribes the chief who destroyed more of his property than the other chiefs was the most powerful" (*C* 193–4). Self-destruction is thus still something one can succeed at—the self-destruction of the devout, of the committed, of the religious zealot or the terrorist, the *potlach* chief who knows better than others how to bring it all down.

Finally, there is, as we have already seen in *Love-Lies-Bleeding*, what we call "assisted suicide," though the debate over how to end the life of another begins already in *Great Jones Street*, when someone asks, "Does NTBR mark the true beginning of the killer state?" (*GJ* 156). Fears of the slippery slope are thus only magnified when we get to assisted suicide or euthanasia, which is at the center of *Love-Lies-Bleeding*. Toinette, Alex's former partner, says to Sean, his son: "We're here to help him die" (*LL* 24). The idea is to ease Alex, the father, into death with "sublingual morphine" (*LL* 72), using what Sean, the son, calls "a child's syringe" (*LL* 79). He will "apply a few drops at a time. His system will absorb them and he will begin to fade" (*LL* 69). It seems fairly easy and unobjectionable, and Sean has learned exactly what to do from a perfectly reliable source—the internet (*LL* 74). "Doctors everywhere do this. Trust me. They increase morphine dosage in the name of pain reduction. In fact they are hastening the moment of death. It's called terminal sedation and it's an act of mercy" (*LL* 73).

But questions inevitably arise. At a certain point, the one being "treated" will no longer be able to voice his or her wishes: "If he were conscious, if he could tell us what he wants. He wants the Nembutal, the Seconal, the applesauce" (*LL* 45). Yes, the applesauce, because maybe the Nembutal has given him Seconal thoughts about applesauce and living a little longer, though now it is up to another to determine and execute those supposedly final wishes—a son or a wife, for example, who is never a wholly disinterested party. And maybe it's applesauce because that's what Marshall Applewhite, the leader of the cult Heaven's Gate, apparently used to make the lethal medicine go down in that infamous 1997 mass suicide just outside San Diego.

Though one always dies, in some sense, alone, there are nonetheless all these attempts, more or less innocent and well-intentioned, to accompany the dying in their solitude, to share their death with them. Lia, for example, with her husband Alex: "I was with him through the night. I think we're ready" (*LL* 70). We see something similar in *Zero K*, though there it's the husband, Ross Lockhart, accompanying—and then eventually joining—his wife, Artis, into a kind of death, or at least a suspended life. These questions from *Zero K* could well be asked of the most loving and well-meaning attempts to help another die: "Is it outright murder? Is it a form of assisted suicide that's horribly premature? Or is it a metaphysical crime that needs to be analyzed by philosophers?" (*ZK* 114). There are any number of questions that emerge when one person gets involved in the death of another. Like this one from *The Day Room*:

> "I'm going to California to help a friend commit suicide."
> "You just get on a plane? I'm trying to picture this. How do you pack for a suicide?"
>
> (*DR* 60-1)

What all these situations have in common, of course, is that they are limit situations, contraband situations, on the razor's edge between life and death. They are situations on the verge, *in extremis*, which DeLillo always likes, beginning with that very phrase *in extremis*: "O recite a litany in extremis" (*RS* 176), "Solitude in extremis" (*ZK* 67); Murielle Chapman entitles her review of Lauren's performance art piece "*Body Art in Extremis*" (*BA* 103); and Alex Macklin, already in the list of characters in *Love-Lies-Bleeding*, is described as "*in extremis*, a helpless figure attached to a feeding tube" (*LLB* 1).

We thus perhaps need to nuance just a bit that theory from *White Noise* that, in short, to the murderer go the spoils of his murder in the form of accumulated energy, a renewed life force. It went, we recall, something like this:

> In theory, violence is a form of rebirth. The dier passively succumbs. The killer lives on. What a marvelous equation. As a marauding band amasses dead bodies, it gathers strength. Strength accumulates like a favor from the gods.
>
> (*WN* 290)

"In theory," it seems, because it turns out that there is another theory, a contraband theory—especially in DeLillo's later novels—that suggests that what accumulates through violence and death is not more life but more death, that the *goal* of life itself is death. When Jeffrey thinks of his father going into the Convergence after Artis, he wonders:

> Was it simply love that made him want to join her? Maybe I prefer to think that he was driven by a dark yearning.... A dark yearning, I liked that.... Because this is the song-and-dance version of what happens to self-made men. They unmake themselves.
>
> (*ZK* 145)

There is a law that dictates that what is made will eventually be unmade. Okay, we can understand that, but this law seems to correspond to a yearning, to a desire. And it is perhaps not only the individual but the whole species, individual species but then perhaps all of life itself, that shares this desire. There is the pleasure principle, as that "looming figure" who is Freud would say (*WN* 289), or the pleasure principle in conjunction with the reality principle, and then, as that same looming figure would say—and here's the counterband—the death drive that always seems to accompany both. As Richard Elster says in *Point Omega*, we have a "dream of extinction" (*PO* 36; see 20), "we want to be the dead matter we used to be" (*PO* 50).

> Matter. All the stages, subatomic level to atoms to inorganic molecules. We expand, we fly outward, that's the nature of life ever since the cell.... Armies carry the gene for self-destruction. One bomb is never enough. The blur of technology, this is where the oracles plot their wars. Because now comes the introversion. Father Teilhard knew this, the omega point. A leap out of our biology.... Back now to inorganic matter. This is what we want. We want to be stones in a field.
>
> (*PO* 52)

The reference here is to the early twentieth-century French philosopher and theologian Teilhard de Chardin. But whereas the universe in de Chardin's work comes to greater and greater consciousness and self-awareness in conformity with the Christian logos, the point of *Point Omega* is that everything is moving toward greater and greater unconsciousness, toward death, toward stone, toward the inorganic, in short, toward a very different vision of last things (see *PO* 51).

It is surely no coincidence that almost all of DeLillo's theorists—Kinski, Elster, the waste guru in *Underworld*—are thinkers of destruction. For each of them, a life drive, a creative drive, is always shadowed or haunted by a death or destructive drive. We saw this earlier when we were looking at technology's death wish. In the end there may be little difference between the radiance by which things become self-conscious and an omega point where consciousness turns to stone. Listen to Richard Elster again, speaking in the desert, against the backdrop of his daughter who will go missing and will never be found, perhaps turned to stone herself:

> Consciousness accumulates. It begins to reflect upon itself. Something about this feels almost mathematical to me. There's almost some law of mathematics or physics that we haven't quite hit upon, where the mind transcends all direction inward. The omega point.... Paroxysm. Either a sublime transformation of mind and soul or some worldly convulsion. We want it to happen.... Think of it. We pass completely out of being. Stones. Unless stones have being. Unless there's some profoundly mystical shift that places being in a stone.
>
> (*PO* 73)

There is an omega point, an end toward which all energy and life are headed, as if gathered at the point of a knife:

> I thought of his remarks about matter and being, those long nights on the deck, half smashed, he and I, transcendence, paroxysm, the end of human consciousness. It seemed so much dead echo now. Point omega. A million years away. The omega point has narrowed, here and now, to the point of a knife as it enters a body.
>
> (*PO* 98)

It is perhaps in terms of such self-destruction or such a death drive, such an omega point, that we must rethink that famous phrase of DeLillo's about all plots tending toward death. In *Libra* the plot that is initially designed simply to make an *attempt* on the life of Kennedy and then implicate the Castro government ends up getting away from the authors of it (see *L* 122–3, 138–9). As things progress, the principal architect, Win Everett, experiences the "sensation of the eeriest panic" as he begins to see the implications of the fictions he has been devising "living prematurely in the world" (*L* 179), heading in directions he had not imagined. It is in this sense, perhaps, that we should understand the claim that "plots carry their own logic," that "there is a tendency of plots to move toward death," that "the tighter the plot of a story, the more likely it will come to death" (*L* 221). Plots carry their own logic and, perhaps, their own future, that is, "the future inside the present, the little cartoon at the heart of events" (*L* 46). This can be explained not only by the fact that all lives tend in exactly the same direction, or that a sort of death drive seems to be inherent to all lives, or that all the things we do and all the schemes we produce seem to facilitate this drive, or that, as we all know, guns introduced in the first act always have to go off by the last, but by the fact that in contrabanded narratives one of the bands is *already there*, already at the death point, the omega point, just waiting for the other band to catch up.

We find the same notion in *White Noise*—only with an extended definition of *plot*: "All plots tend to move deathward. This is the nature of plots. Political plots, terrorist plots, lovers' plots, narrative plots, plots that are part of children's games. We edge nearer death every time we plot" (*WN* 26; see *WN* 199). Michael in *Valparaiso*, who *tries* to commit suicide by strangulation in an airplane bathroom (what a way to go!), is a good case in point, at once actor in and narrator of his own little plot: "I realized I was improvising a journey that had its own stone logic. Meant to end one way only…. In an airline toilet. With my shitmost self" (*V* 98). All plots move deathward, then, toward the inorganic, the omega point, or some "tightly confined space"—like a coffin or the can.

7

Counterworlds

Space

It's the size of things that worries people. No reason for the universe to be so large. It contains more space than I deem absolutely necessary. More time as well.

RS 193

I walked randomly for a time, seeing a woman open a door and enter whatever kind of space was situated there.

ZK 121

All the amazement that's left in the world is microscopic. But I can live with that. What scares me is have they thought it through completely?

WN 161

Yes, it's true that geography has moved inward and smallward. But we still have mass graves, I think.

U 788

Just as DeLillo's characters at one point or another try to pare things down to the minimum, to the basic elements of living, so DeLillo breaks down writing to its most minimal elements, to its two most basic parameters: space and time. For while it is easy to forget, with all the plots and characters and intrigue getting in the way, that everything takes place in space and time, DeLillo is always there to remind us of these basic parameters. After DeLillo as a writer of plots, as a thinker of history, war, ruin, the apocalypse, and so on, after the cosmopolitical and, often, comic DeLillo, there is the cosmic DeLillo, a thinker and writer of space and time on macro- and micro-levels and on all the contrabanded levels in-between.

And so for all his writing about travel and movement, coast to coast, east to west, and West to East, DeLillo is par excellence a thinker and writer of rooms—and of all the little lifetimes that transpire within them. He is a writer of space, to be sure, but it is almost always a space that has been worked, inhabited, configured. Sure there is the desert, but we usually move pretty quickly—in contraband, precisely—from the desert to the city or the village, and then to the chamber, the cell, the room. Because almost everything happens, in the end, in a room. There are entire novels that take place in large measure in a room, apartment, or house, like *Great Jones Street* (see *GJ* 90) or *The Body Artist*, places where one can live, as Jeffrey in *Zero K* says of his time in the Convergence, an "extreme sublifetime" (*ZK* 153).

The room is the place where things take place, but it is also the place where they are narrated, made sense of. In *Libra*, Branch's room, a writer's room, the room of the man trying to make sense of the entire Kennedy assassination, is described as "the room of dreams, the room where it has taken him all these years to learn that his subject is not politics or violent crime but men in small rooms" (*L* 181); it is "the room of theories, the room of growing old" (*L* 59), "the room of history and dreams" (*L* 445), "the room of lonely facts" (*L* 378). It is a writer's room, the connection between Branch and the writer being reinforced by an association to Joyce that Branch himself—a retired CIA agent—entertains as he tries to find a proper analogy for the twenty-six volumes of the Warren Report: "Branch thinks this is the megaton novel James Joyce would have written if he'd moved to Iowa City and lived to be a hundred.... This is the Joycean Book of America... the novel in which nothing is left out" (*L* 181–2).

As DeLillo suggests in several places, there are only two places in the world, where we are and the place, whether inside or outside, that is other to that place. We often take this for granted until something like an earthquake shakes us out of our complacency and we recognize that "everything in the world is either inside or outside" ("IA" 71; see 57, *EZ* 230, *N* 269, *C* 182, *BA* 48, *ZK* 3). And when something is inside it is usually in a room—a point that is so obvious we are liable to forget it, liable to forget that "The purpose of a room derives from the special nature of a room. A room is inside" (*WN* 306). DeLillo is thus a writer of rooms like Keith in *Falling Man* is a denizen of poker halls; both spend some time elsewhere, but they find themselves more inside than out. When Keith sees Las Vegas from afar, "He wondered why he'd never thought of himself in the middle of such a thing, living there more or less. He lived in rooms, that's why. He lived and worked in this room and that" (*FM* 226–7).

It is not so surprising that DeLillo's plays would place such an emphasis on place, and particularly on the room: the first act of *Valparaiso* takes place in the "living room of the Majeski house" (*V* 11), "a man and woman in a walled space" (*V* 46; see 57). *The Day Room*, of course, as its name suggests, takes place essentially in a room, a hospital room, while *Love-Lies-Bleeding* takes place in a series of rooms, not the least of which is the room in which

Alex is to be eased into death by his son, leaving unfinished a final art project that consists simply of "A room, a cube," that is, "A chamber, a cubical room. Fashioned out of solid rock.... A large empty room.... A bare room without a signature" (*LL* 59, 61). Lia latter says of the room in which Alex lay dying: "We're in a room, hidden away from all that sky and light, and this is where everything is.... Everything that matters is pressed between these walls" (*LL* 90).

It is not surprising that DeLillo would concentrate so closely on the room in theater. More surprising perhaps is the amount of space his novels devote to rooms or confined spaces, which can be either familiar and comforting or else, more often than not, rather threatening. In "Baader-Meinhof," we follow a couple who has just met in an art gallery to a restaurant and then back to the woman's apartment, where the space further contracts and things get scary, the woman having to lock herself up in her own bathroom until the acquaintance/intruder leaves (see also "S" 183, *P* 24, 138).

As a writer of rooms, of the world boiled down to a single room, DeLillo could obviously not but be interested in prison, in the prison experience, and, especially, in the phenomenon of solitary confinement, those "special punishment facilities called the hole, the box, the cage—names with a vivid history familiar from the movies" (*L* 95; see 99, *N* 290–1). There is, for example, the room of the hostage in Beirut in *Mao II*, and, elsewhere, the room of the POW, the room of the torture victim. Richard Elster would end up writing an article entitled "Renditions"—an analysis of the word *renditions* in light of those extraordinary renditions after 9-11 that placed people for a long, indefinite time in one very small room where everything happens:

> Within those walls, somewhere, in seclusion, a drama is being enacted, old as human memory, he wrote, actors naked, chained, blindfolded, other actors with props of intimidation, the renderers, nameless and masked.
>
> (*PO* 34)

Beyond its social and political significance, prison—the prison cell—teaches us the very meaning of being in an enclosed space and, in a sense, the very meaning of being in the world: "They took him back to the cell.... A cell is the basic state, the crude truth of the world" (*L* 418). "Men in small rooms, in isolation. A cell is the basic state. They put you in a room and lock the door. So simple it's a form of genius. This is the final size of all the forces around you. Eight by fifteen" (*L* 196). And, of course, to return to what we looked at just above, such small rooms are practically designed to push one over the edge: "In prison there's nothing that can't drive a person to self-destruction. This is the purpose of jails" (*P* 181).

On the one hand, then, the prison is a unique space, uniquely designed and lived; on the other hand, it is continuous with all other enclosed spaces: the room, the home, the basement, the underworld, even the world if you want to look at it that way. When Oswald is arrested in Dallas, he finds himself in a room, a cell, the kind of room he had dreamed of all his life: "The cell was the same room he'd known all his life.... There was strength for him here. Everything about this place and situation was set up to make him stronger" (*L* 426). In that holding cell after the assassination, Oswald thinks of the fame he has already achieved and the fame that still awaits him, his image leaking out of the cell and spreading out into the world: "The more time he spent in a cell, the stronger he would get. Everybody knew who he was now. This charged him with strength" (*L* 435; see "HS" 157). In short, prison changes you—like a religion: "Maybe the brig was a kind of religion too. All prison. Something you carried with you all your life, a counterforce to politics and lies.... It carried a truth no one could contradict" (*L* 100–1). The truth of prison that no one can contradict has to do with this supreme control over and knowledge of space, whether on the part of those incarcerating or those being incarcerated. It is space in its purest form, though at some point the inevitable question will get asked, "how much time did you get?" and the second of Kant's two pure forms of sensible intuition will enter in.

Time

Digital clocks, he felt, told time too bluntly…. But it was more than that. Digital clocks took the "space" out of time.

RS 384

I watched the numbers change, the progression of digital minutes, odd to even. They glowed green in the dark.

WN 224

How deep is time? How far down into the life of matter do we have to go before we understand what time is?

U 222

There is nothing but time. Time is the only thing that happens of itself. We should learn to let it take us along. The Collier woman is a fool.

A 196

There is a certain narrative about time in DeLillo's novels, and it goes something like this: we begin without time, or at least without time in the usual sense, that is, in childhood, and the end of childhood coincides with our awareness of and our insertion into another kind of time, a time of before and after, the kind that makes narrative possible. It is not necessarily the case that there is no time without human narrative but there are no human narratives, no humans strictly speaking, without time. As someone asks in *Zero K*, "How human are you without your sense of time?" (*ZK* 68). It is a narrative about time that is thus inseparable from the time of narrative, which is why time is so central to the novel.

The first time, then, the time without regular time, is the time of childhood:

> Children find a way. They sidestep time, as it were, and the ravages of progress. I think they operate in another time scheme altogether.... Time as we know it now had not yet come into being.
>
> (*U* 673)

In other words, the time that is measured, that is "the agent of our particular ruin" (*WN* 177), begins sometime after childhood. Before this, events are lived and then easily forgotten—or so it seems:

> I liked being with Wilder. The world was a series of fleeting gratifications. He took what he could, then immediately forgot it in the rush of a subsequent pleasure. It was this forgetfulness I envied and admired.
>
> (*WN* 170)

In short, "the child is yet to grow into the deep shadow of his own memories" (*FM* 218).

But then there is the time that we ourselves are complicit in making happen and that ends up taking us down. That is adult time, grown-up time, the time we all grow into. Here are Albert Bronzini's meditations on the subject—complete with a reference to that other Albert who knew a thing or two about time and who will return in *The Silence*:

> We eventually succumb to time, it's true, but time depends on us. We carry it in our muscles and genes, pass it on to the next set of time-factoring creatures, our brown-eyed daughters and jug-eared sons, or how would the world keep going.... He thought that we were the only crucial clocks, our minds and bodies, way stations for the distribution of time. Think about it, Einstein, my fellow Albert.
>
> (*U* 235)

This time of our everyday lives can go more or less quickly, and pass more or less unnoticed. It's a lived human time, but it can look in retrospect like the time of books:

> Seasons ran together, the years were a stunned blur. Like time in books. Time passes in books in the span of a sentence, many months and years. Write a word, leap a decade. Not so different out here, at his age, in the unmargined world.
>
> (*U* 236)

It takes something like an event, then, as we have seen and will see again, to break the regular sequence of this time. It can be a joyful event, a moment of ecstasy, or else a catastrophe—like 9-11—an event, a time, that marks a rupture, a before and an after: September 11, 2001. As the narrator says, "Everything now is measured by after" (*FM* 137-8). People like Lianne thus need to do their best to give a sequence to these "after-days," to reestablish a sense of time that was lost, which is why "she wanted to stay focused, one thing following sensibly upon another" (*FM* 127).

It is only in extreme states, then, that yet another sense of time appears to adults. For example, to the hostage in Beirut in *Mao II*, confined to a basement room, knowing nothing of what awaited him in the long or short term, "Time became peculiar, the original thing that is always there" (*M* 107). While time typically falls into the background, there in that basement room it "permeated the air and food" (*M* 107; see 110). When the hostage "spat up blood he watched the pink thing slug into the drain and it carried time quivering in it" (*M* 107). In such an extreme case, "time and pain became inseparable" (*M* 108). The description there goes on for pages, as if it were a test of survival not just for the hostage but for the narrator, for Bill Gray. Here, for example, is a sentence that itself moves insect-like, inching ever forward while doubling back on itself: "Time moved tormentingly, carried by insects, all-knowing, if we can say it moves, if we can call it time" (*M* 202; see 107-10, 160-1, 204, and *BA* 7). As Omar says earlier in *Mao II*, "The littler the shithole, the more it takes up your life" (*M* 152).

But the desert can do it too—though differently. The most enclosed spaces and the most open ones can change our sense and experience of time. Richard Elster says in *Point Omega*: "It's different here, time is enormous, that's what I feel here, palpably. Time that precedes us and survives us" (*PO* 44). "Time slows down when I'm here. Time becomes blind.... I never know if a minute has passed or an hour. I don't get old here" (*PO* 23-4; see 64). The time of the desert is thus itself "enormously old." It is "deep time, epochal time" (*PO* 72). James Axton in *The Names* gets a similar sense from the mountains in southern Greece: "The mountains here contained a sense of time, geologic time. Rounded, colorless, unwooded. They lay in embryo, a process unfolding, or a shriveled dying perhaps. They had the look of naked events" (*N* 180). There is clock time, then, one form of human time, and then a time that seems to belong to the elements—the desert, the mountains, the earth, the universe. Benno Levin says in *Cosmopolis*: "I don't own a watch or clock. I think of time in other totalities now. I think of my personal timespan set against the vast numerations, the time of the earth, the stars, the incoherent light-years, the age of the universe, etc." (*C* 59–60). It's a little pretentious and he is perhaps providing just a little bit too much context to justify his need to kill Eric Packer, but his point still stands.

Mr. Tuttle of *The Body Artist* is like an experiment unto himself in altered time, perhaps one that has gone astray, perhaps one that successfully teaches us what something is through its withdrawal. Originally nameless and so named by Lauren herself (see *BA* 120), he is the name of someone who lives in a time without name: "His future is unnamed. It is simultaneous, somehow, with the present" (*BA* 77). For Mr. Tuttle seems to lack "the time cues," the "grades of emphasis," the tempo, pauses, and gestures that make sustained conversation possible (*BA* 65–6). "He didn't know how to measure himself to what we call the Now" (*BA* 66–7). He says, for example:

> Being here has come to me. I am with the moment, I will leave the moment. Chair, table, wall, hall, all for the moment, in the moment. It has come to me. Here and near. From the moment I am gone, am left, am leaving. I will leave the moment from the moment.
>
> (*BA* 74)

Lauren thus begins to wonder whether Mr. Tuttle even experiences time, or whether it's another kind of time that he experiences, one that is "unoccurring":

> Time is supposed to pass, she thought. But maybe he is living in another state. It is a kind of time that is simply and overwhelmingly there, laid out, unoccurring, and he lacks the inborn ability to reconceive this condition.
>
> (*BA* 77)

It seems that Mr. Tuttle exists in a time that is without any "reassuring sequence, passing, flowing, happening… with names and dates and distinctions" (*BA* 77; 83, 91). He still lives in time, perhaps, but in a time that is not Lauren's. "Alone and unable to improvise" (*BA* 90), unable to "distinguish one part from another, this from that, now from then," unable to make "arbitrary divisions" (*BA* 91), he seems fully exposed to time if not undone by it: "He was scared.... Here he was in the howl of the world. This was the howling face, the stark, the not-as-if of things" (*BA* 90). Without the everyday categories of understanding that give sequence and meaning to events, he lives in something close to what William James called that "booming, buzzing confusion."

The Body Artist tries to rethink, perhaps unlike any other DeLillo novel, the relationship between time and narrative, the sense of a before and an after, of a minimal temporal span that allows identities to be formed and recognized. Insofar as Mr. Tuttle seems not to experience time as others do, he disrupts this notion of identity and thus of narrative. Lauren suspects that he lives "in a kind of time that had no narrative quality" (*BA* 65). The novel thus works through a kind of time in which the narrative quality is, though not completely missing, fractured and distributed in non-linear, intricately contrabanded ways. As a result, it is difficult if not impossible to distinguish between what is being narrated in the present and what is memory, what is live and what is not, what is Rey or Lauren and what is Mr. Tuttle.

Without time to give order and sequence, Mr. Tuttle seems not so much to drift or float but, precisely, to "seep" from one time to the next, unable to organize himself or the world into a coherent narrative (*BA* 92). *The Body Artist* is thus a narrative about a character who, in being outside of time—or else purely within time—seems to lack the possibility of narrative.

> Time is the only narrative that matters. It stretches events and makes it possible for us to suffer and come out of it and see death happen and come out of it. But not for him. He is another structure, another culture, where time is something like itself, sheer and bare, empty of shelter.
>
> (*BA* 92)

Whether wholly without time or awash in it, Mr. Tuttle seems to lack the minimal requirements for such narrative. He lacks all the tenses—or at least the tenses in their proper order. And it is because he is unable to experience time as usual that he is unable to use or to have language as usual. Lauren cannot help but think that Mr. Tuttle is an escapee from some institution, that there is "something psychotic about him," that there is something wrong with him (*BA* 97), just as Jeffrey at the end of *Zero K* will think that the young boy shouting in wonder at the setting sun may be abnormal in some way. And yet it is just this contrabanded temporality that allows one to become, like Mr. Tuttle, someone "who remembers the future" (*BA* 100). Through a whole series of future anterior constructions, we are able to remember, in the present, what will have been, memories—perceptions—of Rey in the house, of

Rey the dead husband, there and yet not there (*BA* 122–3). It gives one access to the time of a future anterior where the past is no longer simply past and the future has already come: "They will already have slept and wakened and gone down to breakfast, where they muddle through their separate routines, pouring the milk and shaking the juice" (*BA* 123). It is as if Mr. Tuttle were living in the Nyodene-contaminated world of *White Noise* (*WN* 125-6), the main symptom of which (or the false symptom of which—whatever a false symptom may be) is déjà vu, that is, "visions of the future," "precognitions" that cannot be fit "into our system of consciousness as it is now structured" (*WN* 151). Mr. Tuttle lives, in short, in a world where time bands overlap.

A being who blurs differences, Mr. Tuttle "violates the limits of the human" (*BA* 100). He is at once child and adult, male and female, human and animal (Lauren wonders whether he sees what the blue jays see (*BA* 50)), human and machine (a sort of living tape recorder), a human being and "a piece of found art" (*BA* 81), a kind of readymade. He is thus either a great exception to the laws of time or else—perhaps the same thing but different—someone able to perceive and live for a time in a time that we all somehow experience or undergo without knowing it. Lauren thinks: "Maybe there are times when we slide into another reality but can't remember it, can't concede the truth of it because this would be too devastating to absorb" (*BA* 114).

Mr. Tuttle is like an older version of several different misshapen or malformed children in DeLillo's work, from the kid who lives in the same building as Bucky Wunderlick on Great Jones Street, a kid who, according to his mother, "don't have a name" (*GJ* 134; see 161), to a young boy in the Convergence, "head turned left, eyes swiveling up and to the right, where I was standing... thinking his way into my presence here" (*ZK* 94). But Mr. Tuttle, perhaps better than any of these others, teaches us this fundamental truth, expressed here in the words of Artis in the Convergence: "Time. I feel it in me everywhere. But I don't know what it is" (*ZK* 157). In the end, Artis comes to learn what Lauren has learned from Mr. Tuttle: "What did she know? Nothing. This is the rule of time. It is the thing you know nothing about" (*BA* 99). Nothing except this, from "The Ivory Acrobat," a story about an earthquake in Athens: "The pitiless thing [is] time" ("IA" 69).

Space-Time

I approached a young man, a stocky fellow with a mailman's cap and beer belly, wearing a down vest, and he looked at me as if I didn't belong in his space-time dimension but had crossed over illegally, made a rude incursion.
WN 90

> *It was not a street anymore but a world, a time and space of falling ash and near night.*
>
> *FM* 3

> *In my room I wrote a long hysterical letter on the subject of space-time.*
>
> *EZ* 207

Finally, after space and time, and in anticipation of *The Silence*, we come to space-time. It's a pretty heady subject, far "outside my range," to cite *Point Omega* (*PO* 20), so let me simply string together a few citations in time and space in order to try to make a little sense of the sense DeLillo makes of it.

It is the physicist Mohole in *Ratner's Star* who gets us started on understanding what started it all: "Except for the first one thousandth of a second, we can trace the evolution of the universe from the big bang to the present moment" (*RS* 180). Assuming that's true, or at least coherent, what can be said about the universe after that point? Well, there is speculation about the universe expanding and then contracting, only to start up again, or perhaps not, and then speculation about the nature of a mohole (*RS* 181–2, 185), which "has little or nothing in common with a black hole" since "a mohole is part of the innate texture of space" (*RS* 357; see 410). But all this seems to require "an alternative to space and time" (*RS* 102, 355), "a fundamental reconstruction of our ideas about space and time, or space-time, or space-time sylphed" (*RS* 49). For example, "Time and space will be replaced by the nameless dimension of the whirl. They will be purified, if you will. Pure time. Pure space" (*RS* 106; see 109). The whirl: it is as if science fiction or advanced scientific research had brought us back to the beginnings of Western philosophy, to Democritus or Empedocles in dialogue with Heraclitus. It is as if the further we advance the deeper we end up digging into our ancient past. And that is perhaps one of the lessons of a "Mohole" (of a mole hole in space, like *rats* in *stars*). And if all this sounds a little too science-fictiony for DeLillo, then it is worth recalling that Project Mohole was a real thing (taking its name from Croatian Seismologist Andrija Mohorovicic), a serious scientific project undertaken between 1952 and 1964 by a number of leading scientists acting under the aegis of the American Miscellaneous Society. The goal of the project was to counter or to complement the efforts to explore space by drilling into the earth so as to discover the properties of so-called Moho discontinuity between the earth's crust and mantle. So whereas NASA went up into space, the idea behind Project Mohole was to dig down into the earth, a mirror image, as it were, of the two parts of *Ratner's Star* we spoke of in the preface to this work, "Adventures: Field Experiment Number One" and "Reflections: Logicon Project Minus-One," the two parts of the novel themselves mirroring the structure of the research facility in which most of the novel takes place, an enormous cycloid above ground that is mirrored by a subterranean cycloid of the same size below, in other words, "Same shape upside down" (*RS* 282), a shape that then determines both the space and the time of the novel, the fact that the further we go up the further we must go down, as we learn that those radio signals that seemed to be coming to us from out of the future near Ratner's Star were actually produced by an ancient, terrestrial civilization.

So, it's science fiction, though the fiction is informed by science and the science all by itself sounds more and more like fiction. And it provides us with an understanding of the universe that is perhaps similar to the one expressed, albeit in rather different language, by Ratner in his parting words to little Billy Twillig: "The universe is the name of G-dash-d. All of us. Everything. Here, there, everywhere. Time and space. The whole universe. It all adds up to the true name of G-dash-d" (*RS* 230). The question that is asked earlier in the novel echoes here and throughout, "Are we dealing with physics or metaphysics?" (*RS* 49). But it seems that we are being asked to refrain from seeing these as mutually exclusive. Science, fiction, physics, metaphysics— Ratner's words to Billy Twillig seem to suggest that we should probably throw religion into the mix as well.

Religion

I've been doing a lot of reading. I was never much for religion but there's something there.

A 86

"He is everywhere," I said. "Who?" "Supreme being of heaven and earth. Three letters."

EZ 8

"If the man upstairs wants it that way, that's good enough for me. He has his reasons."
"Is the man upstairs supposed to be synonymous with God or what? Because either way it's an outmoded concept."

EZ 97–8

We lost our manhood, our sense of pride and honor, our belief in God and Dick Nixon, our deepest dreams, hopes and ambitions. It's no coincidence that God died in the late sixties, early seventies.

AZ 207

When it comes to last things, to the themes of life, death, time, the afterlife, the end of the world, and what have you, it is impossible not to want to turn to religion—or at least to religion in DeLillo. For DeLillo always treats religion with a mixture of genuine reverence and healthy skepticism, honest admiration and good-hearted fun, a double-banded treatment, as we have come to suspect, that always plays one band off another, religious dogmas and established religions, with all the opportunities they offer for amusement, and the possibility of another kind of faith, a faith not in God, exactly, but in the human, or, more precisely, as we will see, in human language, which may itself come from God.

On the one hand, then, DeLillo's characters are inveterate skeptics. Jack Gladney says to one of his x-wives and the mother of Heinrich, Janet Savory, now Mother Devi, living on an ashram in Montana: "If Heinrich wants to visit you this summer, it's all right with me. Let him ride horses, fish for trout. But I don't want him getting involved in something personal and intense, like religion" (*WN* 273). Many of DeLillo's characters share this skepticism for religion, whether organized or not. But they all also seem to share an interest in it and in the fundamental questions it poses. Here, for example, is James Axton in *The Names*, thinking of how he might answer his nine-year-old son's questions on the topic:

> We were doubters, I might have told him. Skeptics of the slightly superior type.... The quasi-stellar object, the quantum event, these were the sources of our speculation and wonder. Our bones were made of material that came swimming across the galaxy from exploded stars. This knowledge was our shared prayer, our chant. The grim inexplicable was there, the god-mass looming.
>
> (*N* 92)

It's a theme or an attitude that runs throughout the work. When Axton asks his boss, George Rowser, who has just said he could spend hours in a mosque, "Are you religious?" George responds, "Get away from me. I like the awe, that's all" (*N* 45). Later, the same James Axton walks by all the shops in the Plaka in Athens "full of religious souvenirs, rows of mass-produced objects" and thinks: "It was all a reproach to my ardent skepticism. It crowded me, it pressed and shoved. So I tended to look with a small ironic measure of appreciation at the trashy objects in the shop windows" (*N* 146). Bill Gray in *Mao II* thinks something similar as he walks through the same Plaka and sees "votive tokens" to particular saints for every imaginable form of cancer (*M* 168). And here is how Lianne in *Falling Man* initially thought of religion:

> Lianne struggled with the idea of God. She was taught to believe that religion makes people compliant. This is the purpose of religion, to

return people to a childlike state. Awe and submission, her mother said. This is why religion speaks so powerfully in laws, rituals and punishments.... We want to transcend, we want to pass beyond the limits of safe understanding, and what better way to do it than through make-believe.

(*FM* 62–3; see 232–4)

How can you believe when your own mother calls it "make-believe"? And yet Lianne herself also wanted "to snuff out the pulse of the shaky faith she'd held for much of her life" (*FM* 65). She seems to see that there is a power and a danger in both belief and nonbelief (see *FM* 235). There is the same or a similar view in *Amazons*, a respect for religious beliefs and the religious people who hold them and yet always just enough of an ironic distance to suggest that the speaker or the narrator would never be one of those true believers, even when they are doing all the right things and with the purest of intentions: "After I unpacked the box, I always put Baby Jesus in the manger first, to get the most important out of the way so I could relax a little" (*AZ* 294).

This religious skepticism—or this belief in skepticism—goes way back in DeLillo. David Bell in *Americana* tells us that in his prep school, St. Dymphna ("Patroness of Those Afflicted with Nervous Disorders and Mental Illness. 'The Nervous Breakdown Saint'" (*A* 156)), "the student body was composed almost wholly of cynical little anti-religious boys" (*A* 155). There were, however, some exceptions, like the Irish Catholic kid with "an early-Christian lust for martyrdom," who attracted other kids to "meet illegally in his room after lights-out to hear him discourse on the transubstantiation and papal infallibility" (*A* 156) or "to engage in a fiery conversation about science, religion and eternity" (*A* 157). It's pretty clear that our narrator could be counted among those cynical or at least skeptical anti-religious boys at St. Dymphna prep, and that this early skepticism about Catholicism laid the foundation for a more ecumenical skepticism later in the novel:

On Sundays, in the wide rows of light, it's as though all the torpor of Christianity itself is spread over all the land. In the blaze of those moments, men in tight collars and the neat white shoes of little girls on the steps of churches, one feels all the silence of Luther, of Baptist picnics, divinity students playing softball, popes on their chamber pots, scary Methodists driving jalopies over cliffs; of teen-age Jehovah girls handing out leaflets, of Greek archbishops, revivalists fondling snakes in the Great Smokies, Calvinists blowing bagpipes, Gideon bibles turning yellow all over Missouri. All these, in a river of silence, remember to rest on the seventh day.

(*A* 179)

There are organized churches, impromptu churches, and then—a leitmotif of *Underworld*—preachers out there in the wild or on the street, a man who "stands on the corner preaching to the wind" (*U* 350), talking about the coming of the end of the world.

There is both reverence and skepticism, then, both seriousness and humor, in all of DeLillo's treatments of "the world's great religions." While claims to offering a glorious afterlife are typically scoffed off, other benefits of organized religion or of religious education are not. There's good grammar, for instance, taught by Sister Edgar in *Underworld* as a series of riders, as it were, to the ten commandments: "Never end a sentence with a preposition and never begin a sentence with an And" (*U* 729), "transitive verbs, *i* before *e* except after *c*" ("AE" 81). She is saying to them, in short, "if you let me teach you not to end a sentence with a preposition, ... I will save your life" ("AE" 82; see *U* 244). Already in *Players* we get a similar lesson, both about grammar and how to save your life: "Never end a sentence with a preposition. That's the other thing I learned when I was with the Marists. They're a teaching order. Those were the two things they taught us. Chastity and how to end sentences. Which one did me less good I bet you can guess" (*P* 46).

Now there is, of course, a dogmatic or doctrinal version of this rote learning; it's called the Baltimore Catechism, "True or false, yes or no, fill in the blanks" (*U* 244): "Who made us? God made us. Those clear-eyed faces so believing. Who is God? God is the Supreme Being who made all things" (*U* 815; "AE" 91). "It had all the questions and all the answers and it had love, hate, damnation and washing other people's feet" (*U* 716). It's the type of education that marks you for life. Matt Shay, for example, out west working in a weapons research facility, would think of "Sister Edgar in sixth grade talking about desert saints, pillar saints, stylites" (*U* 413; 449). Something similar happens in *Zero K*, as Jeffrey, the narrator, thinks many years later of his mother, and then of an Ash Wednesday from his childhood: "A little ash, at minimum expense, and a Wednesday, here and there, she said, becomes something to remember" (*ZK* 16). Owen Brademas in *The Names*, albeit a very different character, reacts in a similar way to having been exiled from his religious roots in the United States, which are Protestant, this time, indeed Pentecostal. After wandering among Jains, Muslims, Sikhs, and Buddhists, Brademas finally begins to think of himself again, fundamentally, as *Christian*: "How strange it sounded. And how curiously strong a word it seemed, after all these years, to be applied to himself, full of doleful comfort" (*N* 281). Of course there are different kinds of Protestants and different ways to wear your Protestantism. Tweedy Browner, another of Jack Gladney's former wives, provides a good counter-example: "She wore a Shetland sweater, tweed skirt, knee socks and penny loafers. There was a sense of Protestant disrepair about her" (*WN* 86).

But a special paragraph has to be reserved here, perhaps not surprisingly, for Jesuits. Here is how J. Kinnear, domestic terrorist, answers a tough question in *Players* (it doesn't really matter which one): "I don't confirm, I don't deny. Yes and no, but don't quote me on that. I'm a little bit of a Jesuit ... Jebbies know how to play position. They don't leave you with a good shot" (*P* 115). Theology and basketball: the Jesuits are often good at both. We recall that Nick Shay, a public school kid, ends up getting sent to the Jesuits, "at the wintry end of the world, somewhere near a lake in Minnesota" (*U* 512; see 88), after his crime, and when he returns "his brother Matty would call him 'the Jesuit'" (*U* 450). That's because what Nick gets from the Jesuits is much less doctrine or religion than a certain seriousness: "One of the things we want to do here is to produce serious men.... Someone, in the end, who develops a certain depth, a spacious quality, say, that's a form of respect for other ways of thinking and believing" (*U* 538). Already back in *Americana* the pedagogical prowess of the order of Saint Ignatius is celebrated: "Educated by Jesuits for eight years, Warren was able to regard his money, his notoriety, his four ex-wives with a combination of dispassionate wit, profound distress and a monumental Thomistic sense of the divine logic behind it all" (*A* 95). There's a similar encomium of the Jebbies in *Players*, this time of "another Fordham or Marquette lad. Studied languages and history. Played intermural sports. Revered the Jesuits for their sophistication and analytical skills. Voted for moderates of either party. Knows how to strangle a German shepherd with rosary beads" (*P* 130).

Besides all these Christian religions, there are little glimpses of Judaism, Jack Ruby in *Libra*, for example, or, in *End Zone*, Anatole Bloomberg, the three hundred pound football player who wants to un-jew himself (*EZ* 47), beginning with his name, "its Europicity," because he didn't like the way it "smelled": "It was like a hallway in a tenement where a lot of Bulgarians live" (*EZ* 187). Though he's attending Logos College, he is not unjewing himself in order to Christianize himself: "I reject the wrathful God of the Hebrews. I reject the Christian God of love and money, although I don't reject love or money itself" (*EZ* 77). He cuts a strange figure, overweight and yet somehow reminiscent of Socrates in the painting by Jacques-Louis David: he "appeared mad, an imprisoned prophet or a figure in a very old painting, a man about to die, his last word spoken to a finger tip of light" (*EZ* 77–8).

In *The Names* there is talk of Yezidis and Muslims (*N* 295) and, of course, in *Falling Man* there are multiple references to Islam, to people in New York City after 9-11 suddenly "reading the Koran.... *This Book is not to be doubted*" (*FM* 231). These great monotheisms are, however, just the beginning of a long list of religions or religious movements in DeLillo. Just in *Americana* there's everything from "Zoroastrians, Zen cowboys, soothsayers and the like" (*A* 47) to those Eastern theologies where "all the minor deities have the same name as the big guy" (*A* 52). Elsewhere, there are references to the *Upanishads* (*GJ* 9), to doctrines of "non-attachment," to the body as "an illusion" (*GJ* 237; see 6), to "pure mystery" (*PO* 83), aspirations "to total emptiness" (*ZK* 89), and so on. There is also Zen, if anyone wants to call it a religion, from an enlightened teenage grocery bagger in *White Noise* who "*sees* the items arranged in the bag before he touches a thing" (*WN* 281), to kids on the Lower East Side throwing bottles from rooftops in *Players*:

> "Who's the target, I wonder."
> "The bottle is the target. They're breaking the bottle."
> "That's Zen."
>
> (*P* 144; see AZ 241)

There are also, of course, cults—as distinct from religions, though there may be more than just a bit of overlap (see *M* 9)—as in *Mao II*, for example, where the Reverend Moon, "a man who lived in a hut made of U.S. Army ration tins," had "come to lead them to the end of human history" (*M* 6). "He is the messianic secret," the answer, it seems, to the question: "when the Old God leaves the world, what happens to all the unexpended faith?" (*M* 7). As the narrator says in the opening scene of the novel depicting the mass-marriage in Yankee Stadium: "He answers their yearning, unburdens them of free will and independent thought. See how happy they look" (*M* 7). The narrator, who is sitting in the stands, as it were, with the families and on-lookers, is obviously on the side of the skeptics and unbelievers, but he is able to get far enough into the skin of the converted to imagine what they must be thinking: "They're all around us, parents in the thousands, afraid of our intensity. This is what frightens them. We really believe. They bring us up to believe but when we show them true belief they call out psychiatrists and police" (*M* 8). And what really drives the parents crazy is "that our true father is a foreigner and nonwhite" (*M* 9).

But here's where the contraband comes in, the contrast between the religious message or the messianism and its daily practice. There is, first, the power of an individual faith supported by crowds and chants:

> His voice leads them out past love and joy... past miracles and surrendered self. There is something in the chant, the fact of chanting, the being-one, that transports them with its power.... He leads them out past religion and history, thousands weeping now, all arms high. They are gripped by the force of a longing.... The chant brings the End Time closer. The chant is the End Time.
>
> (*M* 15–16)

There's the oneness of the crowd, as we have already seen, thousands sharing the same "unconditional belief" that "the messiah is here on earth" (*M* 69). But then there is the question of just how this End Time is being financed. Karen, for example—married by the Reverend Moon in Yankee Stadium—travels the US selling carnations in decrepit American downtowns (*M* 12). That's why she needs saving and deprogramming, even if this will sound like a rerun of the original programming: "They forced her to agree that he church had made a drone of her. She chanted, Made me a drone, Made me a drone" (*M* 82).

In DeLillo's work the contraband voice of radio or TV can be replaced, and often is replaced, and to good effect, by memory. That is what's known as indoctrination, or simply doctrine, depending upon your perspective. Here is Karen evangelizing in Tompkins Square Park, no longer traveling with the Moonies but still obviously carrying their water: "We will all be a single family soon. Because the day is coming…. She had Master's total voice ready in her head" (*M* 193–4).

It is thus a very short step from Moon to Mao. Though the former has a religious message about the end of the world and the latter teaches only about transforming this world, they move masses by means of the same internal contraband: "Incantations. People chanting formulas and slogans," "The Little Red Book of Quotations" (*M* 162). That is how Mao became "the history of China written on the masses. And his words became immortal. Studied, repeated, memorized by an entire nation" (*M* 161). The story of Mao is the story of how a single story can become internalized by countless others, the narrative of a single individual that of an entire people:

> This is the unchanged narrative every culture needs in order to survive. In China the narrative belonged to Mao…. So the experience of Mao became… the living memory of hundreds of millions of people…. It was a call to unity, a summoning of crowds where everyone dressed alike and thought alike. Don't you see the beauty in this? Isn't there beauty and power in the repetition of certain words and phrases?
>
> (*M* 162)

Between religion and cult, or cult and political ideology, or ideology and brainwashing, the difference is often a little murky. The least one can do is try to keep the names straight—and not confuse, for example, Sun and Moon. Here is Jack in *White Noise* helping Orest Mercator to distinguish between the two:

"He's a Sunny Moslem," Orest said.
"Iron City has some Sunnies out near the airport."
"The Sunnies are mostly Korean. Except mine's an Arab, I think."

I said, "Don't you mean the Moonies are mostly Korean?"
"He's a Sunny," Orest said.
"But it's the Moonies who are mostly Korean. Except they're not, of course. It's only the leadership."

(*WN* 267)

There is, in addition to all this skepticism, a fervent atheism in some of DeLillo's characters, Oswald, for example, who proclaims his atheism on both sides of the Iron Curtain, his belief that "communism was the one true religion" (*L* 100). Here is his conversation with a KGB agent trying to understand his reasons for defecting to Russia:

"Do you believe, I wonder, in God?"
"No."
Smiling. "Not even a little? For my personal information?"
"I consider it total superstition. People build their lives around this falsehood."

(*L* 158)

Here he is back in the United States, being asked a similar question by David Ferrie:

"Do you practice a religion? Do you go to church?"
"I'm an atheist."
"That's dumb," Ferrie told him. "How could you be so stupid?"

(*L* 320)

It's a thought echoed by Bill Gray's literary agent in *Mao II*: "Only shallow people insist on disbelief. You and I know better. We understand how reality is invented" (*M* 132). And then there's this, after Oswald's arrest on November 22, 1963, in Dallas:

They asked him if he believed in a deity. He told them he was a Marxist.
But not a Marxist-Leninist.
It was pretty clear they didn't get the distinction.

(*L* 415)

Perhaps the most visible, daily manifestation of religion in all of DeLillo's novels is prayer, at once individual and collective. There's Lee Harvey Oswald at a lunch in Texas, learning that "Quakers say grace" and that "each person is supposed to recite a silent prayer," "although it was clear to Marina," Lee's wife, "that Lee's silence was not the prayerful kind" (*L* 389; see 298). There's the kind of prayer

Sister Edgar would recite (see "AE" 102), and then there's the kind one utters to end a vacation gone awry—"God, if you exist, please get me off this island" ("C" 11). There are daily prayers, such as "*verily*—the most familiar of everyday prayers" (*U* 237; see "HS" 150 and "AE" 73 for "amen"), and then there's the kind of prayer that accompanies a fingering of beads, like the woman in *Underworld* who was "saying her rosary in the basement room" when she "looked up from her beads and saw a saint standing in the doorway, Saint Anthony" (*U* 755), or Nick Shay's mother Rosemary—not far from Rosary—"doing her beadwork... her piecework. Sweaters, dresses and blouses" (*U* 676; see 696), a sort of secular prayer that has the added advantage of bringing in extra income.

Throughout *Falling Man* there are reflections on all the gestures and rituals, all the practices, of prayer, particularly in Islam: "Say the same prayers, word for word, in the same prayer stance, day and night, following the arc of sun and moon" (*FM* 68; see 77, 173). And then of course there is the sound of prayer, "men breathing in urgent rhythmic pattern, a liturgy of inhale-exhale... voices in recitation, women in devotional lament, mingled village voices behind hand drums and hand clasps" (*FM* 70), "songs of desert mystics in the hallway" (*FM* 217; see 93), "men in chanted prayer, voices in chorus in praise of God. *Allah-uu Allah-uu Allah-uu*" (*FM* 38; see 173, 175, 184). There is the sound of prayer everywhere in *Falling Man*, including a building's laundry room, with its two industrial-sized dryers turning like "a pair of giant prayer wheels beating out a litany" (*FM* 151; see *WN* 38, 288, *ZK* 87). In *Ratner's Star* there are also, in addition to long discourses on cults, names, totems and taboos (*RS* 38) and a mini-lecture on comparative religion (*RS* 386–7), many reflections on prayer: "True prayer is scientific. The answer to prayer is in the prayer when it is prayed" (*RS* 58; see 161). So it's either that or, in *Underworld*, something much more matter-of-fact: "Prayer is a practical strategy, the gaining of temporal advantage in the capital markets of Sin and Remission" (*U* 237). Whether aimed only at itself or at some material gain, prayer can be seen to be operating more or less everywhere in DeLillo. And for the truly nonreligious, there is always therapy, itself a sort of prayer with its rituals or repetitions, an effective but often more costly "countermeasure" to damage and suffering (*FM* 40):

> Even the program of exercises [Keith] did for his postsurgical wrist seemed a little detached, four times a day, an odd set of extensions and flexions that resembled prayer in some remote province, among a repressed people, with periodic applications of ice.
>
> (*FM* 59; see 235)

As we have had plenty of occasions to see already and as we will see again, DeLillo often compares everyday human reactions to religious experience.

Here, for example, are people in a crowded airport with too many passengers and not enough flights coming away from a ticket counter with boarding passes: they "seemed propelled by some deep saving force. A primitive baptism might have been in progress" ("C" 5). But the humor here is more at the expense of the passengers than religion. For religion is always more than a laughing matter in DeLillo's work, even though there are always a lot of laughs to be found there at religion's expense.

In the end, religious belief does not seem to be wholly incompatible with a certain skepticism or secularism. And belief or faith in any particular religion seems less important than belief itself, even if this latter can always be perverted or led astray (*WN* 27, "MD" 126, 131). This becomes clear in a long conversation between Jack Gladney and a nun in the hospital to which he has brought Mink and himself. When Jack insists that she must "believe in tradition. The old heaven and hell, the Latin mass. The Pope is infallible, God created the world in six days. The great old beliefs. Hell is burning lakes, winged demons" (*WN* 318), the nun counter-insists that these are really his beliefs, *Jack's* beliefs, and that, in the end, it is the nonbelievers who "need the believers. They are desperate to have someone believe," because "Hell is when no one believes" (*WN* 318). In other words, Jack is among those who, she says, "spend their lives believing that *we* still believe," and such belief in these old beliefs is necessary to everyone: "The devil, the angels, heaven, hell. If we did not pretend to believe these things, the world would collapse" (*WN* 318). There are thus those who believe in those who pretend to believe, and those who allow themselves to be believed in this way. And while this would seem to be an empty belief on all sides, that's not where the conversation ends: "Someone must appear to believe. Our lives are no less serious than if we professed real faith, real belief" (*WN* 319).

But Jack's truly "religious moment," if we can call it that, seems to happen not as a result of this theological discussion about faith but in what follows, in the nun's German words that Jack "failed to understand," "a storm of words" in which he "began to detect a cadence, a measured beat. She was reciting something, I decided. Litanies, hymns, catechisms. The mysteries of the rosary perhaps. Taunting me," he says, "with scornful prayer. / The odd thing is I found it beautiful" (*WN* 320). It is close to speaking in tongues.

Perhaps we can now understand DeLillo's emphasis on prayer; it is obvious but it nonetheless bears repeating: prayer is a thing of *language*. It may be accompanied—or not—by faith or belief, by a certain conception of God or the holy (*L* 15), but it is first of all an event of language. This helps explain why *The Names* revolves around a group of "monks," "secular monks," who "want to vault into eternity" (*N* 203; see 205) through language, through a cult of the alphabet, in short, through "lips moving to the endless name of God" (*N* 92). As we read later in the same novel, "It is religion that carries a language. The river of language is God" (*N* 152; see 181). There is thus belief attached to God, but then there is a faith or belief in language and the everyday, a belief in the world that God made for humans or that humans made for themselves: "Isn't it the world itself that brings you to God? Beauty, grief, terror, the empty desert, the Bach cantatas" (*FM* 234).

Belief and unbelief, belief *as* unbelief, and vice versa—that is perhaps one of the central lessons of *The Cloud of Unknowing*. Here is Nick Shay in *Underworld*:

> A long time ago, years ago, I read a book called *The Cloud of Unknowing*. Written by an anonymous mystic.... A priest gave me this book... it made me think of God as a force that withholds himself from us because this is the root of his power. I remember one sentence.... "Pause for a moment, you wretched weakling, and take stock of yourself."
>
> (*U* 295)

This is, of course, not the only cloud in DeLillo—one will recall the billowing cloud of the airborne toxic event in *White Noise*—and it is not even the only reference to the cloud of unknowing, for it too is in *White Noise*, a description of Wilder, the Wilder child: "A cloud of unknowing, an omnipotent little person" (*WN* 290). But in *Underworld* this cloud of unknowing becomes something like the ultimate secret, the ultimate promise or ultimate threat, that which makes all religions believable and, insofar as they profess any true knowledge, suspect. Here is Nick Shay, attending a conference on waste management in LA, confessing his most intimate secrets in a hotel room to a woman attending a swingers convention:

> And I read this book and began to think of God as a secret... This is what I respected about God. He keeps his secret.... Maybe we can know God through love or prayer or through visions or through LSD but we can't know him through the intellect.... We approach God through his unmadeness. We are made, created. God is unmade.... *The Cloud* recommends that we develop this intent around a single word.... I became preoccupied with this search for the one word, the one syllable. It was romantic. The mystery of God was romantic.
>
> (*U* 295–6)

Nick goes on to tell the woman from the swingers conference to whom he is confessing about his search for an appropriate prayer, an appropriate word "to penetrate the darkness," a word like *help*, for example, though he says he soon realized that he needed "to change languages," to "find a word that is pure word, without a lifetime of connotation and shading," and so he came upon the Italian word for help, "*Aiuto*," "a great and profound word," he says, but he couldn't use it (*U* 296). And that's when he came upon the prayer of St. John of the Cross:

> I knew I was right to abandon English. And finally I came upon a phrase that seemed alive with naked intent. Alive with something I knew and felt from my own experience. A beautiful spontaneous prayer. Five syllables but so what.... It came from another mystic, a Spaniard, John of the Cross, and for that one winter this phrase was my naked edge, my edging into darkness, into the secret of God. And I repeated it, repeated it, repeated it. *Todo y nada.*
>
> (*U* 296–7)

Todo y nada, everything and nothing—the ultimate contraband, not so much a contradiction in terms but a contrapuntal truth. It's everything and nothing, everywhere and nowhere.

On the last day of the conference on waste management, Nick and a colleague are walking through their Los Angeles headquarters when the colleague turns to Nick and asks "You believe in God?" "Yes, I think so," answers Nick. And the colleague responds. "We'll go to a ball game sometime" (*U* 303). A ball game, it seems, because it was there, decades earlier, in a stadium on the east coast, that Cotter Martin, a teenager from Harlem skipping school, came to see the true meaning of belief in the person of Bill Waterson who had not given up on his New York Giants even though they were trailing the Dodgers by three runs going into the ninth inning on that fateful day in the Polo Grounds in October 1951: "Cotter likes this man's singleness of purpose, his insistence on faith and trust. It's the only force available against the power of doubt" (*U* 31; see 42). A ball game because it was at the end of that same game on October 3, 1951, that Giants announcer Russ Hodges, after witnessing the everyday miracle of Bobby Thomson's game-winning homerun, came to express his most profound belief, that is, his utter disbelief, in a series of utterances worthy of a sixth-century negative theologian: "He shouts, 'I don't believe it.' He shouts, 'I don't believe it.' He shouts, 'I do *not* believe it'" (*U* 44; see 249, 417).

Miracles

The Giants didn't come from thirteen and a half games back just to blow it on the last day. This is a miracle year. Nobody has a vocabulary for what happened this year.

U 18

Miracles share the landscape with death.

N 285

Don DeLillo is, as we have seen, a writer of dangers and threats, disasters and catastrophes, apocalypse and ruin—everything from the Kennedy Assassination to 9-11 to the airborne toxic event to the threats of nuclear war. But he is also, and in these very same works, and usually near the end, in what can be taken as a moment of ultimate contraband, a writer of miracles, secular miracles, if that means anything, that is, a writer of events that somehow escape for one radiant moment all skepticism and doubt, all death and destruction.

There is, for example, in *White Noise* the "miracle" of Wilder, the Gladney toddler, crossing a highway on his tricycle, the same Wilder who, earlier in the novel, had returned transformed, beatified, from a seven-hour crying fit in his suburban desert: "They watched him with something like awe. Nearly seven straight hours of serious crying. It was as though he'd just returned from a period of wandering in some remote and holy place" (*WN* 79). At the end of the novel, this same Wilder gets on his plastic tricycle, rides it around the block, and then is somehow able, without suffering injury, "to pedal across the highway, mystically charged" (*WN* 322)—a modern, secular, American miracle if ever there was one. We are talking about a tricycle, notice, not the trinity, but they might not be so different, for the tricycle is also Endor's symbol in *Ratner's Star* (*RS* 190, 196), a work that ends with Billy Twillig riding Endor's white tricycle, as "mystically charged" as Wilder, it seems, producing a noise "resembling laughter, expressing vocally what appeared to be a compelling emotion, crying out as he was, gasping into the stillness, emitting as he was this series of involuntary shrieks, particles bouncing in the air around him, the reproductive dust of existence" (*RS* 438). It seems that whenever anyone is about to pass beyond opposites in DeLillo, some sort of three-wheeled, three-circled, or three-pointed thing, whether a tricycle, a coat hanger, a boomerang, a bat, or a v-shaped nuclear-powered submarine, will be somewhere in the vicinity (*RS* 340-1).

But then there is the miracle of Esmeralda in *Underworld*, which is not about the holy trinity, exactly, though it does get set up earlier in the novel when Lenny Bruce tells a weird, convoluted story-slash-joke about a young Puerto Rican prostitute who begins to get famous by blowing smoke rings out of her vagina, a trick that some interpret as supernatural, as a miracle, when the rings begin to look like the Greek letter Omega or, even more, when she comes close to intertwining the three rings, "either a symbol of the Blessed Trinity, Father, Son and Holy Ghost" or "the Ballantine beer logo—Purity, Body and Flavor" (*U* 631). It is crude and tasteless and it seems to be going nowhere until we see it becoming intertwined with the story of Esmeralda: "Let's tell the truth.... She fled the whorehouse on her own initiative.... She never worked in a whorehouse at all.... You take the subway to the South Bronx, where she lives with her junkie mother" (*U* 632). Hence the girl in the Lenny Bruce bit slowly morphs into the young girl we will have been following in the novel. "Let's make her human. Let's give her a name" (*U* 633). Lenny doesn't do it but the narrator does: her name is Esmeralda Lopez.

This is the Esmeralda Lopez, a young girl from the Bronx who was raped and thrown off a rooftop and then memorialized by a spray-painted graffiti angel, "a winged figure in a pink sweatshirt and pink and aqua pants and a pair of white Nike Air Jordans with the logo prominent" (*U* 815), with the epitaph below: "Esmeralda Lopez/12 year/Petected in Heven" (*U* 816).

If religion is a buffer against the terrors of contingency, the death of Esmeralda Lopez seems to push both Sisters Edgar and Gracie to the edge. The first says to the latter, as if she knew what the other was thinking: "You wonder if we make a difference. You can't understand how the last decade of the century looks worse than the first in some respects" (*U* 811). It's a kind of doubt to which everyone—Sister Edgar included—seems vulnerable. Indeed "she believes she is falling into crisis, beginning to think it is possible that all creation is a spurt of blank matter that chances to make an emerald planet here, a dead star there, with random waste between" (*U* 817; see "AE" 93). Actually, it's not a loss of faith she's experiencing but something worse, the birth of another faith, more ancient and more terrifying: "It is not a question of disbelief. There is another kind of belief, a second force, insecure, untrusting, a faith that is spring-fed by the things we fear in the night, and she thinks she is succumbing" (*U* 817; see 251). When things are this tenuous, when faith is this fragile and uncertain, something is needed to keep one from falling into complete abjection or despair. As the narrator puts it, "sometimes faith needs a sign," because sometimes "you want to stop working at faith and just be washed in a blowing wind that tells you everything" (*U* 757). For Florence on 9–11, trying to escape one of the towers, this appeared in the form of a "dog, a blind man and a guide dog, not far ahead, and it was like something out of the Bible.... The dog was like some totally calming thing. They believed in the dog.... The dog would lead them all to safety" (*FM* 57–8). In *Underworld* it's the appearance of a human face, the miraculous appearance of Esmeralda Lopez, not in a church or out in the desert but on a billboard in the Bronx, "an advertising sign scaffolded high above the riverbank and meant to attract the doped-over glances of commuters on the trains that run incessantly down from the northern suburbs into the thick of Manhattan money and glut" (*U* 818; "AE" 94). It could be just a rumor, or an illusion, but Sister Edgar sees "a radiant grace in the girl ... a source of personal hope, a goad to the old rugged faith" (*U* 811). It is this openness to radiance and grace that makes her so open to the possibility of revelation, that is, of a miracle. Here is the moment itself—or else the moment just before the moment itself:

> *The train.* / She feels the words before she sees the object. She feels the words although no one has spoken them. This is how a crowd brings things to single consciousness…. The headlights sweep the billboard and she hears a sound from the crowd, a gasp that shoots into sobs and moans and the cry of some unnameable painful elation. A blurted sort of whoop, the holler of unstoppered belief. Because when the train lights hit the dimmest part of the billboard a face appears above the misty lake and it belongs to the murdered girl…. *Esmeralda.* / *Esmeralda.* / … Women holding babies up to the sign, to the flowing juice, let it bathe them in baptismal balsam and oil.
>
> (*U* 821; see "AE" 97–98)

It is short-lived, momentary, minute-made and then quickly gone, but it is no less miraculous or compelling for Sister Edgar. Accompanied by its own incense—the smell of jet fuel from the planes taking off and landing at nearby La Guardia (*U* 824; "AE" 101)—it's a total kinesthetic experience, absolutely immediate and then immediately gone:

> She sees Esmeralda's face take shape under the rainbow of bounteous juice and above the little suburban lake and there is a sense of someone living in the image, an animating spirit—less than a tender second of life, less than half a second and the spot is dark again.
>
> (*U* 822; see "AE" 99)

Once again the lights of a New York City train reveal things. But whereas in *Libra* Oswald in the subway watched as the "beams picked out secret things" (*L* 13), like rats in the tunnels beneath the city, here, in *Underworld*, the beams reveal or make miraculous things appear, right there on the surface of the everyday. Instead of a moving image being produced by the projection of light upon a screen, the projector and the screen both unmoving, it is the moving lights of the train that here illuminate or reveal the image of Esmeralda, though just for moment, the time for the first car of the train to pass by, there and then gone in a New York minute.

For Sister Edgar it is a moment of grace. She thus believes, overcomes her own skepticism, though her partner, Sister Gracie, despite her name, sees nothing miraculous here at all, "just a trick of light. Not a person at all. Not a face but a stab of light" (*U* 821; see "AE" 97–98). She remains skeptical, suggesting that "it's just the undersheet. A technical flaw that causes the image underneath, the image from the papered-over ad to show through the current ad" (*U* 822; see "AE" 98). But Sister Edgar continues to believe, to have faith, a faith, at the very least, in the faith of others if not in the revelation of Esmeralda herself: "People go there to weep," says Sister Edgar, "to believe" (*U* 819; see "AE" 95). And *that*, perhaps, is the real miracle here, not the appearance of Esmeralda's face on a billboard but the fact that the germophobic Sister Edgar is able not only to mingle with the crowd but to embrace it and be embraced by it, the fact that she is able to take off her latex gloves, finally, without fear of contamination:

> They see her and embrace her and she lets them. Her presence is a verifying force—a figure from a universal church with sacraments and secret bank accounts and a fabulous art collection.
>
> (*U* 822; see "AE" 99)

It is here that Sister Edgar, with all her hard edges, lets herself be transformed into liquid:

> Everything feels near at hand, breaking upon her, sadness and loss and glory and an old mother's bleak pity and a force at some deep level of lament that makes her feel inseparable from the shakers and mourners, the awestruck who stand in the tidal traffic—she is nameless for a moment, lost to the details of personal history, a disembodied fact in liquid form, pouring into the crowd.
>
> (*U* 823)

Of course it ends at some point, "peters out," like all miracles, even Catholic ones, must (*U* 823), but the question then remains of what remains of it all, what remains not of Esmeralda, exactly, but of Sister Edgar's momentary faith:

> And what do you remember, finally, when everyone has gone home and the streets are empty of devotion and hope, swept by river wind? Is the memory thin and bitter and does it shame you with its fundamental untruth—all nuance and wishful silhouette? Or does the power of transcendence linger, the sense of an event that violates natural forces, something holy that throbs on the hot horizon, the vision you crave because you need a sign to stand against your doubt?
>
> (*U* 824; see "AE" 101)

For Sister Edgar, who has perhaps been waiting for this moment all her life, "There is nothing left to do but die and this is precisely what she does, Sister Alma Edgar, bride of Christ, passing peacefully in her sleep, the first faint snow of another dim winter falling softly on the unknown streets" (*U* 824). But for the rest of us, what remains is not nothing; in fact, it could be the opposite of nothing, the contraband of nothing, the blank space where anything can still happen: "The next evening the sign is blank.... The sign is a white sheet with two lonely words, *Space Available*, followed by a phone number in tasteful type" (*U* 824). In other words, what remains is a blank page, a blank screen, a place for other faces to be projected or other stories to be written, other strokes on the white, snowy surface: not the end of the world but a new beginning.

It all happened because two light beams had somehow picked out an angelic face on a billboard advertising orange juice—which comes from oranges, sometimes fresh-squeezed, as one might say in an ad, and that is perhaps not insignificant because you also "squeeze a baseball. You kind of juice it or milk it" (*U* 131). Throughout *Underworld* this *orange*, at once the thing and the name, the color and the fruit, mobilizes all the terms and oppositions we have previously seen. There is the "orange juice mixture" used to clean graffiti from subway station walls (*U* 433) and there is agent orange, stored in drums that "resembled cans of frozen Minute Maid enlarged by a crazed strain of DNA" (*U* 463; see 534, 824, "AE" 101, *DR* 87, *L* 156 and 164). Good orange bad orange, like good apple bad apple, but then "how can you tell the difference between orange juice and agent orange if the same massive system connects them at levels outside your comprehension?" (*U* 465). There is the orange that harnesses the power of the sun and then the orange moon that fills the night sky for the appearance of Esmeralda, that "madder orange moon [that] hangs over the city" as people look up at "a vast cascade of orange juice pouring diagonally from top right into a goblet that is handheld at lower left" (*U* 820; "AE" 96)—a glass that is perhaps not unlike the one Rey in *The Body Artist* will eventually pour his juice into after his morning ritual to prepare it:

> He went to the fridge and got the orange juice and stood in the middle of the room shaking the carton to float the pulp and make the juice thicker.... He shook it longer than he had to because he wasn't paying attention... and because it was satisfying in some dumb and blameless way, for its own childlike sake, for the bounce and slosh and cardboard orange aroma.
>
> (*BA* 10)

The billboard of the Minute Maid ad is a Madison Avenue fresco illuminated by the New York City Transit Authority, just one little corner of the vast cathedral that is American consumer culture, a symbol of hope and resurrection to thwart the triumph of death.

> What a lavishment of effort and technique, no refinement spared—the equivalent, Edgar thinks, of medieval church architecture. And the six-ounce cans of Minute Maid arrayed across the bottom of the board, a hundred identical cans so familiar in design and color and typeface that they have personality, the convivial cuteness of little orange-and-black people.
>
> (*U* 820; see "AE" 96–97)

That's the miracle in the Bronx, which is recounted, interestingly, not directly or even through memory but through a website that Nick's son Jeff, living with his parents in Phoenix (talk about resurrection), is following. It is thus just after the miracle of Esmeralda that we encounter the miracle of the internet, which allows us to click back and forth, effortlessly, between good and bad, creation and destruction. We click on one Edgar and jump almost immediately to the other, the other germophobe, J. Edgar, the other Cold War Edgar, the two united now on the internet through a kind of apocalyptic vision they also shared:

> Shot after shot, bomb after bomb, and they are fusion bombs, remember, atoms forcibly combined.... A click, a hit and Sister joins the other Edgar. A fellow celibate and more or less kindred spirit but her biological opposite, her male half, dead these many years.... Everything is connected in the end. / Sister and Brother. A fantasy in cyberspace and a way of seeing the other side and a settling of differences that have less to do with gender than with difference itself, all argument, all conflict programmed out.
>
> (*U* 826)

There is the orange, then, round like the sun, capturing the sun in its orbit and transforming it into juice, into an orange that is about the size of a baseball or the uranium core of a nuclear bomb. All those opposites—that world of opposites that we have been exploring with DeLillo from the beginning—are brought together on the web.... Science and religion, destruction and creation, war and peace. The miracle is not always some good, shining vision on the horizon; it can also be some explosive, genuinely destructive force. For who can tell the difference between a miracle and a nuclear explosion when "miracles and visions" are but "the supernatural underside of the arms race"? (*U* 452)

Baseball, orange, plutonium core… but then also earth, moon, sun: these are the circles or circuits of DeLillo's novels, the three everyday orbs around which everything inevitably revolves.

The Everyday

I'm the type of person who's willing to confront moderately awesome phenomena. Beyond that I lose my bearings.

RS 67

The shock, the power of an ordinary life. It is a thing you could not invent with banks of computers in a dust-free room.

U 308

DeLillo is, as we have just seen, a writer of the extraordinary, the miraculous, a writer of the event that tests and challenges experience. He is a writer of an event that is, as we have been able to bear witness to with Sisters Edgar and Gracie, never simply itself but always doubled, contrabanded by its narrative, or its lack of narrative, or the hole it leaves in those who try to recount or understand it. He is also, as we have seen, a writer of large-scale historical events, events that DeLillo did not himself invent but constructed narratives around, events such as the Kennedy assassination and 9–11. They are the kinds of events that blow a hole in the understanding of an entire nation, the kinds that require serious effort to make a people "whole again," to "restore sensation," "to grid the world" anew (*L* 414).

In works of DeLillo an event is thus anything unexpected and unexplainable, something that comes out of nowhere, that doesn't "fit the known world as recently constructed… a peculiar element in a series of events otherwise joined in explainable ways" (*RD* 81; see 31, *EZ* 5, 45, 112, 124, *M* 6, *FM* 69, *P* 158, *PO* 31). Like when birds suddenly fly off all at once because "they read a message in some event outside the visible spectrum" (*BA* 53), an event is something that eludes "the standard sun-kissed chronology of events" (*BA* 83). Unexpected and unrepeatable, "singular" (*PO* 9), a "sting of pure transcendence" (*C* 81), it's the kind of thing that often requires the look of another to be confirmed: "They glanced at each other wide-eyed as if to confirm the dimensions of the event" (*RD* 116–117).

There are thus historical events around which DeLillo will weave his narratives, and then there are the fictional events, like the famous airborne toxic event of *White Noise*. As Jack thinks at one point, after having just been diagnosed with Nyodene exposure as a result of this event, "I feel enmeshed, I feel deeply involved. It's no wonder they call this thing the airborne toxic event. It's an event all right. It marks the end of uneventful things" (*WN* 151). "The end of uneventful things": that's the perfect albeit tautological definition of the event. The event marks the end of uneventful or everyday things—even when it's an everyday thing that is occurring, like the arrival of another living being in a room. The event makes a hole in perception or in the everyday; it is an interruption of life as such, which is why every event seems to be tinged by the intimations of death.

In *White Noise* Winnie Richards, a psychobiologist at College-on-the-Hill, speaks of an event "so electrifyingly strange that it gives you a renewed sense of yourself, a fresh awareness of the self—the self in terms of a unique and horrific situation" (*WN* 229; see 248). We find a similar description in *Ratner's Star*: "Billy was stirred to relive some elemental moments separately blessed within the flow of past events.... They could be named and listed, the places he'd hidden from danger, the nights he thought would never end" (*RS* 276). Perhaps that's another way to think of it: if you cannot name it or list it—whether right off the bat or after some reflection—then it's not an event.

While such an event is singular, it can sometimes take time to unfold or unravel, its implications made manifest. Because sometimes one needs "to travel an event to its final unraveling" (*RD* 56; see 192). An event is thus never really perceived in the present but only recognized retrospectively, that is, recognized, processed, put into a pattern, made into the event it *will have been*:

> Moments before noon something happened near post 12. To Lyle it seemed at first an indistinct warp, a collapse in pattern. He perceived a rush, unusual turbulence, people crowding and looking around. He realized the sharp noise he'd heard seconds earlier was gunfire.
>
> (*P* 28)

As singular, unforeseeable and unrecognizable, the event is disquieting, destabilizing. One will thus eventually try to domesticate or "neutralize" it, to erase or remove what is uncanny within it. During the Moonie wedding in Yankee Stadium, for example, there are "whole families" snapping their cameras "anxiously, trying to shape a response or organize a memory, trying to neutralize the event, drain it of eeriness and power" (*M* 6).

Whatever its origin or its cause, the event seems to defy all explanation—at least for a time. There is an "unresolvable heart" within the event (*U* 454); those who were there do not quite know what they saw and those who were not there thought they were witnesses to it. We are reminded in *Underworld*, for example, of how many people who were nowhere near the Shot Heard

'Round The World "honestly insisted they were there because the event had sufficient seeping power to make them think they had to be at the Polo Grounds that day" (*U* 94).

In the short story "The Runner" a child's sudden abduction in Central Park—by his father or a stranger, it is unclear—is an event that initially makes no sense and yields no interpretation: "Now that I've had some time to think, there's no explanation. A hole opened up in the air. That's how much sense it makes" ("R" 53). The same incomprehensibility accompanies Elster's daughter's disappearance in *Point Omega*, or, far less ominous but still rather dramatic, in *Americana*, the appearance of a nearly naked secretary in the office of one of Bell's business associates: "It had been one of those moments for which an explanation evades the mind forever, an underwater moment tilted and warped by a rapture of the deep" (*A* 92).

There are events, then, what we might be tempted to call major historical events, world events or, for someone, world-shattering events, whether blessed or catastrophic, and then there are micro-events, not everyday events, exactly, but events within the everyday: "He stands at the window and sees what's happening in the street. Something is always happening, even on the quietest days and deep into night, if you stand a while and look" (*FM* 66). Things are indeed happening everyday in this way, seemingly minor events—like the arrival of a stranger in a house—events that are perhaps just as inexplicable and potentially just as earth-shattering or earth-shaking for those involved as those major historical events. Such is the sudden arrival, the mysterious appearance, of Mr. Tuttle in *The Body Artist*, an arrival that seems just as mysterious to Mr. Tuttle as it is to Lauren, "the breathless shock of his being here" (*BA* 69). It happens everywhere, every day, a stranger walking into a room, the sudden emergence of a living being. But it takes a certain heightened perception in order to see it for what it is. *The Body Artist* seems to make a plea for seeing or transforming such an everyday thing into a genuine event:

> Is the thing that's happening so far outside experience that you're forced to make excuses for it, or give it the petty credentials of some misperception?
>
> Is reality too powerful for you?
>
> Take the risk. Believe what you see and hear. It's the pulse of every secret intimation you've ever felt around the edges of your life.
>
> They are two real bodies in a room.
>
> (*BA* 122)

Narrative would apparently be an attempt to make sense of the event, to put it into perspective, to find it a frame, a structure. Few people can live outside such narrative structures, live a life outside the recognizable patterns, a life of the pure event. The arrival of Mr. Tuttle in Lauren's house would seem to be one of those events, an inscrutable thing that happens and then needs to be unfolded, interpreted. For events do not simply yield their meaning of their own accord. That is why, in order to think the event, the unique event, one must begin to understand its repetition, its reproduction and mediatization, its recording and its filming.

The event seems to elude all explanation and narrative, all comparison and analogy, even if it also calls for these things, for a counternarrative to give shape or meaning to it:

> The event itself has no purchase on the mercies of analogy or simile.... People falling from towers hand in hand. This is part of the counternarrative, hands and spirits joining, human beauty in the crush of meshed steel. In its desertion of every basis for comparison, the event asserts its singularity. There is something empty in the sky. The writer tries to give memory, tenderness and meaning to all that howling space.
>
> ("RF")

The event stands in a contraband relation to ordinary time, just like the "swerve" (of Lucretius) evoked in "The Power of History," the "free veer from time and place and fate" ("PH"). It is perhaps no coincidence, then, or else the perfect coincidence, a sign of the law of coincidence, that at the heart of the Convergence there is the *veer*: "Artis was down there somewhere, at veer's end, counting the drops of water on a shower curtain" (*ZK* 139).

But then there are events, special events, that seem to be like the irruptive and inexplicable event of narrative itself. Here is one from *Americana*, a first narrative, it seems, about the promise of narrative itself: "You go for long walks that are like episodes of French novels. You feel that some great encounter is about to take place, something that will change the course of your life" (*A* 181). This something may be momentous, as we have seen, an earthshaking event of some kind, registered on a world-historical scale, or it may be something rather ordinary. David Bell is reading a baseball magazine on the porch while his mother is "looking at a tray of French pastries" when, all of a sudden, out of nowhere, totally out of the blue, a pack of motorcycles roars down Bell's suburban street:

> They were gone in seconds and it was as though a hurricane or plague had struck the town.... I could almost feel every man and woman in town looking from windows down that street and experiencing a strange

mixture of longing and terror. We were all in one piece. But we were not quite the same people we had been ten seconds before.

(*A* 182–3)

It's an event in its own right, it seems, but it also seems to be leading up to something else, to an event—and there is no better definition of the event—that will feel like "the beginning of time."

> I did not move. I felt close to some overwhelming moment. In the dim light her shadow behind her consumed my own. I knew what was happening and I did not care to argue with the doctors of that knowledge. Let it be. Inside her was something splintered and bright, something that might have been left by the spiral passage of my own body. She was before me now, looking up, her hands on my shoulders. The sense of tightness I had felt in my room was beginning to yield to a promise of fantastic release. It was going to happen. Whatever would happen. The cage would open, the mad bird soar, and I would cry in epic joy and pain at the freeing of a single moment, the beginning of time. Then I heard my father's bare feet on the stairs. That was all.
>
> (*A* 196–7)

It happens just like that, an event that changes everything. Bell is able to look back on it, already aware of a certain itinerary, and see that he had been destined to go from high school at St. Dymphna's to college at Leighton Gage to something that has not yet been defined.

> I would be going into senior year at St. Dymphna's, where I would amble along the gray lanes in my tweed sportcoat. And yet something was coming to an end, not just summer but something like the idea of what I was, the time I occupied like space, that private time in which one moves and thinks and knows the questions.
>
> (*A* 198)

There are thus events that change one's life, exceptional events, unforgettable moments, not world historical events but events that nonetheless change everything. And then there are the moments, the most ordinary moments, that often go unnoticed but that are themselves exceptional when we come to take a look at them. A writer of the exceptional and the everyday, of the exceptional in the everyday, DeLillo seems to believe what is said by one of the architects of the JFK assassination attempt in *Libra*: "We lead more interesting lives than we think. We are characters in plots, without the compression in numinous sheen" (*L* 78). As Jeffrey Lockhart, the narrator of *Zero K*, recalls about his mother, Madeline, a name that itself might be read as a remembrance of things past if one wants to give a name (*madeleines*) to those little "French pastries" in *Americana* that David Bell's mother brought out on one of those days when "you go for long walks that are like episodes of French novels":

> Ordinary moments make the life. This is what she knew to be trustworthy and this is what I learned, eventually, from those years we spent together.... What I failed to know before is clearer now, filtered up through time, an experience belonging to no one else, not remotely, no one, anyone, ever.
>
> (*ZK* 109)

As his mother—not his rich, successful father—had taught him, it is "minor matters that define us" (*ZK* 172): "Things people do, ordinarily, forgettably, things that breathe just under the surface of what we acknowledge having in common.... These are the soporifics of normalcy, my days in middling drift" (*ZK* 209). The last two chapters of *Zero K* (*ZK* 265–74), after Jeffrey's return to NYC, are a series of disjointed observations of everyday life, some seen for the first time, like a man kneeling on a sidewalk outside a taxi—turns out he is "the driver of the taxi and that the direction is Mecca, he is bowing toward Mecca" (*ZK* 265; see 271)—and some familiar but only now recognized as such, like that "contemporary pattern of declarative sentences that slither gradually upward into questions" (*ZK* 265).

There is a certain death in "routine things" (*WN* 248), as Jack says to his father-in-law, but much of the richness of life is to be found in those same routine things. There is the extraordinary, therefore, and then there is the familiar, the ordinary, which becomes remarkable because it is ordinary, because of the way it allows us, rather miraculously, to settle into things:

> This talk we were having about familiar things was itself ordinary and familiar. It seemed to yield up the mystery that is part of such things, the nameless way in which we sometimes feel our connections to the physical world. *Being here.*
>
> (*N* 32)

Just before the assassination attempt, even Lee Harvey Oswald does some of the simplest things in the world, like watch his wife in their bedroom. "He was watching her. She put the nightdress over her head and rolled back the bedcovers. Ordinary in every way, simple moments adding up, with rain falling on the lawn" (*L* 390). "They were the same as anyone, completely ordinary, saying what people say" (*L* 202). But the juxtaposition, the contraband, is always there, between what Oswald is seeing and what he is thinking, plotting, between the normal life he is apparently leading and the extraordinary actions we know he is planning to take.

In *Underworld* there is even an argument made for the significance of the everyday over against the extraordinary and world-shaking, the importance of a simple baseball game—even if it was a playoff game, and even if it did end with a game-winning homerun—over against world historical events and geopolitics:

> Isn't it possible that this midcentury moment enters the skin more lastingly than the vast shaping strategies of eminent leaders, generals steely in their sunglasses—the mapped visions that pierce our dreams? … This is the thing that will pulse in his brain come old age and double vision and dizzy spells—the surge sensation, the leap of people already standing, that bolt of noise and joy when the ball went in. This is the people's history and it has flesh and breath that quicken to the force of this old safe game of ours.
>
> (*U* 59–60)

That game, Russ Hodges thinks, would have been part of "another kind of history," a "people's history," and he thinks that those who witnessed it "will carry something out of here that joins them all in a rare way, that binds them to a memory with protective power" (*U* 59). And yet, as a baseball announcer would be the first to know, the problem with preserving the ordinary or the everyday is not its nonexceptionality but its extraordinary variety, its endless shadings, difficult to see but then even harder to capture in words, "The sandgrain manyness of things that can't be counted," a thing so rich and nuanced "it is all falling indelibly into the past" (*U* 60).

A people's history would thus have to include everyday impressions of a momentous thing like a game-ending homerun, because "when you see a thing like that, a thing that becomes a newsreel, you begin to feel you are a carrier of some solemn scrap of history" (*U* 16). But it would also have to include everything that is special, spectacular even, about being "home alone, surrounded by all the things and textures that make you familiar, once again, to yourself" (*U* 482). It would have to include the kind of everyday expressions that come and go, suddenly emerge and then just as suddenly perish: "People weren't saying *Oh wow* anymore. They were saying *No way* instead and she wondered if there was something she might learn from this" (*U* 382; see 496).

Part 6 of *Underworld*, "Arrangement in Gray and Black, Fall 1951-Summer 1952," follows Albert Bronzini, pushing forty, and Nick, sixteen or seventeen, through their everyday lives and their everyday encounters with ordinary things (*U* 661–781), everyday encounters that require a kind of genius to retain or even to recognize in the first place: "Bronzini thought that walking was an art. He was out nearly every day after school, letting the route produce a medley of sounds and forms and movements, letting the voices fall and the aromas deploy in ways that varied, but not too much from day to day" (*U* 661). "This is the only art I've mastered," he says, "walking these streets and letting the senses collect what is routinely here" (*U* 672).

Everyday things, everyday words, and then not so everyday words to describe the everyday. Father Paulus has this little exchange with Nick:

> "Everyday things represent the most overlooked knowledge. These names are vital to your progress. Quotidian things." "Quotidian." "An extraordinary word that suggests the depth and reach of the commonplace."
>
> (*U* 542)

Everyday things, then, quotidian, even when they come every couple of weeks, everyday things like a haircut, from an old-time barber rather than a hairdresser. It's one of those things money cannot buy, not even for a multi-billionaire currency trader living in a forty-eight room penthouse on the 89th floor of a Manhattan high-rise. Everyday things like sitting at the kitchen table, a day like any other, maybe more mundane than most, except that your husband is about to walk out the door and commit suicide:

> She sat there and finished her tea and thought of what she thought of, memory traces and flary images and a friend she missed and all the shadow-dappled stuff of an undividable moment on a normal morning going crazy in ways so humanly routine you can't even stop and take note except for the Ajax she needs to buy and the birds behind her, rattling the metal frame of the feeder.
>
> (*BA* 24–5)

Everyday things, like how people smoked back in the day, since people don't smoke the same way today. Lee Oswald, for example, being escorted "to a green-and-white squad car" where there was "a cop behind the wheel" who "drove with one hand, keeping the hand that cupped a cigarette down between his knees" (*L* 10), because people don't do that anymore, and it takes a novel to remind us of it, the way an officer, years later in another novel but in that same "green and white vehicle," it seems, might be driving along, "cupping a smoke between his knees" (*U* 333). It's the kind of thing that makes an impression if one is open enough to receive it, an impression that then bears repeating, for if a quotidian gesture like cupping a smoke can fall into forgetfulness then nothing is safe. The point of writing would thus seem to be to preserve those miracles of the everyday, without getting too pious about it, to preserve them through the contraband of writing, everyday writing, the writing of the everyday, beginning with the day itself.

Earth, Moon, Sun

I began in the dark and would no doubt end the same way. But somewhere between beginning and end there would have to be an attempt to explain the darkness, if only to myself.

A 206

The night sky appeared, the scattershot of blazing worlds.

N 298

"What's the best thing you ever learned in school? Going back to the beginning, to the first days." ... "The sun is a star."

FM 186

Secrets, rumors, plots and conspiracies, historical events, wars, disasters, and catastrophes—these are the stock and trade of the DeLillo novel. How surprising is it, then—how much of a contraband—that so many of DeLillo's novels would also revolve, in the end, not just around such momentous events in human history, events created by humankind, but around some kind of natural or even meteorological event, like rain or snow, or a sunset, or an eclipse, or, precisely, a meteor, such as the one that landed in Chelyabinsk, Siberia, in 2009, the event around which *Zero K* revolves (*ZK* 42; see 128)?

No doubt the most common contrabanded phenomenon in our everyday lives is the simple alternation of day and night, light and darkness, waking life and dreams. Both of these are abundantly represented in DeLillo, and precisely as contrabanding opposites. In *Libra* we read of how, in the night, "dreams sent terrors you could not explain" (*L* 148), and how these then begin to cast their shadow into waking life, making both night and day inexplicable and terrorizing in their own ways. For "the dark had a power," says the narrator on behalf of the young Oswald, riding the New York subway (*L* 13; 46), the power to break down our everyday distinctions, to sink everything we know or think we know into obscurity: "I have a feeling about night. The things of the world are no longer discrete. All the day's layers and distinctions fade in the dark" (*N* 81). It is a daily wonder—and a nightly source of terror. As someone asks in *Valparaiso*, "Do you lie awake sometimes and feel the genius and terror of night?" (*V* 79) For darkness has a power, the darkness of night, and even more so the "darkness outside ordinary night" (*L* 424, see *A* 270 and *ZK* 199, 264), for example, the darkness of caves: "This dark had a special presence. It was far from empty. It was not just nonlight. It had a nature that dated back. It had intrinsic characteristics. It was animal" (*RS* 391). "This is why," as we read again in *Valparaiso*, "we have daytime," a separate time "to interpret the night" (*V* 68).

The darkness has a power and an attraction for Oswald; and yet at the moment of his greatest trial, the assassination attempt, "the light was so clear it was heartbreaking" (*L* 400). The image is echoed in *The Names*, when the narrator, living in Greece, speaks of "the clear light before sundown that just about breaks my heart" (*N* 112). Elsewhere in the same novel, the light of Greece is described as "surgical" and "binding" (*N* 9; see 71), a "sun-cut clarity" (*N* 119; see 172, 176) that draws out "the cut-paper brightness of doors and flowers" (*N* 74; see also *N* 169, 179, and "IA" 59). Act Two of *Love-Lies-Bleeding* is itself set in a room "open to late-afternoon light, a sense of blazing sky" (*LL* 51), the perfect setting for Alex Macklin, who quotes the Italian poet Giuseppe Ungaretti, "*M'illumino d'immenso*. I glow, I shine, I bathe myself in light. I turn luminous in this vast space" (*LL* 64).

The theater, of course, is made for these dramatic alternations between darkness and light. The day room of *The Day Room* is "painted pure white, coat after coat after coat" (*DR* 25). "The whole room's fluorescent. You hear the sizzling lights" (*DR* 26; see 37, 59). Here, in contrast, is the final scene of *Valparaiso*: "*Stillness. Then lights up bright on Chorus, flanking members still suspended in mid-gesture. / BLACK*" (*V* 107). And the final scene of *Love-Lies-Bleeding*: "*The sitting figure in isolation. Black*" (*LL* 97).

There is, then—setting aside gray and black and orange, DeLillo colors all, or brown, a Murray Jay Siskind color, so much so that "if there was such a thing as the Citizens' Committee for the Color Brown, they could have used Murray in their commercials" (*AZ* 154)—white, the white of white noise, of white light (*DR* 48), of white snow and the white page, these latter conjoined in *Underworld* in the dual image of snow shovel marks and the markings on a white page. Nick says of his time in a correctional facility:

> All that winter I shoveled snow and read books. The lines of print, the alphabetic characters, the strokes of the shovel when I cleared a walk,

the linear arrangement of words on a page, the shovel strokes, the rote exercises in school texts, the novels I read, the dictionaries I found in the tiny library, the nature and shape of books, the routine of shovel strokes in deep snow—this was how I began to build an individual.

(*U* 503)

White snow, the white page, and the strokes of pen or shovel upon or against them. There is something about snow and shoveling snow that brings DeLillo back to the origins of writing, to a memory that goes all the way back to *Americana*: "When I command snow to fall once again on the streets of Old Holly, my father's hands curled about a shovel, I can't be sure I'll get the precise moment I want.... We are what we remember" (*A* 299; see 222). Bell is, it seems, trying to summon up the "sound of men with shovels" down the street (*A* 133; see 222, 248, 290, *GJ* 91, *WN* 109, 171, "MD" 119). It is the sight of snow that brings us back, or else the sound of snow, from *Americana*'s Old Holly to *Amazons*' Badger, Ohio, the safe, reassuring sound of "people shoveling snow—the sound of shovels on a brick sidewalk" (*AZ* 38). It is the very same image that sticks with Oswald from his time in Russia, "broadbacked women shoveling snow" (*L* 156; see *U* 358 and 362), the whole city of Moscow "stunned, dream-white" (*L* 159). There is something about that snow, as if rain were to sex what snow is to literature—the medium that helps it take root, a contrast, a cover, or a contraband, a surface on which to make one's mark. Day and night, light and dark, blinding white snow and the black marks of a shovel on the pavement—these are the meteorological coordinates of Don DeLillo's writing, a writing that so often takes us from these everyday, earthy phenomena to the heavenly bodies that produce them, bodies like the earth, the moon, and the sun, the three bodies around which our daily lives revolve.

They are everywhere, those three spherical bodies. The short story "Human Moments in World War III" ends with a vision of the earth itself, of the world at war, seen from the window of an orbiting spacecraft ("HM" 43–4). Near the end of *The Names* there is a moon rise, which begins in silence, the moon orange, then silver, in contrast with the blood-colored earth, though the scene is abruptly curtailed, the silence interrupted, by the sound of a telephone ringing, a sound that forebodes danger for the narrator:

A silence seemed to fall. I watched a glow appear behind the mountain, a shower of light, brick orange, climbing. Then the topmost arc of the moon showed over the ridge-line. It rose in degrees, fully illuminated, a calculus-driven model of pure ascent. Soon it was free of the mountain's dark mass, beginning to vault toward the west, to silver and glint, a cold

object now, away from the earth-blood, the earth-burn, but beautiful, hard, bright.
The phone rang twice, then stopped.

(*N* 320; see *AZ* 239)

This is just one of the many moons in DeLillo, from man's landing on the moon and the graffiti artist Moonman 157 in *Underworld* to the thousands of Moonies in *Mao II*.

As for the sun, it is worth repeating because it is so self-evident and thus so easy to forget: "The sun is a star. When did she realize this herself and why didn't she remember when? The sun is a star. It seemed a revelation, a fresh way to think about being who we are, the purest way and only finally unfolding, a kind of mystical shiver, an awakening" (*FM* 187). And this too is obvious and yet also worth stating, the sun, as a star, radiates from within: "A star makes its own light" (*FM* 232). And to top it all off, "We are at the mercy of our star" (*ZK* 65). Once again, what is furthest away echoes and reminds us of what is closest, since we ourselves have our origin in the stars:

> We come from the stars. Our chemicals, our atoms, these were first made in the centers of old stars that exploded and spread their remains across the sky eventually to come together as the sun we know and the planet we inhabit…. We're stellar cinders, you and me. We come from the beginning or near the beginning. In our brain is the echo of the little bang…. We're part star, you and me. Our beginning and end are made in the stars.
>
> (*RS* 218, 224)

A star, what is furthest away, teaches us what we are deep inside. As the venerable Lazarus Ratner says from inside his "ultrasterile biomedical membrane environment" (*RS* 211), "The sun within us, the source of all mystical bursts, is perfectly counterbalanced by the physical sun that presses outward, swallowing up the orbits of the nearest planets" (*RS* 223).

But then we come to eclipses, the overlapping—the contrabanding, as it were—of moon and sun. The predicting of eclipses, the mathematics and astronomy behind those predictions and human reactions to them, are at the center of several DeLillo novels. As *Ratner's Star* recalls, "calendar-making is one of our earliest cognitive labors and evidence of interest in lunar cycles, eclipses, so on" (*RS* 318). We learn by the end of that novel that the code supposedly sent by extraterrestrials on a planet near Ratner's Star was actually sent by evolved earthlings of a much earlier time and that the code indicated the time of a total eclipse of the sun, one that had not been anticipated by contemporary astronomers. We thus come to understand in retrospect the many preceding references in the novel to light and shadow (see *RS* 40, 225, 258). That is, we come to see these references as foreshadowing, as it were, the eclipse of the sun that occurs at the end of the novel, an eclipse that is ultimately forecast by someone named "Skia Mantikos"—a name that "sounds like a Greek-American soccer team" but means "the shadow prophet" (*RS* 423). The secret of the code supposedly from near Ratner's star—the sequence fourteen, twenty-eight, fifty seven—ultimately means that at twenty-eight minutes and fifty-seven seconds after two p.m. Greenwich mean time on the day in question, which turns out to be the day the code is finally interpreted, there would be an unexpected or unforeseen eclipse (*RS* 385, 429), a "lunar shadow" that would slowly cover India, Bangladesh, and China (*RS* 430–3).

Now it is true, as the philosopher David Hume would have been the first to affirm, that "an unforeseen eclipse is no more startling, logically, than an eclipse predicted decades or centuries earlier," since the taking place of even the latter is also only "sheer conjecture" (*RS* 435). And yet this unforeseen eclipse is something of a miracle at the end of *Ratner's Star*. It is the ultimate convergence or boomeranging of past and present, up and down, high and low, light and dark. Moreover, as this exceptional astronomical event takes place in the sky above, Endor, the first to have discovered the meaning of the code, uses a coat hanger to dig deeper and deeper into the earth: "It was still light, still light. Some forewarning mechanism made him begin to crawl, knowing, everywhere, feeling it, a sense of violated space, the air itself infused with this infrared surprise" (*RS* 437).

Hence *Ratner's Star* concludes with a solar eclipse, just like *The Names* (see *N* 280), as well as the play *The Day Room*, which ends with instructions being given by a voice from a TV (a box of sorts) on how to create a box (a room or space of sorts) in order to watch a solar eclipse:

Some people like to keep the box on their head even after the eclipse is over. Some people never remove the box. Some people live out their days with the box on their head, waiting for another eclipse, or just looking at the sheet of white paper on the inside of the box.

(*DR* 100)

Yet another white sheet of paper, yet another snowy page to be shoveled, another "space available."

We have spoken throughout this work about doubles and double takes, about isolation and retrospection, about closed eyes, the sun and its eclipse; here's a little passage that combines them all: "She heard a plane cross the sky and then the light blinked off and on, the sunlight, the sunray, an event she assembled through closed lids, and she knew the fog had finally lifted" (*BA* 73-4). The "she" in question here is Lauren Hartke, who has just lost her Rey, and who is thus very susceptible to the mini-eclipse of her sun. And then there's Sunny, the granddaughter of Nick Shay—his last name a co-mingling, it can now be heard, of Shade and Gray—"My granddaughter is with me, Sunny, she is nearly six now" (*U* 809). She is, of course, the great-granddaughter of Jimmy Costanza, who went out to buy a pack of cigarettes one day and simply disappeared, that is, "went under."

There are thus sunsets, spectacular sunsets, natural phenomena par excellence, but which sometimes get a little boost from human technology. For there is nothing like a bit of toxic residue, Nyodene Derivative, for example, to cause an "aesthetic leap from already brilliant sunsets to broad towering ruddled visionary skyscapes, tinged with dread" (*WN* 170). It's not quite an "atomic sunset" (*ZK* 186), but close, the great sun "going down like a ship in a burning sea": "Another postmodern sunset, rich in romantic imagery" (*WN* 227). Later in *White Noise* the sunset becomes a veritable tourist attraction: "We go to the overpass all the time. Babette, Wilder and I. We take a thermos of iced tea, park the car, watch the setting sun" (*WN* 324). It's an event that "transcends previous categories of awe," like Wilder crossing the highway in his tricycle, though they don't know whether they are "watching in wonder or dread" (*WN* 324). It's a miracle of sorts, and yet nothing could be more familiar, more everyday: "Something golden falls, a softness delivered to the air. There are people walking dogs, there are kids on bikes, a man with a camera and long lens, waiting for his moment" (*WN* 325). It's an everyday thing, an everyday spectacle, and so a little ho-hum, though it can also scare the living daylights out of you: "Some people are scared by the sunsets, some determined to be elated, but most of us don't know how to feel, are ready to go either way" *(WN* 324). It is just as Richard Elster would have prognosticated: "To Elster sunset was human invention, our perceptual arrangement of light and space into elements of wonder" (*PO* 18).

Yes, it all comes down to wonder (see *N* 339)—to awe, or reverence, or "astonishment" (*ZK* 9). It's a word or a notion that appears frequently in DeLillo. In *Love-Lies-Bleeding* Lia recalls Alex, incapacitated, being taken outdoors, into the desert, "His head raised up and he was in awe, I know he was—purest living wonder" (*LL* 14).

"Wonder": that is also the very last word of *Zero K*, and everything that comes before can be read as preparation for it. Early on in the novel Jeffrey describes Artis's hopes to achieve through the Convergence "a purer aura," a "transcendence, the promise of a lyric intensity outside the measure of normal experience" (*ZK* 48). At the end of the novel, that vision seems to be realized, not by the Convergence, however, not in the future, not thanks to science, and not by someone at the end of their life, but in New York City, in the present, in nature—though it's a nature that has been framed by human construct (buildings on one end, a bus on the other)—and by a child, a boy on the back of a bus with his mother (of course). It is the kind of fictional event that actually sometimes happens, Manhattanhenge, this one on July 13, 2011, apparently:

> We were in midtown, with a clear view west, and he was pointing and wailing at the flaring sun.… It was a striking thing to see, in our urban huddle, the power of it, the great round ruddy mass, and I knew that there was a natural phenomenon, here in Manhattan, once or twice a year, in which the sun's rays align with the local street grid.
>
> I didn't know what this event was called but I was seeing it now and so was the boy, whose urgent cries were suited to the occasion, and the boy himself, thick-bodied, an over-sized head, swallowed up in the vision.…
>
> The boy bounced slightly in accord with the cries and they were unceasing and also exhilarating, they were prelinguistic grunts. I hated to think that he was impaired in some way, macrocephalic, mentally deficient, but these howls of awe were far more suitable than words.
>
> The full solar disk, bleeding into the streets, lighting up the towers to either side of us, and I told myself that the boy was not seeing the sky collapse upon us but was finding the purest astonishment in the intimate touch of earth and sun.
>
> I went back to my seat and faced forward. I didn't need heaven's light. I had the boy's cries of wonder.
>
> (*ZK* 273–4)

The scene begins with the narrator taking a bus not west, toward the setting sun, but east, so that he first notices the sunset's glow not through the bus's windshield in front of him but on his hands picking up the light from behind. It is then that he turns around, sees the sun and hears the young boy's cries. It is thus a sunset that elicits the wonder, the sun setting in the west, though the true miracle, once again, seems to be language, language at its limits, which seems to be, for DeLillo, all the wonder we need in the world.

Radiance

There's a huge body of work, yet to be written, on the subject of brightness. "Brightness falls from the air." This is the only thing they've written so far, of all the things that could be written, on a subject so vast and dazzling.

DR 15

Suddenly what do I see? A thing beyond naming. Not a thing at all. A state. I am falling into a state. Radiance everywhere. An experience. I am having an experience.

RS 226

The en-sof is the unknowable. The hidden. The that-which-is-not-there. The neither-cause-nor-effect. The G-dash-d beyond G-dash-d. The limitless. The not-only-unutterable-but-by-definition-inconceivable. Yet it emanates. It reveals itself through its attributes, the sefiroth.

RS 217

It is everywhere in DeLillo, though most often it is concentrated at the end: an event, a miracle, and then a moment of radiance. While DeLillo writes everywhere of secrets and hidden plots, of underworlds, of things concealed behind or within other things, of the power of darkness, he is also, ultimately, a writer of light, of radiance, of light seen or experienced anew.

Hence moments of revelation punctuate DeLillo's novels. It's usually some everyday thing, and even when it's miraculous there is usually an everyday thing—an ad for orange juice, for example—behind it. Anyone who has ever gone to a baseball game has seen it, coming up out of the tunnels of the stadium to see the luminous colors of the field, an "unfolding vision of the grass," "the excitement of a revealed thing" (*U* 14), and then, later, under the lights, the field and the stands with "the glow of first-time things" (*U* 20). Later still, "with advancing dark the field is taking on a deeper light. The grass is incandescent, it has a heat and sheen" (*U* 53). These are moments of illumination that we all know, everyday moments of incandescent wonder.

Revelation, incandescence, radiance: whatever one wants to call it, the emphasis here is on the revealing rather than the revelation, on the way things light up from within, becoming themselves to such an extent that they are nothing but their own revelation, their own self-revealing. Already back in *Americana* Sullivan speaks in an apocalyptic tone of the way "all energy runs down, all life expires, all except the force of all in all, or light lighting light" (*A* 330). *Players* too ends in sunlight, with a sort of cinematic light falling upon Lyle in a motel room, a light that reminds one of the opening in-flight movie depicting a terrorist attack, already a foreshadowing of the attack Lyle is about to carry out:

> There's a splatter of brightness at one edge of the window. Minutes and inches later, sunlight fills the room.... The angle of light is direct and severe, making the people on the bed appear to us in a special framework.... The whole room, the motel, is surrendered to this moment of luminous cleansing.
>
> (*P* 212)

Even the moment of catastrophe is a moment of radiance. On November 22, 1963, for example, "Everything looked so painfully clear. / The President had chestnut hair and the First Lady was radiant in a pink suit and small round hat" (*L* 395; see 391). That clarity and radiance are then transferred to everyone around the first couple, so that "it wasn't only Jack and Jackie who were riding in a fire of excitement" but the people around them, the crowd itself being brought "into heat and light" (*L* 394).

In *Great Jones Street* the radiance appears in the form of fruit—not oranges, this time, but strawberries: "I understood what strawberries really are, not that I could put it in words. They were inconceivably beautiful, so rich and plump and alive, actually glowing from within. Of course I was probably stoned on something" (*GJ* 84). In *White Noise* Jack Gladney again sees a living, glowing, vibrant red that comes not from strawberries but spilled blood: "I knew what red was, saw it in terms of dominant wavelength, luminance, purity. Mink's pain was beautiful, intense" (*WN* 312).

In *The Names* one speaks of a light that comes out of things rather than shining upon them, a "charged luminescence, a stormlight that does not fall upon objects so much as it emanates from them" (*N* 232). The light or radiance of objects here appears related to the contrabanding or doublebanding of experience in memory: not the repetition of what has already happened but, more interesting, the memory of what has not yet taken place but will have or should have. Owen Brademas says about his time on the Greek island: "I realize finally what the secret is. All these months I've wondered what it was I couldn't quite identify in my feelings about this place.... These are all things I seem to *remember*" (*N* 112). It is the kind of memory that first makes things what they are through their doubling, their contrabanding, through a sort of *déjà vu* of the very form of things. This time it's not an orange or a strawberry but a fig: "You eat a fig and there is something *higher* about this fig. The first fig. The prototype. The dawn of figs.... I feel I've known the particular clarity of this air and water, I've climbed these stony paths into the hills. It's eerie, this sense. Metempsychosis" (*N* 113; see *P* 150, *BA* 122). It's an odd kind of memory, one where the event itself seems to coincide with the memory of it, as band and contraband. It is this doubling that gives things not only their radiance but, it seems, their mortality: "Here I am again, standing by the bed in my pajamas, acting out a memory.... The moment referred back to itself at the same time as it pointed forward. *Here I am*. A curious reminder that I was going to die" (*N* 81).

It's a transformation that can be located in either the perceiver or the perceived, or, really, always, in both at once. Artis Martineau in *Zero K* recalls how her perception had changed—and how the world had changed along with it—after an eye operation:

> When I woke up I removed the shield and looked around and everything looked different. I was astonished. What was I seeing? I was seeing what is always there. The bed, the windows, the walls, the floor. But the brightness of it, the radiance. The bedspread and pillow cases, the rich color, the depths of color, something from within. Never before, ever.
>
> (*ZK* 44–5)

It is as if there were a world beneath the world—a contraband world—now suddenly revealed. As if we spent our lives fabricating a less real world to cover over a world that is too vibrant, too cutting or lacerating for everyday living:

> I don't know the details or the terminology but I do know that the optic nerve is not telling the full truth. We're seeing only intimations. The rest is our invention, our way of reconstructing what is actual, if there is any such thing, philosophically, that we can call actual.
>
> (*ZK* 45)

In certain extreme states, human invention and fabrication give way to something else, the experience not of some supernatural vision but of the things right there before our eyes—like the color white, the white of shoveled snow or a blank page or, since it's a matter of looking, a window frame:

> I became mesmerized by the rug and then by the window frame, white, simply white, but I had never seen white such as this... I thought, Is this the world as it truly looks? Is this the reality we haven't learned how to see?... Is this the world that only animals are capable of seeing?
>
> (*ZK* 46)

Artis thus experiences this extraordinary radiance of things for a time, only to have the everyday, ordinary ordering and vision of things eventually return:

> My vision was improved but only ordinarily so. The experience was gone, the radiance in things.... Or the experience hadn't drifted away and the

radiance hadn't faded—it was all simply re-suppressed.... I returned to see the doctor a few days later. I tried to tell him what I'd seen. Then I looked at his face and stopped.

(*ZK* 46)

The promise of the Convergence is, it seems, nothing other than this radiance, only generalized, stretched out into time and space. As Artis puts it: "I have every belief that I will reawaken to a new perception of the world.... I will be reborn into a deeper and truer reality. Lines of brilliant light, every material thing in its fullness, a holy object" (*ZK* 47).

Earlier in the novel, Jeffrey, the step son, visits Artis, now frozen in the Convergence, and sees something like the radiance that she saw in the things around her after her eye surgery in Artis's own body, that is, in the art her body now is:

Her body seemed lit from within. She stood erect, on her toes, shaved head tilted upward, eyes closed, breasts firm.... It was a beautiful sight. It was the human body as a model of creation. I believed this. It was a body in this instance that would not age. And it was Artis, here, alone, who carried the themes of this entire complex into some measure of respect.

(*ZK* 258)

We mentioned earlier the way in which the Convergence of *Zero K* seems to have a predecessor in the Kramer cube of *Amazons*. Well, just as the totally shaven Artis in the Convergence appears lit up from within in this later novel, so the recuperating Shaver glows from within his Kramer cube in that much earlier one: "He sort of glows, doesn't he?" (*AZ* 353).

Strawberries, a Greek village (*N* 49), a brick façade in New York City (*U* 387)—these ordinary things, lit up from within, all look and sound pretty spectacular. They are moments of heightened perception that seem to coincide or overlap with an iridescent, self-perceiving quality in the things themselves. Here is an early appearance of such a phenomenon, this one sports-related and drug-induced, in *End Zone*:

I sensed knowledge in the football. I sensed a strange power and restfulness. The football possessed awareness. The football knew what was happening. It knew. I'm sure of it.... The football knew that this is a football game. It knew that it was the center of the game. It was aware of its own footballness.

(*EZ* 37)

It is meant to be funny, and it is funny, this zen football, but it will lead to more serious moments of self-awareness—like the kind one encounters in the fruit section of a supermarket: "I took Wilder along the fruit bins. The fruit was gleaming and wet, hard-edged. There was a self-conscious quality about it" (*WN* 170). We saw earlier how Jack Gladney's perception is heightened in his encounter with Mink. It is a heightened perception in the observer that coincides with a radiance and self-presentation of the things themselves, a duplicity that leads to things finally becoming what they are, what they have always been:

> I continued to advance in consciousness. Things glowed, a secret life rising out of them.... I knew for the first time what rain really was. I knew what wet was.
>
> (*WN* 310)

Things somehow become themselves at such moments, coincident with their definitions, their names: "The weapon was gun-shaped, the little pointed projectiles reassuringly bullet-shaped" (*WN* 297). "I went out and watched him take the stairs two at a time. / I had an insight. He is a man who takes stairs two at a time" (*N* 74). Things become what they are. A certain redundancy is thus the ultimate insight: "The room was small and featureless. It was generic to the point of being a thing with walls. The ceiling was low, the bed was bedlike, the chair was a chair. There were no windows" (*ZK* 20).

Things thus come to be self-referring (*L* 23), which means that they have no outside: "this is my vision, a self-referring world, a world in which there is no escape" (*N* 297). This moment of self-reference is then *either* the point where everything closes down, where everything is snuffed out, *or* the place where things open up completely to what is outside them. It is the moment when things fold back into themselves not to disappear but to radiate, to become themselves—only better: "Mother used to stand in the arbor with an armful of cut flowers. Just stand there, being what she was" (*WN* 89). So it is that things concealed during a storm reappear afterwards as themselves, as existing, as if for the first time: "The power of storms to burnish and renew, he thought, had never been more clearly evident. The sky was flawless. Things *existed*. The day was scaled to pure tones of being and sense" (*RD* 244). In the end radiance seems to coincide with things not simply glowing from within but actually becoming self-aware, self-referring, lit up from within by "a stab of awareness" (*C* 72; see *N* 280, *U* 230, 752, 821). And it can happen to the least thing, "the smallest falling leaf," for example, "stabbed with self-awareness" (*BA* 7). Things become like the haiku that evokes them, a haiku that "means nothing beyond what it is" (*PO* 29; see *FM* 32).

Such radiance is related to the opposites or the contraries we have seen throughout. It is what happens when one goes "beyond" opposites, as band and contraband produce not contradiction but a sort of conflagration:

> When I go into mystical states, I pass beyond the opposites of the world and experience only the union of these opposites in a radiant burst of energy. I call it a burst. What else can I call it? You shouldn't think it's really a burst. Everything in the universe works on the theory of opposites.
>
> (*RS* 218–19)

On the final page of *Ratner's Star*, this radiance returns, coinciding with Endor's descent into the earth and his loss of language, as least becomes best and radiance becomes release:

> He continued to dig the hole's hole. The sounds he uttered became by degrees more rudimentary and crude. He crawled, knowing, he scratched at dirt, he clawed the hard earth, everywhere, feeling it, a sense of interlocking opposites, the paradox, the comedy, the fool's rule of total radiance.
>
> (*RS* 438)

Water dropping to the ground, the setting sun—ordinary events seen anew, unfolding or manifesting from out of themselves, that is, from out of nothing, or nothing more than the language that doubles or contrabands them, marking them with the silence from which they emerged.

Conclusion
Silent Mode (The Future of Contraband)

That whereof we cannot speak, thereof we must remain silent.
                                    Ludwig Wittgenstein, *Tractatus*

What cannot be said above all must not be silenced, but written.
                                    Jacques Derrida, *The Post Card*

All writers repeat themselves, the good ones in interesting and the lesser ones in uninteresting ways. In lesser writers repetition is often the sign of a lack of creativity or a waning imagination, while in the better ones it is the way to create a motif or a theme. In the very best, however, it can be the sign of a preoccupation or an obsession that gives meaning, coherence, and texture to a corpus. At 116 pages, published in large type—and in typewriter font—with lots of space around the text (an imitation facsimile, it would seem, of DeLillo's original typescript), *The Silence* (2020) is a novel-novella that repeats many of the themes and topoi and even words of DeLillo's earlier works. Almost everything we have looked at here in *Apocalyptic Ruin and Everyday Wonder in Don DeLillo's America* is to be found there, America—and once again New York City—as well as what lies beyond it, starting with France, but then also sports and gambling, air travel and tourism, the academy, philosophy and religion, science and technology, and, of course, destruction, catastrophe, apocalypse, and war.

The Silence thus repeats, but with some telling differences and in ways that should interest us, the DeLillo corpus that has been at the center of this analysis and, indeed, this celebration of DeLillo's work. In this conclusion, we will look at this most recent work of DeLillo's in order to see how it overlaps with or confirms DeLillo other works and, especially, how it diverges from or breaks with them. All that in an attempt to say something about the *future* of contraband in DeLillo's work.

More like a play than a novel in many respects, *The Silence* could be staged and performed in two relatively brief acts, the first requiring just a few changes in décor and the second no more than in a single set representing a single living room. There are just five main characters throughout these two acts, two couples and an uncoupled fifth person. This is writing stripped down to its bare essentials, to its "basic parameters," to use the subtitle of a course Babette taught at the Congregational Church (*WN* 171), two to five people in a room, talking, working the space, biding their time, people with nothing but time, space, language, and a looming catastrophe between them.

While the exact nature of this catastrophe will remain unspecified, any reader living in the age of COVID-19 will have no difficulty "identifying" with certain aspects of it. Released in October 2020, though apparently finished well before, *The Silence* seems to have "carried the virus of the future" within it, to cite *Mao II* (*M* 119), with its talk of "virus, plague, the march through airport terminals, the face masks, the city streets emptied out" (*S* 88), people "escorting each other through the mass insomnia of this inconceivable time" (*S* 78).

Whatever the actual chronology of DeLillo's writing, the time of the narrative itself is clear. It's early February 2022 (February 6, if you Google it), Super Bowl Sunday, and the Tennessee Titans are taking on the Seattle Seahawks in Super Bowl LVI (it actually turned out to have been the LA Rams against the Cincinnati Bengals, with the Bengals beating the Titans in the divisional playoffs and the Seahawks, at 7–10, not even making the playoffs), the game being played in the newly opened SoFi Stadium in Inglewood—where else?—California. The first of the two couples is Jim Kripps (pronounced, presumably, like "crypts," as in "cryptocurrencies," but written with a "K," of course) and Tessa Berens, returning by plane to New York (or Newark, really) that afternoon from a two week vacation in Paris. Jim is a claims adjuster for an insurance company (*S* 39) and Tessa, his "dark-skinned" wife of "Caribbean-European-Asian origins," at once a "poet" and "an editor with an advisory group that answered questions from subscribers on subjects ranging from hearing loss to bodily equilibrium to dementia" (*S* 7). Their plan is to make their way upon arrival to the apartment of two friends in Manhattan to watch the game. With the kickoff at six-thirty and the plane scheduled to arrive at Newark at "sixteen thirty" (*S* 11), they should have plenty of time, they think (especially since, smart travelers that they are, they didn't check in any luggage), to make it to their friends' apartment for the beginning of the game.

On the ground, waiting in their upper East Side Manhattan apartment for Jim and Tessa to arrive and for the Super Bowl to begin are Max Stenner, a building inspector, and Diane Lucas, a retired college professor of physics. The couple has two grown-up children, both girls, one married and living in Boston, the other on holiday in Europe (*S* 29). The fifth and final figure, waiting for the game to begin with Max and Diane, is Martin Dekker, a former student of Diane's, now working as a high school physics teacher in the Bronx (*S* 20). Mid-thirties, "neatly dressed" and "clean shaven" (*S* 22)—a little detail we will want to hold on to—Dekker has been for the past year "lost in his compulsive study of *Einstein's 1912 Manuscript on the Special Theory of Relativity*" (*S* 22–3). Of course, just Dekker's name is enough to tell us that, in a DeLillo novel, he will play a key role, for it sports not just one "k" (like Kripps) but two (like Kierkegaard, who is not mentioned in *The Silence* but figures prominently in *Falling Man*, and like Kafka, who is not mentioned either but does appear in *Ratner's Star*, alongside Einstein, who, wouldn't you know it, may have actually met Kafka, possibly in Prague, in 1911, right around the time Einstein was lecturing on the theory of relativity (see *RS* 89)). Martin has joined Max and Diane in front of their "superscreen TV" (*S* 19) in order to watch, like most of America, the big game.

The novel thus begins with a quintessentially DeLillo back-and-forth, a perfectly DeLillo contrabanded narrative, between, on the one hand, Jim and Tessa's flight from Paris to Newark, including (spoiler alert) the eventual crash landing, and, on the other, the New York apartment where Max, Diane, and Martin are waiting for the game to begin and Jim and Tessa to arrive, a narrative back-and-forth that is punctuated by the time left in the flight, posted minute by minute on the inflight screens in the cabin, and the "six-thirty kickoff" (*S* 8).

We thus have two narrative lines, one moving forward in space and time, the other advancing only in time. It's not unlike *Falling Man*, where Keith Neudecker and his colleagues are stationary on the morning of 9-11, waiting unknowingly in the South Tower for impact, as the hijackers, in flight from Boston, are headed for that same tower. Just as in *Falling Man*, then, we will see how both narrative lines, both sides of the equation, as it were, are interrupted at more or less the same time by catastrophe.

The Silence is essentially the contrabanding of these two catastrophes, the local or localized catastrophe, if it can be called that, the plane crashing with Jim and Tessa in it, and then the generalized catastrophe responsible for it, the one we first witness with Max, Diane, and Martin when the electricity goes out. Hence chapter 1 of Part One revolves around Jim and Tessa aboard the plane; chapter 2 focuses on Max and Diane in their Manhattan apartment with Martin; chapter 3 brings us back to Jim and Tessa, this time in a van taking them to a clinic to get Jim's head cut bandaged up after the crash at Newark; chapter 4 takes place back at Max and Diane's; chapter 5 brings us back to Jim and Tessa, now at that clinic somewhere in Manhattan, within walking distance from Max and Diane's; and chapter 6 brings us back to Max, Diane, and Martin, who are finally joined by Jim and Tessa in the East Side apartment. ("I was hoping it was you." "It's us, barely," says Jim Kripps as they are greeted at the door (*S* 70).)

Apart from a brief reconnaissance mission by Max into the streets of Manhattan to find out what the hell is going on (*S* 98–9), the apartment of Max and Diane will be the setting for all of Part Two, which has no chapter divisions, only section breaks, each one marked by what looks like seventeen underlined spaces, and a shifting number and configuration of characters, sometimes all five, sometimes three (when Jim and Tessa are resting in the bedroom), and sometimes just two (when Max leaves the apartment to find out what is happening).

Everything we have seen in this work concerning DeLillo's multiple and varied uses of "contrabanded" narratives and themes can be found on full display in *The Silence*, beginning with air travel as a sort of contraband life, a life within or outside or beyond life as we typically live it. One could imagine a DeLillo-inspired ad campaign that would use these words as their ironic slogan: "Filling time. Being bored. Living life" (*S* 10). Once again, DeLillo has depicted the life lived miles above the ground as a parallel life, one disconnected for the most part from life down below. "Here, in the air, much of what the couple said to each other seemed to be a function of some automated process, remarks generated by the nature of airline travel itself" (*S* 7). On planes, talk is "free-floating," "sentences trimmed, sort of self-encased... every word forgotten the moment the plane sets down on the tarmac" (*S* 7). Indeed every word is not only self-encased but prepackaged and just waiting to be reheated, with phrases like, "Children on this flight. Well-behaved." That's Jim speaking to Tessa, the two of them flying business class for once, which provokes the DeLillo-inspired add-on about these kids: "They know they're not in economy. They sense their responsibility" (*S* 15). As for their other fellow passengers, they, like their language, are also self-encased, living lives of the flying dead: "images of sleeping people bundled into airline blankets, looking dead"—and then, in contraband—"the tall attendant asking if she could refill his wine glass" (*S* 8).

Now if most of Jim and Tessa's flight aboard their jumbo jet returning from Paris resembles other DeLillo narratives of travel and tourism (see *S* 13, 41, 43), the landing is a little more turbulent. First, there's the seemingly more than just choppy air, followed by "a massive knocking somewhere below them." It's at this point that the inflight screen—the one that gives you all the information on the flight, time to destination and so forth—"went blank. Pilot speaking French, no English follow-up" (*S* 16). Because you know it's serious when they don't even bother to translate. Jim thus quickly goes

Conclusion: Silent Mode (The Future of Contraband) 223

from looking ahead to the Super Bowl to imagining that "every passenger was looking straight ahead into the six o'clock news, at home, on Channel 4, waiting for word of their crashed airliner" (S 16–17).

Throughout the ordeal Jim and Tessa gauge their own feelings, their fears and their expectations, by looking at one another—just as we would have expected from other DeLillo works. When that massive knocking sound begins, for example, Tessa asks Jim, "Are we afraid?" (S 17). It's a real question because "life can get so interesting that we forget to be afraid" (S 37), and so we need confirmation or reminding of just how bad things really are. Same thing after the crash, in the van taking them to the clinic, "Jim waited for Tessa to look at him so they could trade looks" (S 37; see 45). To find out what you think and feel, even who you are, even whether you are still alive, the idea is, as always in DeLillo, to look not inside (since no one in there knows anything) but at others around you. That is particularly necessary, it seems, when you have survived a crash landing: "'We have to remember to keep telling ourselves that we're still alive,' Tessa said, loud enough for the others to hear" (S 39).

DeLillo's interest in sports, and particularly football, is also on striking display in *The Silence*. It's Super Bowl Sunday, after all, the yearly sporting event that draws more people in America to their TVs than any other during the year. And they are there not just for the game but also for the commercials: "One hundred commercials in the next three or four hours" (S 21). Diane is exaggerating the number, but only just slightly, as when she wonders aloud whether the game is being played in "The Benzedrex Nasal Decongestant Memorial Coliseum" (S 24). Because it's hard not to be cynical about all the hype, though it is even harder not to watch. So if you are planning an attack on the electricity grid, you could not pick a better day.

Whereas Martin says he prefers that other kind of football known as soccer—"Ancient traditions. Entire countries involved to the core. A shared religion…. People gathered in huge public squares in country after country, the World Cup, cheering, weeping" (S 24)—Max, like every true-blooded American, endorses America's surprisingly *less* Puritanical version of the game: "What kind of sport is it where you can't use your hands? Can't touch the ball with your hands unless you're the goaltender. It's like self-repression of the normal impulse" (S 25). Moreover, American football is simple to follow. Beyond all the intricacies of prevent defenses and T or I formation offenses, it's a simple game of simple numbers, as Max reminds us: "two teams, eleven players each time, rectangular field one hundred yards long, goal lines and goal posts at either end, the national anthem sung by a semi-celebrity, six U.S. Air Force Thunderbirds streaking over the stadium" (S 19). That's all you need to know to enjoy the game.

The Super Bowl is also the most betted-on sporting event of the year, and Max has a few dollars riding on the game. As Diane says: "I am waiting for him to die first so he can tell me in his final breath how much money he has pissed away in the years of our something-or-other partnership" (*S* 21). Just how much Max has put down on this game we do not know, but we can bet it's enough to make the game interesting to the end, with point spreads and under-overs, a whole world of calculation ruled by desire: "Let the impulse dictate the logic. This was the gambler's creed, his formal statement of belief" (*S* 19). Because you can bet on almost anything these days, as we already knew from *Zero K*, where Stak, Emma's teenage son, frequents "online wagering sites" to bet not on sports but "plane crashes, real ones, various odds, posted depending on the airline, the country, the time frame, other factors" (*ZK* 193–4). (Had he, for example, placed a bet on Jim and Tessa's plane crashing, a perfectly ordinary flight from a perfectly respectable country in perfectly unexceptional weather, he would have made a killing.)

Here is how the catastrophe—the big one—is first signaled on the ground, that is, in Max and Diane's apartment. It is not, like most catastrophes these days, like the ones talked about in *White Noise* and elsewhere, brought to us through the magic of television. This time, the catastrophe *is* the TV, that is, the fact that it stops working.

> Something happened then. The image onscreen began to shake. It was not ordinary visual distortion, it had depth, it formed abstract patterns that dissolved into a rhythmic pulse, a series of elementary units that seemed to thrust forward and then recede. Rectangles, triangles, squares…. Then the screen went blank.
>
> (*S* 25–6)

So first it's the inflight screen on Jim and Tessa's flight, then it's the TV in Max and Diane's apartment. No matter how much Max plays with the remote control the screen stays blank. And then they realize it's not just the TV: "He and Diane checked their phones. Dead. She walked across the room to the house phone, the landline, a sentimental relic. No dial tone. Laptop, lifeless" (*S* 26).

When it eventually becomes clear that the problem is more widespread than their apartment or even their building, that it's bigger, much bigger, though no one knows exactly how big, we hear Diane saying to herself: "Think of the many millions of blank screens. Try to imagine the disabled phones. / What happens to people who live inside their phone?" (*S* 52).

That seems to be one of the central questions or challenges of *The Silence*. As we read later in the novel about these particular devices that, today, seem to tell us who we are:

> In other times, more or less ordinary, there are always people staring into their phones, morning, noon, night, middle of the sidewalk, oblivious to everyone hurrying past, engrossed, mesmerized, consumed by the device, or walking toward him and then veering away, but they can't do it now, all the digital addicts, phones shut down, everything down down down.
>
> (S 99)

The argument about science and technology that we looked at in some detail in the pages above here seems to reach its ultimate conclusion with a worldwide breakdown in the systems that supposedly link us: not just phones, computers, and TVs but the entire electrical grid. "Seemingly all the screens have emptied out, everywhere" (S 80). "Stove dead, refrigerator dead" (S 66). It's the whole "grid system, all emptied out," "no street lights, store lights, high-rise buildings, skyscrapers, all windows everywhere" (S 70). With the breakdown of all the systems around them, people begin wondering again just who they are without their devices: "All the people watching intently or sitting as we are, puzzled by science, technology, common sense" (S 29). It's a cross between the great Blackout of 1965 and 9–11, though the catastrophe seems to reach well beyond New York City.

There's the loss of power on the plane, in the apartment, and then in the clinic where Jim and Tessa have gone to get Jim's head wound taken care of:

> The overhead lights blinked and dimmed and then went out. There was instant silence throughout the clinic. Everyone waiting. A sense also of fear-in-waiting because it wasn't clear yet what this might mean, how radical, how permanent an aberration in what was already a drastic shift of events.
>
> (S 60)

It is not long thereafter that the woman administrator in the clinic delivers one of the morals of the story. The more we rely on these systems the more we are in trouble when they fail us. In short, "The more advanced, the more vulnerable. Our systems of surveillance, our facial recognition devices, our imagery resolution. How do we know who we are?" (S 61). At least she still has a sense of being someone and living somewhere beyond her screens and her job. As she says, wondering how she will get home: "I love my cubicle but I don't want to die here" (S 62).

At first, there are searches for the cause of it all, speculations, hypotheses. Martin wonders, half-seriously, whether it was the Chinese (no mention, curiously, of Russian hackers): "They've initiated a selective internet apocalypse. They are watching, we are not" (S 27). Max's neighbors, with whom he consults on the matter, a bit like Jack Gladney at the beginning of the airborne toxic event, have other explanations: "Something technical. Nobody blamed the Chinese. A systems failure. Also a sunspot. This was a serious response. A guy smoking a pipe" (S 34). As we remember from *White Noise*, in emergencies like this the first thing you do is solicit the opinions of those who are just as much in the dark as you are. And so, says Max, "We stood in the hallway becoming neighbors for the first time. Men, women, nodding our heads" (S 34).

By Part Two of the novel, certain things can be said with a little more certainty about what is not happening, though no one really knows what is: "It is clear by now that the launch codes are being manipulated remotely by unknown groups or agencies. All nuclear weapons, worldwide, have become dysfunctional. Missiles are not soaring over oceans, bombs are not being dropped from supersonic aircraft" (S 77). So it's not Armageddon, at least not yet, or at least it's not the one we have been prepared to expect, though that only fuels the speculation and unleashes the onslaught of language: "Cyberattacks, digital intrusions, biological aggressions. Anthrax, smallpox, pathogens. The dead and disabled. Starvation, plague and what else?" (S 77) "Power grids collapsing. Our personal perceptions sinking into quantum dominance" (S 77).

Maybe it's war and maybe it's climate change, or maybe some combination of the two: "Are the oceans rising rapidly? Is the air getting warmer, hour by hour, minute by minute?" (S 77). It's as if all the ills or plagues or dangers of the world were cascading down into this one small room in Manhattan: "Dark energy, phantom waves, hack and counterhack.... Mass surveillance software that makes its own decisions, overruling itself at times" (S 80). "Internet arms race, wireless signals, countersurveillance" (S 85), not to mention "Satellites in orbit that are able to see everything. The street where we live. The building we work in. The socks we are wearing" (S 90). (And we haven't heard the last of socks.) "The drone wars. Never mind country of origin. The drones have become autonomous" (S 93). "Plastics, microplastics. In our air, our water, our food" (S 94).

It is unclear what is a genuine threat and what is not, what is threatening and what is protecting us, what threats are existential and what are just major inconveniences. It's all so unknown that people soon seem to grow nostalgic for the good old days of war and terrorism when the sides were clearly demarcated—and, most important, things could still be seen on TV: "Do people experience memories of earlier conflicts, the spread of terrorism, the shaky video of someone approaching an embassy, a bomb vest strapped to his chest? Pray and die. War that we can see and feel. / Is there a shred of nostalgia in these recollections?" (*S* 78).

Without news or images to feed their speculations, the characters begin to turn less toward geopolitical questions—Was it China? What is our government doing or saying about all of this?—and more toward physics and cosmology. Diane recalls Martin as a student: "In class you quoted footnotes. You vanished into footnotes. Einstein, Heisenberg, Gödel. Relativity, uncertainty, incompleteness" (*S* 29). Diane and Martin, teacher and student, will thus begin talking physics, and particularly Einstein. "Einstein and black holes in space. He said it and then we saw it…. His universe became ours. Black holes. The event horizon. The atomic clocks" (*S* 30). Martin recalls on a couple of occasions "The Large Synoptic Survey Telescope" in Chile (*S* 30; see 100), that is—and it's a real thing—the super-telescope at the Vera C. Rubin Laboratory in the Andes Mountains, operational only since 2021. He thinks of this because the global or terrestrial catastrophe they seem to be experiencing may have an extraterrestrial cause. As Martin says: "Asteroids that become meteorites as they approach a planet…. Why not us. Why not now" (*S* 90).

We are now well beyond the hypothesis of a simple power outage. But, again, none of this can be confirmed or verified because all the screens are blank, all the news sources silent. The most we can learn about what is going on comes from Max, who first ventures out into the hallway of his apartment building and then into the neighborhood. When he returns and the others in the apartment ask him, "What is happening in the streets?", asking him for themselves but also for us, the reader, who is just as curious, he simply replies, "You don't want to know" (*S* 101).

But Martin, filled with the language of Einstein, whose words about World Wars III and IV are the epigraph to the entire novel, has yet another hypothesis. In a section of Part Two that consists of a single line, Martin speculates: "Nobody wants to call it World War III but this is what it is" (*S* 79). The theme of war is already evoked earlier, indeed already in the military flyover at the Super Bowl, when Max, continuing DeLillo's argument in *End Zone*, rejects the common comparison between war and sports: "We've gone beyond all comparisons between football and war. World Wars in Roman numerals, Super Bowl in Roman numerals. War is something else, happening somewhere else" (*S* 28).

If war in *Zero K* was total projection, with all of the wars, real and imagined, being combined and then screened, projected, in the Convergence, *The Silence* represents none of these wars, none of the deaths or the violence, not through narrative (Diane surmises that Max has seen the "bedlam" on the streets, but Max himself is not talking) and not through images (since all the screens are blank). With all the devices silent, everything—whatever it may be—is taking place off-screen. We do not know just how bad it is (there has already been one crash landing at Newark), so in the absence of any concrete information the speculation turns from the geopolitical to the cosmological and then even the metaphysical:

> Are we an experiment that happens to be falling apart, a scheme set in motion by forces outside our reckoning? This is not the first time these questions have been asked. Scientists have said things, written things, physicists, philosophers.
>
> (*S* 88–9)

Whatever it is, whatever the cause, it all seems headed toward that Omega Point that, as we have seen, DeLillo seems to have been talking about for decades now. Max was already heading in this direction when he came up on his own, with all the screens blank, with this brief commercial announcement: "*Perpetual Postmorten Financing. Start your exclusive arrangements online*" (*S* 48). Or in his introduction to the big game itself: "*Super Bowl Fifty-Six. Our National Death Wish*" (*S* 48). For the idea is that some of us, maybe all of us, had a sense that it was coming. Tessa says, "It was always at the edges of our perception. Power out, technology slipping away, one aspect, then another" (*S* 88). And Diane: "Didn't this have to happen? Isn't that what some of us are thinking? We were headed in this direction. No more wonder, no more curiosity" (*S* 105). For Martin, it's not just a premonition but a secret desire: "All my life I've been waiting for this without knowing it" (*S* 103). It's something that we have all been at once dreading and desiring—dreaming about in contraband: "The semi-darkness. It's somewhere in the mass mind. The pause, the sense of having experienced this before…. People in the grip of serious threat" (*S* 65). Time for a reckoning, as it were, but with no devices to guide or enlighten us, we, vulnerable earthlings, are left to our own devices, left to figure it out—ourselves and our predicament—all by ourselves:

> And isn't it strange that certain individuals have seemed to accept the shutdown, the burnout? Is this something that they've always longed for, subliminally, subatomically? Some people, always some, a minuscule

number among the human inhabitants of planet Earth, third planet from the sun, the realm of mortal existence.

(*S* 78)

This is not the first time DeLillo will have spoken this way of planet earth. One novel before, in *Zero K* again, the earth has a similar definition and is the place for a similar search for meaning: "They were clinging to the surface, weren't they, both of them? Earth in all its meanings, third planet from the sun, realm of mortal existence, every definition in between" (*ZK* 242).

There is, then, in *The Silence*, in the narrative as a whole and in the progression of the narrative, a steady whittling away or narrowing down from page 1 to 116 (the upside down inverse of 911, if anyone is interested, an observation that seems less of a stretch when considered in the light of these reflections about the number 101 in *Ratner's Star*: "One zero one. Not only the lowest three-digit prime but the smallest three-digit palindrome. Not only reads the same forward and back but rightside up and upside down" (*RS* 99)). At a certain point we are reduced to the basic elements of drama: a handful of people on the third planet from the sun, in a single room, with only time, space, and language between them, giving them time to reflect on one another and themselves: "Was each a mystery to the others, however close their involvement, each individual so naturally encased that he or she escaped a final determination, a fixed appraisal by the others in the room?" (*S* 72–3). We are talking here about people in a room—and there's that "encased" again—people in space and time, though we could be talking about elementary particles. Martin quotes from Einstein's manuscript of 1912, "The beautiful and airy concepts of space and time," before then adding, "Space and time. Spacetime" (*S* 29). Those are the things of physics but also, as we have seen, the things of literature, especially when the narrative is stripped down, like *The Silence*, to a handful of people in a room over the course of a single afternoon and evening in February 2022. People lost in space and time, people in spacetime: those are the basic elements of literature.

For in addition to being a novel about some unknown global catastrophe, *The Silence* is, like all of DeLillo's novels, essentially about literature, or rather about language and writing. Though it is titled *The Silence*, it begins with words, that is, with "words": "*Words, sentences, numbers, distance to destination*" (*S* 3). Those are the first words of the novel, and soon thereafter Jim Kripps begins speaking or narrating to himself the words and numbers he is reading off his inflight screen: "He began to recite the words and numbers aloud because it made no sense, it had no effect, if he simply noted the changing details only to lose each one instantly in the twin drones of mind and aircraft" (*S* 3–4). On the flight from Newark to Paris, there was "no bilingual screen" (*S* 13), but on the way back there is, and Jim is happy, or at least intrigued—"You like your screen," says Tessa (*S* 13)—until it suddenly goes blank.

That is just the beginning of a novel whose implicit or silent theme— beyond the global catastrophe suggested there—is language, and names, beginning with English, indeed very English names, like *scone*, the kind they might serve as a snack before landing in Newark: "I like to pronounce the word properly. An abbreviated letter *o*. As in scot or trot. Or is it scone as in moan?" (*S* 5). Before all the German (through Einstein) there is thus English, and already with English some French. Jim asks Tessa, who speaks French, about the meaning of one of the words on his inflight screen: "What about vitesse. What does vitesse mean?" "Vitesse. Speed," she said (*S* 5).

The Silence is thus yet another DeLillo novel about letters and names, about speaking names, translating names, and first of all remembering names, whether with or without the mnemonic supplement of some device. Early on in the novel, on the same inflight screen, there are a few more French words, followed by English and a letter: "Température extérieure minus fifty-eight C." It is Tessa again who knows the French and knows what the C stands for but cannot remember, at least not at first, the first name: "Celsius. Cap *C*. It was someone's name. Can't recall his first name" (*S* 5). Moments later she remembers that Celsius was "Swedish," and, no, she didn't "sneak a look at [her] phone" (*S* 6). For such things can "come swimming out of deep memory" (*S* 6), the last name first, the easy part, but then eventually the first: "'I remember now.... Came out of nowhere, Anders.... The first name of Mr. Celsius.... Anders Celsius.' She found this satisfying. Came out of nowhere. There is almost nothing left of nowhere" (*S* 14). Almost nothing comes out of nowhere anymore because everything is already stored in our devices, all the memories we will ever need or want. Just turn it on and you will see that C is for Celsius in *The Silence*, like K is for Kelvin in *Zero K*.

But there are still times, it seems, when words come "swimming out of deep memory," or out of dreams, as with one of Martin's students: "It was a dream of words, not images. Two words. He woke up with those words and just stared into space. *Umbrella'd ambuscade. Umbrella* with an apostrophe d. And *ambuscade*" (*S* 69). An umbrella, then, at once protector from rain and a sort of sunscreen, an eclipser of the sun, though maybe also, in the underworld of Martin's student, a shadow of some terrorist act, whether in the past or to come.

Even the religion of *The Silence* seems to be, as we have seen elsewhere in DeLillo, a question less of cult or doctrine than of words and names. After Max utters a series of "Jesus"-laced invectives motivated by the fact that he has no idea how his bet is going, Diane completes the name, "Jesus of Nazareth," anticipating that Martin will fill in the Einstein reference: "The radiant name," says Martin, and then, quoting Einstein, "I am a Jew but I am enthralled by the luminous figure of the Nazarene" (*S* 42; see 53). So there's that radiance again, the one that we saw emanating out of so many DeLillo novels, particularly near the end. Here the radiance and the power seem to be attached to the name:

> She knew that the name Jesus of Nazareth carried an intangible quality that drew him into its aura. He did not belong to a particular religion and did not feel reverence for any being of alleged supernatural power. / It was the name that gripped him. The beauty of the name. The name and place.
>
> (*S* 43)

And as with religion, so with sex. While waiting in the clinic to get the cut on Jim's head bandaged up, Jim and Tessa are able to find an empty bathroom for a quickie (*S* 56). It's a little odd and unexpected, coming, as it does, just after a crash landing, but what's less unexpected is the fact that it is language that turns them on or gets them off: "Tessa whispered a list of nationalities as they completed the act" (*S* 57). Later, it is Martin's use of the term "Cryptocurrencies" that seems to get Diane, his former teacher, into the mood for a different kind of physics lesson after Max leaves the apartment to find out what's going on outside. "Cryptocurrencies.... Money running wild.... No government standard. Financial mayhem" (*S* 85). Diane "builds the word in her mind, unhyphenated.... 'Crypto,' she says, pausing, keeping her eyes on Martin. 'Currencies'" (*S* 86). Though teacher and student never actually complete the transaction, the "libidinal" overtones seem to remain in the air as long as the language does (*S* 93–4).

The Silence, despite the title, or actually because of the title—since the title is a name—is thus essentially a story about language, about words. Take this description of tourists—a theme we see early and often in the novel—and watch how it veers into language: "In one gallery tourists with headsets, motionless, lives suspended, looking up at the painted figure on the ceiling, angels, saints, Jesus in his garments, his raiment" (*S* 44). It's just another word, a quasi-synonym, for "garments," but Martin can actually see the thing within the word: "His raiment. I try to think of a rumpled garment embedded in the word" (*S* 45). For words and names have here not only sense and meaning but shape and texture, height and girth: "Kripps was a tall man's name and he was tall" (*S* 11). Already in *Ratner's Star*, recall, *kilt* was a more revealing name than *guilt*.

There are English words and French, as we have seen, and references to all the languages we hear when we travel, watching and listening to "others with audio guides hand-held, pressed to their ears. Voices in how many languages" (*S* 45). But then there is German. Martin says near the end, "When we're finished with all this, it may be time for me to embrace a free death. *Freitod*" (*S* 103), and, well before that, he uses world-words like "Weltpunkt" and "Weltlinie" (*S* 31). These are, of course, Einstein's words, but they are also part of DeLillo's world, his *Welt*, from *Underworld*, which feature's Eisenstein's *Unterwelt*, through *Zero K*, where there's "a list, a litany of German words... words in most cases beginning with the syllables *welt, wort,* or *tod*" (*ZK* 77).

Bur it is not just Einstein's theories about space and time or spacetime that somehow get translated into the space and time of literature. It is also his *writing*. The Einstein manuscript of 1912 is interesting, Martin thinks, not only for the ideas expressed in it but for the thinking *inscribed* there: "Yes, the words and phrases that he crossed out. We can see him think.... The nature of the handwritten text. The numbers, letters, expressions" (*S* 31). "This is Einstein, his handwriting, his formulas, his letters and numbers. The sheer physical beauty of the pages" (*S* 32). With the typewriter font of *The Silence*— the one that began the novel with the words "*Words, sentences, numbers, distance to destination*"—the point seems to be that we are not only reading but watching DeLillo write or type, watching him pull one sheet after another out of the Panasonic or whatever it is and stack it in a little pile on his desk. (Some words and letters, we might even see, make more of an impression on the page, have more depth than others, MAX, for example, built out of a series of open-ended triangles, or Vs, as in Vitesse or Vol or Velocity, not to mention Super Bowl LVI and World War IV and, of course, TV.)

As always, it is letters and numbers that give sense to the world: Max "count[ing] the steps as he climbs to the apartment" (*S* 99), Tessa "counting down slowly by sevens from two hundred and three to zero, deadpan, changing languages along the way" (*S* 72; see the epigraph 7 pages earlier). And *The Silence* itself, so slim at 116 pages, Part One, broken into six chapters, and then Part Two, with its unnumbered breaks. None of it means anything, or at least not much, and the same goes for the repetition or the return of all those DeLillo themes from novels past, the references to real life as a movie (see *S* 39, 104), the multiple mirrors (*S* 12, 51, 84), even the drugs Martin has been taking, medications with such possible side effects as "Irrational fear. Distrust of others" (*S* 49), a drug that, unlike Dylar, which was supposed to counteract our (rational) fear of death, brings on an irrational fear. And speaking of fear, there is philosophy, which, for Martin, is also more about the words than anything else:

> Thaumatology, ontology, eschatology, epistemology. He could not stop himself. Metaphysics, phenomenology, transcendentalism. He paused and thought and kept going. Teleology, etiology, ontogeny, phylogeny.
> (*S* 68)

Even Marvin Lundy from *Underworld*, who lives in New Jersey, after all (and so maybe heard the crash), makes a guest appearance in *The Silence* through Martin, who says at one point, "Greenland is disappearing" (*S* 94; see *U* 315–16).

All the old DeLillo themes are thus here, war, technology, tourism, academia, philosophy, and then even things like alcohol, that earliest of contrabanded themes, even though, as always, it is the language that is most intoxicating. Waiting for the TV image to return, Max pours himself "a glass of bourbon called Widow Jane, aged ten years in American oak" (*S* 41). What did he like about it? Probably the taste, but especially the name and description: "Aged ten years in American oak. It was something he liked saying, a hint of irony in his voice" (*S* 42). Indeed, some sixty pages later he's at it again: "'Widow Jane,' he says. 'Aged ten years in American oak. Did I say this before?'" (*S* 101)

But that is not Max's only linguistic turn. With the TV screen blank and the game unwatchable, Max begins providing his own color commentary for an invisible game: "*This team is ready to step out of the shadows and capture the moment…. During this one blistering stretch, the offense has been pounding, pounding, pounding…. Ground game, ground game, crowd chanting, stadium rocking*" (*S* 45–6). Diane, his partner of some thirty-seven years, is astonished by "his use of language… emerging from a broadcast level deep in his unconscious mind" (*S* 46). She is fascinated by these "Half sentences, bare words, repetitions." She "wanted to think of it as a kind of plainsong, monophonic, ritualistic, but then she told herself that this is pretentious non-sense" (*S* 46). Whatever we may think of Max's abilities for broadcasting, he joins the ranks of all the announcer-writers in DeLillo, from Russ Hodges in *Underworld* to Bill Gray in *Mao II*, who saw in the announcer's discourse something like an original form of writing: "When I was a kid I used to announce ballgames to myself. I sat in a room and made up the games and described the play-by-play out loud…. I do batting orders in my head all the time. And I've been trying to write toward that kind of innocence ever since" (*M* 45–6).

And of course, since it's DeLillo, we know that Max will start doing commercials as well—this first one for the very service whose interruption has caused Max to turn up his own volume: "*Wireless the way you want it. Soothes and moisturizes. Gives you twice as much for the same low cost. Reduces the risk of heart-and-mind disease*" (*S* 47). Again Diane wonders whether it is "the bourbon that's giving him this lilt, this flourish of football dialect and commercial jargon," or whether it's "the blank screen" that brought it on, "a negative impulse that provoked his imagination" (*S* 47–8). In other words, is this silence the end or the beginning of language? Is it the mere absence of words or the equivalent of the clean white piece of paper just waiting to be typed up? And just so the questions do not seem too deep, do not weigh us down like a doctoral thesis in linguistics, DeLillo gives Diane a bit of irony in counterpoint: "She was enjoying this, at least she thought she was, based on how much longer he kept broadcasting" (S 48).

Max is not the only one to be taken in and taken up by language, to be tuned in, as it were, to his own channel. If Max is broadcasting from the Fox Sports Network, Martin is channeling Nova or a PBS special on Einstein. He has been quoting Einstein throughout, but sometime after midnight quotation becomes actual imitation: "The way in which time has seemingly jumped forward. Did something happen at midnight to intensify the disruption? And the way in which Martin's voice is beginning to change" (S 81). Speaking about "bioweapons and the countries that possess them" (S 81), Martin suddenly begins speaking the living language of Einstein, but with an accent, "Albert Einstein speaking English" (S 82). It's yet another origin of language, it seems, a sort of speaking in tongues that can be deciphered only by the adept. Diane's Martin Dekker has become a sort of latter-day version of Lauren's Mr. Tuttle, only with a degree in physics (Mr. Tuttle was, after all, the name of Lauren's former science teacher):

> She is not sure that what he is saying is pure fiction. Something about him, his tone of voice, adopted accent, a sense that he has access to world events, whatever that means, however he is able to allow censored news to reach him. He said it himself, people with phones implanted in their bodies.
>
> (S 83)

What was once called glossolalia in DeLillo has become here a sort of "subcutaneous" telephony, the hypothesis of "a form of phone implanted in [our] bodies," tuned in to radio free Einstein (S 80). It can sound like the unfounded fears of anti-vaccinators, or like a QAnon conspiracy theory, but it is here being used to explain how language enters us, how it becomes us—like "organic shrapnel"—and makes us who we are:

> She understands that this is foolish, all of it. She also knows that there is something in her former student's essential nature that makes such speculation possible.... And she doesn't know whether these are terms out of the *1912 Manuscript*, Martin's bible, his playbook, or simply noises floating in the air, the language of World War III.
>
> (S 82–3)

Conclusion: Silent Mode (The Future of Contraband)

Those who have read *White Noise* could probably predict that Martin, Einstein's *doppelgänger*, will begin speaking actual German (we already saw him sprinkling in words beginning in *Welt*): "And now he swings from accented English into living German…. There is no hint of parody or self-parody" (*S* 83). "He sounds either brilliant or unbalanced, Martin does… with Einstein referring to himself in Martin's voice as Albert Einstein" (*S* 83). This is the guy who tells his students—and tells them in physics class, we presume—to watch foreign language films, and to watch them without subtitles:

> Foreign-language films in black-and-white. Films in unfamiliar languages…. Do not read subtitles. I tell them forthrightly. Avoid reading the printed translation of the spoken dialogue at the bottom of the screen. We want pure film, pure language. Indo-Iranian. Sino-Tibetan. People talking. They walk, talk, eat, drink. The stark power of black-and-white. The image, the optically formed duplicate.
> (*S* 51–2)

Word and image: with the narrative stripped down to bare basics, with the "plot" more or less out of the way, the characters of *The Silence* become much less concerned with what is happening outside or outside themselves and more concerned with what is happening to *them*. The fact that, for example, they are still alive. As Martin says, "People"—because it's not just Jim and Tessa—"have to keep telling themselves that they're still alive" (*S* 102).

We've been watching these five characters from the beginning. We have witnessed how each has responded to some technological catastrophe of unknown origin. Here, for example, is Max's first reaction when the TV screen goes blank on the game: "What is happening to my bet?" (*S* 26). And here's Martin: "Look at the blank screen. What is it hiding from us?" (*S* 28). And Martin's former teacher: "The screen. Diane kept edging her head around to make sure it was blank. She could not understand why this was reassuring to her" (*S* 49).

At the end of the novel we get a chance to see how each one, in turn, goes silent. For DeLillo has each character speak one last time, as in the theater, each given a final soliloquy in which each will try to remember or to question how they got where they are:

First to speak—and thus the first to go into silent mode—is Diane:

> Staring into space. Losing track of time. Going to bed. Getting out of bed. Months and years and decades of teaching…. I feel so simpleminded. A college professor who quit too soon. I want to resume teaching and

return to my classroom and speak to my students about the principles of physics. The physics of this, the physics of that. The physics of time. Absolute time. Time's arrow. Time and space.

(*S* 104–5)

With all this talk of the physics "of this and that," it is hard not to think of Father Paulus's lesson for Nick Shay in *Underworld* on "the physics of language." (And not just because of the mention of shoes just a few pages before. When Tessa comes out of Diane and Max's bedroom "fully dressed, wearing low-cut socks but no shoes," Max just has to ask, "What happened to your shoes?" and Tessa answers, "They walked off without me" (*S* 100–1).) For it is not just time and space that are at issue here but language or literature itself. If the connection seems forced, then you have to ask yourself why Diane ends by speaking not of Einstein or Heisenberg but Joyce:

> Before I shut up I will quote a stray line from *Finnegans Wake*, a book I've been reading on and off, here and there, for what seems like forever. The line has stayed secure in the proper mind slot, the word *preserve. Ere the sockson locked at the dure.* Just one more thing to say. To myself this time. Shut up, Diane.

(*S* 105)

And then Diane shuts up—radio silence for the remainder of the novel. But that's quite a way for a former physics professor to go out, quoting Joyce, the author who is cited or referred to more often than any other in *Americana*, DeLillo's first novel, and the one who, in his first published interview, DeLillo cites as providing the key to his writing, a line from the middle of *Portrait of the Artist as a Young Man* that speaks eloquently of silence: "I will try to express myself in some mode of life or art as freely as I can and as wholly as I can, using for my defence the only arms I allow myself to use— silence, exile, and cunning." (And if anyone is looking for more symmetry, *The Silence* is dedicated not just to Barbara, as *Zero K* was, but to Barbara Bennett, just like *Americana*.)

Joyce, then, but not just any Joyce, the Joyce of *Finnegans Wake*, the last Joyce, the Joyce who set the word "SILENCE." in capital letters and put it on a line all by itself, just the word, treated unlike any other, a single word, followed by a period (FW 501); the same Joyce who had earlier in the same work set nearly the same word without caps but with a period in parentheses "(Silent.)," this time between two sets of dates, double dates, mirror-imaged: "1132 ... 566 ... (Silent.) ... 566 ... 1132" (FW 14); the same Joyce who thus played on time and space and on the Einstein who thought them together, for example in "eins within a space and a wearywide space it wast ere whooned a Mookse," a rewriting in space and time of the time with which *Portrait* begins, "Once upon a time and very good time it was there was a moocow...." It's the beginning of language, or the beginning of the English language, simple English, there on the threshold, sixth century AD, let us say, ere the era of the Saxons who, socks on and sons of German stock, looked at the door—knock! lock!—and made it for the duration.

After Diane, Jim tells his story, beginning with the story of the plane crash he and Tessa have just survived. He recalls the look he didn't exchange with Tessa as the plane was about to go down: "I don't think I looked at her because I didn't want to see the look on her face" (*S* 106). He recalls thinking what other people in his position must have been thinking or feeling, all those others in the minutes before they went silent: "This is how it begins, this is how it feels, all those many thousands of passengers before us who have experienced this and then were silenced forever" (*S* 107). The crash promised to silence him forever, but the crash itself is compared to language, "the impact... felt like God's own voice, forgive me, and my head hit the window" (*S* 107).

After Diane and Jim, it's Max's turn at the plate, to mix sports metaphors, beginning with his return from outside and his trek up the stairs to the apartment since all the elevators were out. "I used to do this when I was a kid. Seventeen steps to count.... I'd like to say that I was reliving those earlier years but my mind was more or less blank. Just the stairs and the numbers, third floor, fourth floor, fifth floor, up and up and up" (*S* 109–10). But that's when he was a kid. Now, adult, his name alone says it all: "People today tell me that they can't imagine me as a kid. Was I called Max?... A kid named Max" (*S* 109). His job as a building inspector consists in going into luxury towers to find "violations of the building code." It's satisfying work on many levels: "I love the violations. It justifies all my feelings about just about everything" (*S* 109–10). Max tells us in a couple of pages his story of returning from the streets, a tale mixed with the story of his life, before going, he too, suddenly silent.

After Diane, Jim, and Max, there's Tessa, Tessa Berens, who "studies the backs of her hands" (remember Jeffrey at the end of *Zero K*?) "as if confirming the color, her color, and wondering why she is here and not somewhere else in the world, speaking French or a kind of splintered Haitian Creole" (*S* 112). But then she talks about her writing, or at least her pre-writing, the notes that go into her writing, notes taken in little notebooks:

For years, many years, I've been writing in a little notebook. Ideas, memories, words, one notebook after another.... Means nothing to anyone but me. Could be a line of poetry that I will cross out seconds later. Could be an item on a supermarket shelf, the package design, the name of the product, take out the notebook, take out the ballpoint pen, so on and so on.

(*S* 112–13)

These little notebooks—little blue notebooks—have been there from the very beginning of the novel. For example, on the first printed page, still on the plane, before Tessa even has a name: "the woman nodded faintly and kept on writing in a little blue notebook" (*S* 3). It is that notebook, it seems, that Tessa lost during the crash landing (see *S* 38). But why blue? Because they had to be some color, but maybe also because Wittgenstein is known to have written in blue and brown notebooks, and what is happening here with her, Diane, Max, and Jim feels like a series of language games emerging momentarily out of silence and then returning to that silence.

It turns out that Tessa had been writing about her and Jim's trip to Paris, writing in English, "Elementary English. The cow jumped over the moon" (*S* 9). It's not "once upon a time there was a moocow" but it's close, and it causes Jim to wonder about the origin of it all. "He was watching her write. Was she writing what she was saying, what they were both saying?" (*S* 5). And since we, the reader, are reading what she has written, at least some of it, in a book titled *The Silence*, Tessa Berens has to be for us an image of our author, a sort of portrait of the artist as a young creole woman. Earlier, Tessa had said that she tends to *see* her work, her words, in her mind or on the page before she really understands what she wants to say: "There is a poem she wants to work on… the first line bouncing around in her brain for a while. / *In a tumbling void.* / She will see the line when she closes her eyes and concentrates. See the letters set against a dark background" (*S* 97).

At the end of her narrative, her testimony, Tessa says she just wants to walk home with Jim across Central Park to their upper West Side apartment. All she hopes for is that the sun will rise with the new day, another everyday miracle: "If we have to walk, fine, yes, in daylight. Will the sun be shining? Will the sun be in the sky at all? Who knows what any of this means?… I write, I think, I advise, I stare into space" (*S* 113). Here's the end of Tessa's speech, where she begins resorting to single words, action verbs, this time without pronouns, the "simplest physical things," but also, here too, the beginning and end of language:

Is it natural at a time like this to be thinking and talking in philosophical terms as some of us have been doing? Or should we be practical? Food, shelter, friends, flush the toilet if we can? Tend to the simplest physical things. Touch, feel, bite, chew. The body has a mind of its own.

(*S* 113)

One by one they are shutting up or shutting down, powering down or putting themselves into silent mode. After Diane, Jim, Max, and Tessa, it's Martin's time:

> Time to stop, isn't it? But I keep seeing the name. Einstein. Einstein's Theory of Relativity causing riots in the streets or am I imagining this because it's late and I haven't slept … Einstein speaking beyond our current situation, which I've referred to as World War III. Einstein had no premonition concerning how this war would be fought but he made it clear that the next major conflict, World War IV, would be fought with sticks and stones.
>
> (*S* 114)

And then Martin returns to the manuscript, not so much to the ideas as to the manuscript itself, to its writing, the manuscript as a piece of writing. There is thus time and space, writing, and then, like David Bell in *Americana*, like Selvy in *Running Dog*, like Ross Lockhart in *Zero K*, the need for a shave in order to prepare for what is coming next:

> And the Special Theory, dated 1912, one hundred and ten years ago. Manuscript brown ink, unwatermarked paper and then the paper improves and the ink goes black. This is what I carry in my head, for better or bad or worse. What else? I need a shave. That's what else. I need to look into a mirror and remind myself that it's time for a shave.
>
> (*S* 114–15)

But before ending, Martin too, in his own way, returns us to the origins of writing, moving backward from the language and terms of 2022 back to cave drawings and then, in the company of Einstein, to silence:

> Face in the mirror. Granular surveillance. Techdome. Two-factor verification. Gateway tracking. I can't help myself. The terms surround me. I try to think sometimes in a prehistorical context. A flagstone image, a cave drawing. All these grainy shreds of our long human memory. And then Einstein. The exhilarating language. German, English. "Dependence of mass on energy." I want to walk with him across the Princeton campus. Saying nothing, silent. Two men walking.
>
> (*S* 115)

Here are Martin's final words, Martin's and the last words spoken by any individual in the novel: "The world is everything, the individual nothing. Do we all understand that?" (S 115). After this, there is silence. Everyone has shut up. There is no more talking to be done. Just a few concluding words of writing, a description of Max back in front of his unworking TV. The narrator picks up the narrative at this point to bring it across the goal line:

> Max is not listening. He understands nothing. He sits in front of the TV set with his hands folded behind his neck, elbows jutting.
>
> Then he stares into the blank screen.

(S 116)

The Silence thus ends without the radiance of either *White Noise* or *Zero K*, without sunset or sunlight. The screens are still dark, Max "understands nothing," and, as we saw, there is even a question of whether there will be sunlight when morning comes. Whereas other novels, *Zero K*, for example, end with a miracle, or, maybe the same thing, an astronomical event like a sunset, *The Silence* ends with uncertainty about these very things. It ends, it goes silent, without sun or moon or earth, without the trinity or triangle or tricycle that marks the miraculous conclusion of other novels. The last time we saw triangles it was just as the TV image was blinking off—"Rectangles, triangles, squares" (S 25). Since then, nothing, no image, no signal, no miracle, no wonder, just a blank screen.

Unless, of course, we look at Max's final gesture, "hands folded behind his neck, elbows jutting," as if to form two Vs, two triangles, which come together to form one, one V, like that theory of history in *Ratner's Star*, or like a boomerang, even a coat hanger, the kind that, back in the old days, one would sometimes use to get better TV reception. Max gets himself positioned there, puts up the antenna as it were, and "Then he stares into the blank screen" (S 116).

Part I of the novel, we recall, had ended in almost exactly the same way, with the difference of just a single letter—"Then he stared into the blank screen" (S 73)—but that final "s" perhaps makes all the difference between past and present, the past and a present that is open to a future (Tessa too, recall, says, "I write, I think, I advise, I stare into space" (S 113)), the difference between being closed or locked down and open to receiving something from the future or from the beyond. Whereas at the end of Part I Max poured himself a glass of bourbon and then "put the bottle down and held the glass in both hands" (S 73), here, at the end of the novel, "he sits in front of the

TV set with his hands folded behind his neck, elbows jutting," looking ahead, understanding nothing, emptying his mind, it seems, in everyday lazyboy prayer, ready to receive whatever is to come next.

• * •

In "Human Moments in World War III" two astronauts circle the earth in extraterrestrial contraband and watch as the earth below is in the process of destroying itself in another world war, another that will perhaps be the last or the next to last. It is hard not to think of the epigraph to *The Silence*, the line from Einstein: "I do not know with what weapons World War III will be fought, but World War IV will be fought with sticks and stones." But then suddenly, through some time warp or glitch in the technology, the astronauts begin picking up strange radio signals, stray signals, signals gone astray, German and Japanese voices it seems from the Second World War ("HM" 33, 39), voices that had somehow been suspended in space and time, a bit like that ancient civilization in *Ratner's Star* that beamed "radio signals into space" to be received and decoded millennia later (*RS* 403). Recall that just before the TV goes completely silent in *The Silence* "there was a snatch of dialogue coming from the blank screen" that also seems to come from elsewhere. "It is not earthly speech," says Diane, "It is extraterrestrial" (*S* 27).

Someday, perhaps far into the future, on some distant planet, or on our own planet radically remade, or perhaps just tomorrow, somewhere nearby, someone will happen upon a book by Don DeLillo, an audio version of *Americana* maybe, a digital copy of *The Silence*, and he or she or they may think what those astronauts thought in "Human Moments in World War III": "What odd happenstance, what flourish or grace of the laws of physics enables us to pick up these signals? Traveled voices, chambered and dense" ("HM" 38).

Acknowledgments

Fiction is all about reliving things. It is our second chance.

"PH"

I explained in the postface to *Don DeLillo, American Original*, the prequel, as it were, to *Apocalyptic Ruin and Everyday Wonder in Don DeLillo's America*, that that earlier work was inspired or motivated in large part by the 2016 US Presidential election, which boded so ill for what might happen in and to America that, for me at least, some kind of countermeasure, a sort of reading and writing therapy, became necessary. This work, written almost entirely over the last two years, years that included an impeachment—two impeachments—a worldwide pandemic that touched America in a uniquely horrific way, and an insurrection within our nation's capitol, is being completed in the days just after the Presidential inauguration of 2021, that is, at a time when so many of us hold on to the hope that after coming so close to the precipice America too has been granted a second chance.

Once again, there are many people to be thanked here. First, I must thank my three extremely generous and meticulous readers at Bloomsbury who gave me a great deal of invaluable advice on how to improve my manuscript. Rarely does one find readers who, in addition to knowing DeLillo's corpus backwards and forwards, are able to address at once large organizational or methodological issues and pick up mistakes that somehow crept into the work—everything from the month of Charlie Parker's birth (August 29, not April 29, as I had had it) to the position Willie Mays was playing during that famous game in the Polo Grounds on October 3, 1951 (center field and not right field). I am extremely grateful both for the more general advice on how to reorganize and rewrite my work and for these essential bits of Americana. It is from Russell Ford that I learned everything I know about the real Project Mohole and the equally real American Miscellaneous Society, and it is to him as well—reader extraordinaire—that I owe my remarks in the conclusion about the numbers 116 and 911. Don DeLillo is fortunate to have such a devoted, generous, perceptive, and knowledgeable readership.

Without the support of DePaul University's College of Liberal Arts & Sciences, as well as the DePaul Humanities Center, and especially its director, H. Peter Steeves, I would have never been able to complete this work. The same has to be said of all those who were part of my "pod" or "bubble" during the COVID-19 pandemic of 2020–1, Elizabeth, who can hear and appreciate DeLillo's humor as well as anyone and who has been a constant interlocutor for this work, Jean-Stéphane, who continues to introduce me to other American idioms and embodies all the hope I still have for America, and, of course, Pascale-Anne, for our "thirty-seven years" of life lived together "in states of dire routine" (*S* 21), an everyday wonder every day renewed.

One last thing: this one is for John Walsh, Darrell Gibbs, and Paul (Fritz) Doherty, with whom I got my first taste of the world of opposites, all those many years ago, in Holden, Amherst, and Worcester.

Menton, France
December 2021

www.ingramcontent.com/pod-product-compliance
Ingram Content Group UK Ltd.
Pitfield, Milton Keynes, MK11 3LW, UK
UKHW022121190226
468205UK00006B/33